Human Resource Management

HUMAN RESOURCE MANAGEMENT

(In Two Volumes)

(Volume–1)

H.L. Kaila

Publications

KALPAZ PUBLICATIONS

DELHI-110 052

Human Resource Management
(In Two Volumes)

Rs. 1800 (Set)

ISBN : 81-7835-438-1 (Set)
ISBN: 81-7835-439-X (Vol. 1)

Published in 2005 in India by
Kalpaz Publications,
C-30, Satyawati Nagar,
Delhi-110 052
Email : kalpaz@hotmail.com

Lasertype Setting by: Tact Computer Graphics, Delhi
Printed at: Salasar Imaging System, Delhi

Contents

Foreword 7

Preface 9

1. Definition of Human Resource Management 13
2. Human Resource Planning 23
3. Recruitment 43
4. Motivation at Work Place 63
5. Training In Organizations 99
6. Job Satisfaction and Quality of Working Life 143
7. Employee Counselling 159
8. Managing and Coping with Stress 171
9. Depression among Executives 181
10. Personnel Records, Reports and Audit 203
11. Balancing Work and Life Issues 223
12. Organization Development 281
13. Change Management 295
14. Total Quality Management (TQM) 335
15. Organizational Behavior-Emerging Reality for Workplace Revolution 349
16. Organizational Survey Research 365

Foreword

The new role of the human resource professional is changign fast is this globalizing world. Hence the issues such as human resources training, performance appraisal, managerial leadership, the personnel functions are very important which has been touched in this book.

Managing human resource is the organizations require special skills as people have a lot of expectations from HR department. As a result, the stresses of HR managers have increased and the stress related health problems of HR managers need attention for increased organizational performance and excellence.

HR managers are facing many challenges these days. Managing change is one of the biggest challenges in organizations. Management of human resources requires multiple skills. The role of the HR manager must match the needs of his changing organization. Communication sensitivity is an effective tool for the HR Manager. The management of human resource must emphasize the most important human side of the human resources.

The author had done a very good collections of research material by careful selection, compilation and comprehensive review of researches carried out by India and foreign researchers. This will help the HR students and professional to understand objectively the human resource issues, and how they are being tackled in organizations.

This book 'Human Resource Management' by Dr HL Kaila contains twenth-seven chapters in two volumes based on research review of various aspects in HR development and management across business organizations. This would be useful to organizations interested in managing their human resource in a humane way with an objective to march towards organizational excellence.

P.N. Thakre
Vice President and Head
RIC Learning Centre

Preface

In Indian organizations, the 'field of human resource' has grown over the years from time-keeping to human resource development. The approach has changed from stick to caring. The organizations understood that coercion would lead to compliance but not commitment; instread caring would lead to commitment. For every level whether time keeping of HR, caring is important. Earlier the organizations used the approaches of welfare at the time of selection warfare during the time the employee stayed in the organization and then farewell to him did not take much time. Now the orientations dwell on competence development, motivation, and providing congenial environment. Of course, these orientations are not easy. Recruitment is a different process. Converting potentials into skills is a challenge. Employee's satisfaction, freedom and involvement are important concerns.

Motivational development is a multiplying method. HR is to identify what are the motivators in a particular job. These can be different from job to job. Organizations need to take care of employees; they take care of the business. The Operational people in originations are so busy that some times they don't take care of human side, so HR department should do this.

Job content and training have significant influence on employee attitude and behaviour, and play a pivotal role in job satisfaction. The intrinsic aspect of motivation are important for Indian managers. Managers also consider promotion and growth opportunities significant. The job attitudes and role perceptions at the middle and lower management levels influence the manager's satisfaction with the company. Managers and supervisors should be given adequate training and practice in leadership.

Managers is the positively perceived organizational climate (more conducive) are lower on job anxiety as compared to those in the low perceived organizational climate group.

In order to achieve the increased managerial effectiveness in the organizations, some insights from the studies are as below:

- A periodic analysis and appraisal of managers' on-job activities can accomplish effectiveness of middle level managers. Managerial effectiveness can be improved by redesigning their 'job' content.
- The organization should consider ways of fostering the managers' satisfaction with the company in term of defining the job duties/ responsibilities, minimizing job tasks which conflict with his values and job expectations.
- Indian managers spent significant amout of time in coaching and counseling their subordinates even on personal matters.
- Managers believed that mostly job performance and their influence of past career influenced career success. The 'effective' managers were found to be satisfied with their careers. A large number of personality traits than organizational factors are found discriminating 'effective' managers from 'not so effective' managers.
- Internally controlled managers are found significantly higher or overall managerial effectiveness as compared to externally controlled managers.
- While studing the psychology of management, it is observed that personality development palys a crucial role in high work motivation, good decision-making ability, and better interpersonal interaction.
- There is a tendency among the managers to use an autocratic style of management. Awareness about the democractic decision-making style in the overall effectiveness of the organization is to be developed among managers. As a manager and major decision-maker of an organization, the individual should work towards self-integration and self-motivation.

The two volumes of this book include all the topics that would be desired for a student of human resource management (HRM), a HR manager or a functional/operational manager involved in HR activities. It's an almost complete review of literature on human resource issues that would interest a HR professional. It's based on a bibliographic survey on HRM. It present concepts along with latest researches and case studies.

(DR HL Kaila)

1

Definition of Human Resource Management

Meaning, Nature, Scope and Definition of HRM

Human resource management is a part of the process that helps the organization achieve its objectives. Once the general direction and strategy have been established the next stage is to formulate firm objectives and develop these into action plans. The objective cannot be attained without the required resources, which of course includes people. HRM should be a part of the process, which determines what people are required, how to use them, how to get them and how to manage them. It should be fully integrated with all other management process.

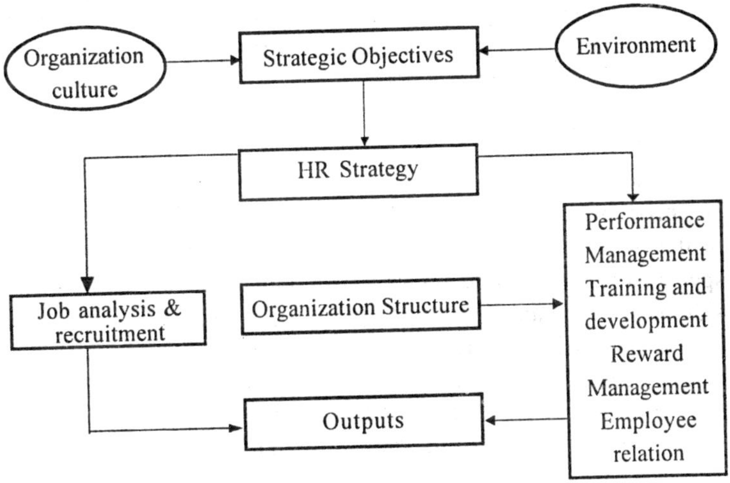

The Human Resource Management Process

Torrington and Hall Defines Personnel Management as: A series of activities which: first enable working people and their employing organizations to agree about the objectives and nature of their working relationship and, secondly, ensure that the agreement is fulfilled.

In this definition more emphasis is placed on the strategic importance of HRM and on the process, because of continues nature of the activities carried out. While there is less emphasis on the need of agreement, it is a fact that some personnel policies are, and perhaps have to be, implemented as a purely managerial exercise, the importance of integrating the two sets of needs is underlined.

It is proposed that we take human resource management to be that part of management concerned with:

- All the decisions, strategies, factors, principles, operations, practices, functions, activities and methods related to the management of people as employees in any type of organisation (including small and micro enterprises and virtual organisations);
- All the dimensions related to people in their employment relationships, and all the dynamics that flow from it (including in the realisation of the potential of individual employees in terms of their aspirations);
- All aimed at adding value to the delivery of goods and services, as well as to the quality of work life for employees, and hence helping to ensure continuous organisational success in transformative environment.

Nature of HRM

The objective of human resource management will vary from organization to organization and will depend on the organization's stage of development. At one extreme, for example, the human resource specialist will be seen as someone who looks after the administrative side of people management, i.e., preparing contracts of employment, maintaining personal files and so on. At the other extreme he or she will be seen as an integral and vital part of business planning process. The objective of HRM, therefore, are many and various and will at different times include some, if not all, of the following:

- Advertising management on the human resource policies required to ensure that the organization has a high performing workforce, has people equipped with change and meets its legal/employment obligations.

- Implementing and maintaining all necessary human resource policies and procedures to enable the organization to achieve its objectives.
- Assisting in development of the organization's overall direction and strategy, particularly with regard to human resource implementations.
- Providing the support and conditions that will help line managers achieve their objectives.
- Handling crises and difficult human relations situations to ensure that they do not get in way of the organization achieving its objectives.
- Providing a communication link between the workforce and the organization's management.
- Acting as a custodian of organizational standards and values in the management of human resources.

Main HRM Activities

The main activities, which make up personnel function, can be considered in terms of those that apply before, during and after the appointment of employees. To put it another way, HRM relates to the acquisition, management and disposal of resources, which in this case happen to consist of people.

Resource Acquisition

- Advertising on the kind of organization structure required to deliver the strategy, i.e., how activities should be grouped together, who should report to whom, how decision should be made and communicated, etc.
- Planning and advising on the number, levels and type of jobs required for the organization to meet its objectives in the most cost-effective way, including the extent to which activities should be resourced from the organization.
- Designing job in terms of duties and responsibilities, reporting lines and supervisory role.

- Advising on the most effective way of acquiring the people required.
- Managing or advising on the selection process to ensure that the applicants selected have the skills, knowledge and experience necessary to be able to carry out the duties required to the appropriate standard and that the process is carried out equitably and is free from bias against minority group.

Resource Management

- Designing performance management process that will help people know what is expected of them and to increase the possibility that they will achieve their identified objectives although it is essential that any such process is owned and managed by the line managers.
- Designing and running training programmes to ensure that employees have the necessary knowledge, skills and approach to carry out their responsibilities effectively.
- Designing and running development programmes to equip employees to undertake more responsible jobs and to assist in career management and succession planning.
- Advising on and administering reward strategies that support the organization's objective and business plan which provides a level of remuneration sufficient to attract and retain employees of the right caliber.
- Consulting and negotiating with trade unions and employee representatives on terms and conditions of employment.
- Advising on the administration of disciplinary and grievances issues.
- Advertising on the most effective means of communicating with employees and of innovating them in the organization's decision-making processes.
- Advising on staff changes, e.g. in terms of revised duties, relocation, transfer of undertakings, etc.
- Advising on staff welfare, health and safety issues.
- Maintaining all necessary administrative and legal processes connected with employment, such as contracts of employment, personal files, etc.

- Formulation and recommending employment policies on issues such as equal opportunities, smoking at work, harassment, etc.
- Advising line managers on all employment policies and on employment law and ensuring that the organization meets legal and social obligations.

Resource Disposal

- Conduct of termination interviews to ascertain the reasons behind any resignation and tie up any loose ends.
- In the event of redundancy, advice on possible alternatives and on the consultation and communication required.
- Design a redundancy and severance policy and advice on its application and on payments.
- Advice on the provision of outplacement counseling.
- Organize any necessary pre-retirement courses and provide advice as required.
- In the event of any appeal on dismissal, advice managers of the action to be taken.

Topical Issues

HRM is a constantly changing and developing area. Some of the keys issues currently being discussed by human resource specialists include the following:

- The extenta to which line managers should undertake activities.
- How those line managers who are taking over personnel activities can be adequately trained to carry them out.
- How the human resource functions can be more closely integrated with the strategy and objectives of the organization.
- The extent to which personnel activities should be outsourced or undertaken by contractor or consultants.
- How the effectiveness of the personnel function can be assessed and demonstrated- a perennial problem this one, compounded by some recent studies, some demonstrating that organizations with a strong personnel function are more effective and others showing that they are less effective.

- How to measure, develop and reward competencies, i.e. those observable and measurable behaviors required for effective or superior job performance.

Change Management

- Advise management on implications of change for employees.
- Co-ordinate & facilitate the change process.
- Facilitate changed relationships.
- Provide support structures for employees during change.
- Deliberate and proactive management of the changing environment and its implications for work and the organisation.

Compensation Management

- Develop compensation strategies and policies in line with legislation and the organisation's business strategy.
- Attach meaningful monetary values to posts in the organisation ensuring that the organisation's compensation is in line with market forces (this may be by means of traditional job evaluation or other methods such as skill or competency based pay).
- Develop appropriate compensation systems for the organisation.
- Manage overall labour costs.

Information Management

- Provide current information regarding employees to be used in the decision-making process and measurement of HRM's contribution to the organisation.
- Advise management regarding trends emerging from the data.
- Conduct HRM research with the aim of solving problems in the organisation.

Administrative Management

- Provide integrated HRM administration that is speedy and cost effective to receiver and administrator.
- Integrated employee data management.

Financial Management

- Manage the budget for HRM functions (Training and development, IR compensation, Employment Equity).
- Negotiate maximal funds for HR.
- Add value to the organisation by demonstrating a sound understanding of the complexity of business.
- Measure the financial impact of human resource systems

Qualities of HR Managers

According to the research carried out by Carrie Shearer following are some of the qualities of an HR manager-

1. **Understand the importance of the family:** To quote Robin Pascoe, noted author and spokesperson for expat spouses, "The IHR manager must recognize the critical role the spouse and family play in the overall success of the assignment."
2. **Empathy**: HR managers should have international experience. Unfortunately, we do not live in an ideal world and such assignments are highly unlikely. When asked why this was so vital, the response was that once you have experienced life in a world turned upside down, you become empathetic.

   Empathy refers to –"putting ones self in other persons shoes." This means thinking not only from ones own perspective but also thinking from others point of view. As a manager it is very important a quality. If a manager possesses this quality he will not only understand his employees but will be successful in involving them as a team.
3. **Integrity:** HR managers have two distinct, and often conflicting, roles according to the European director for a consumer products company. "They support the company to ensure they are optimizing the value of the assignment *and* they support the employee by ensuring they are able to maximize their value to the organization." These roles often require careful assessment and arbitration since they require HR managers to work in the gray zone. It is crucial that they are sensitive to the emotional upheaval.
4. **Flexibility:** HR managers need to be flexible in administering policies and in their own work schedules. Policies are guidelines.

What matters is how to make this relocation successful. HR managers need "good business judgment skills and the ability to draw a delicate line at the right place between policies/procedures that apply to all and those areas where individual circumstances demand and deserve individual treatment.

5. **Communicate effectively:** HR managers must communicate without placing blame and inspire a spirit of cooperation and teamwork. It often takes several people to solve a problem, and HR managers must be comfortable dealing with everyone from the CEO to the mailroom.

To conclude good IHR managers see themselves as allies, not policeman. They view their job as helping employees do their jobs. Employees, needs and situations vary. The best HR managers take the time to get to know each situation so that they can provide the support needed.

Scenarios for India Resource Management

Role of the organization: As there are mounting pressures and developments are possible, organization must be flexible. It may be necessary to allow fundamental shifts in values, strategy, policies and practices of all parties in the organization.

The organization should also take into consideration:

1. The technical aspects of personnel should be viewed as part of the activities to be performed by personnel executives.
2. As HRM is inherent in all management positions, it is a primary function and responsibility of all managers, regardless of the nature of their activities or their place in their organization.
3. The performance of these functions must deal with employees in their actual work environment, and not in any idealistically perceived situation.
4. Since the organizations do not exist in isolation, HRM cannot be understood outside the context of the total economic, technological, political and social environment in which it is performed.
5. At present personnel activities are performed by more capable and professional HR managers than ever before, they should be

treated with greater respect. This is true of managers and employees in other areas as well.

References and Further Reading

1. Barry Cushway (1998). Human Resource Management. Crest Publishing House. New Delhi.
2. http://www.expatica.com/xpat/xpatsite/hr.asp? pad=235,377, & item_id=30568.
3. Jhon P. Wilson. (Ed) (1999). Human Resource Management Learning and Training for individuals and Organisation. Kogan Page limited London.
4. Kaila HL et al (2003). Human factors in organizational management. Himalaya Publishing House, Mumbai.
5. K. Aswathappa. (1998).Organization behaviour. 5th revised edition. Himalaya Publishing House. pp. 478-495.
6. K. B. Akhilesh, D. R. Nagaraj (1990). Human Resource Management 200 Indian Prespectives. Editors Willey Eastern Limited. pp. 33-44.
7. Trevor Botton (2001). An introduction to Human Resource Management. Blackwell Imprint. 1st edition.

2

Human Resource Planning

Human Resource Planning, sometimes called as manpower planning, involves identifying staffing needs, analyzing the available personnel, and determining what additions and/or replacements are required to maintain a staff of the desired size and quality. It may be defined as a strategy for the acquisition, utilization, improvement and preservation of an organization's human resources.

In simple words, Human Resource Planning is a process of identifying human resource requirements in terms of quality and quantity. It is not just the quantity of manpower that matters, but more so the quality of manpower (Vaz Michael and Paralikar Vinayak, 2003).

People are one of the most important national resources. However, systematic approaches to Human Resource planning, forecasting, and action programs designed to provide trained people to fill needs for particular skills are still evolving at the national as well as at the enterprise level.

Human Resource planning systems include several specific, interrelated activities. Talent inventories provide a means of assessing current resources like skills, abilities, promotional potential, assignment histories, etc. Future assessments of Human Resource supply and demand enable planners to predict employment requirements. These together help to determine Human Resource objectives and policies that provide operational meaning and direction for action plans in many different areas. These include recruitment, selection, placement, career management and performance appraisal, as well as numerous training activities. Control and evaluation procedures provide feedback to the system and monitor the degree of attainment of Human Resource goals and objectives.

Ultimate success in Human Resource Planning depends on several factors. Some of these are: (1) The degree of integration of Human Resource planning with strategic planning activities. (2) The quality of the databases used to produce the talent inventory and forecasts of Human Resource supply and demand. (3) The caliber of the action programs established to achieve Human Resource objectives. (4) The organization's ability to implement the programs. The net effect of Human Resource Planning should be a wiser, more efficient use of human resources (Cascio Wayne F., 1998).

Human Resource Planning basically is a two-step process. Primary emphasis is on anticipating and responding to needs emerging within and outside the organization to determine priorities and to allocate resources where they can do the most good.

The analysis of needs leads to the planning of programs to be conducted. Activities and programs, in turn, relate directly to current and anticipated issues and must be evaluated in terms of needs, costs, and expected benefits.

In short, Human Resource Planning reflects three areas of primary concern to management:

1. Needs forecasting: Human Resource Planning personnel should analyze needs of the organization, based on these they should then suggest improvement in planning and control over office staff and organizational requirements.
2. Performance management: Human Resource Planning personnel should suggest means and methods to be adopted to improve the performance of individuals, teams, and the organization as a whole.
3. Career management: Human Resource Planning personnel should suggest guidelines to select, assign, develop individuals and manage their careers in the organization.

A range of external and organizational factors is studied for any linkages. This knowledge can be used in recruitment, development, compensation, performance management and other activities of the organization as an integral part of a dynamic process.

Human Resource Planning can be defined as "An effort to anticipate future business and environmental demands on an organization and to meet the human resource requirements dictated by these conditions". Thus several specific interrelated activities together comprise a Human Resource Planning System. These activities are:

1. Talent inventory–to assess skills, abilities and potentials of employees and analyze their current use.
2. Human resource forecast–to predict future human resource requirement.
3. Action plan–to enlarge the pool of qualified individuals by selection, recruitment, training, placement, transfer, promotion, development, and compensation.
4. Control and evaluation–to provide feedback and monitoring system to analyze the attainment of human resource goals and objectives (Cascio Wayne F., 1998).

Need and Importance of Human Resource Planning

Now-a-days, organizations are becoming more and more dependent upon people. They are increasingly involved in more complex technologies and are functioning in more complex economic, social, and political environments. As a result, the organizations face shortages of the right kind of human resources. Human Resource Planning enables to get the right type of personnel in the organization.

There is a growing importance of Human Resource Planning, due to following reasons:

1. **Personnel Requirements:** Human Resource Planning involves forecasting of personnel requirements in an organization. In other words, human resource planning helps management to anticipate personnel shortages and surpluses and develop ways to avoid or correct problems before they become serious.
2. **Recruitment and Selection:** A proper forecasting of personnel requirements enables the organization to determine proper sources of recruitment. The required personnel can be selected either from internal or external sources.

   The organization can also adopt a proper selection procedure depending upon the needs of the jobs. Proper tests can be designed to select the right candidate for the right job.
3. **Placement of Personnel:** Human Resource Planning facilitates proper placement of the employees in the organization. Placement refers to fitting the right person at the right place of work. Proper

placement brings job satisfaction to the employees and enhances employee's efficiency.

The selected personnel are placed at the right place of work. Persons are placed in those departments or in those areas where there is a shortage of personnel. If there is surplus, then that personnel can be shifted to some other areas or departments as the case may be.

4. **Performance Appraisal:** Human Resource Planning assists in performance appraisal of the employees in the organization. Performance appraisal refers to identification of strengths and weaknesses of the employees, relating to their jobs.

   The performance appraisal is conducted to find out whether the existing work- force has the necessary qualifications and qualities as per the job requirements. If there are weaknesses, then additional training or some other measures can be undertaken.

5. **Promotions:** Human Resource Planning ensures right promotion of the employees in the organization. Promotion involves higher position, higher power and higher pay.

   Human Resource planning involves Performance appraisal. Necessary performance reports are prepared. The organization would be in a position to promote the right person depending upon the performance appraisal reports.

6. **Training:** Human Resource Planning ensures training of the employees in the organization. Training involves imparting knowledge and developing attitudes, skills and social behavior of the employees.

   Human Resource Planning identifies the training needs of the personnel. If the personnel lack knowledge and skills, then necessary arrangements can be made by the organization to provide training.

7. **Transfer:** Human Resource Planning facilitates proper transfer of the employees in the organization. Transfer involves side- ways movement of the employees in the organization.

   There may be a situation where there is surplus personnel in one department and shortage in another department. This situation can be corrected by effecting transfers at the right time.

8. **Career Development:** Human Resource Planning facilitates career development of the employees in the organization. Career development refers to developing career of the employees in the organization.

   Human Resource Planning is conducted taking into consideration the long range plans of the organization. The plans are made known to members of the organization. The employees can plan for their careers within the organization once they come to know of the qualifications and qualities that would be required to implement the long range plans.

9. **Organizational Development:** Human Resource Planning assists in organizational development. Organizational development takes place when there are better results in the form of higher productivity or efficiency.

   Human Resource Planning ensures the development of the organization. It avoids surplus or shortage of personnel in the organization. The organization with qualified and able personnel can easily solve the problem of low productivity, absenteeism, inter- department conflicts, resistance to change, etc.

10. **Motivation of Personnel:** Human Resource Planning is concerned not only with the identification of the personnel in terms of quality and quantity, but it is also concerned with the improvement and motivation of the human resources. The organization would make every possible effort to have dedicated and committed personnel at all levels in the organization (Vaz Michael and Paralikar Vinayak, 2003).

Process of Human Resource Planning

The process of Human Resource Planning begins with a review of organizational strategies and objectives. Such review enables an organization to forecast personnel requirements and the internal supply of personnel.

The following are the steps in Human Resource Planning process:

1. **Review of Organizational Objectives:** The first step in Human Resource Planning is to review the objectives of the organization. Proper review of the objectives will enable the organization to make a proper list of the various activities that would be required to achieve the objectives.

To undertake the activities, the organization can determine the required work- force in terms of quantity and quality. A proper job analysis needs to be conducted at this stage.

2. **Personnel Requirements Forecasts:** The Human Resource Development manager should find out the requirements of human resources to undertake the various activities. The human requirements forecasts must be both in terms of quantity and quality.

3. **Personnel Supply Forecasts:** The Human Resource Development manager should also forecasts the availability of manpower. The required manpower may be available within the company, or they may be required to be hired from the lobour market.

4. **Make Comparison:** The Human Resource Development manager must make a comparison between personnel requirements and personnel supply, to find out whether the required personnel is available or not.

5. **If no Differences:** The comparison between personnel requirements and personnel supply would indicate whether there are any differences. If human resource requirements are equal to human resource supply, then there are no differences and as such no action need to be taken.

6. **If there are differences:** The comparison may reveal differences between the human resource requirements and human resource supply. There may be:

   (a) Personnel surplus, or (b) Personnel shortage

   (a) If there is Personnel Surplus: The management needs to take proper action:

   - Voluntary retirement
   - Lay- off,
   - Termination, etc.

   (b) If there is Personnel Shortage: The management needs to take proper action:

   - Hire
   - Promotion
   - Overtime
   - Training to improve quality, etc.

7. **Motivating the Manpower:** An important aspect of human resource planning is to motivate the personnel by providing monetary and non- monetary incentives.

8. **Monitoring Personnel Requirements:** The organization needs to monitor the requirement of perÿonnel. This is because there is constant need for additional personnel, as some of the existing personnel do leave the organization due to resignation, retirement, and so on (Vaz Michael and Paralikar Vinayak, 2003).

Limitations of Human Resource Planning

Human Resource Planning suffers from the following drawbacks or Limitations:

1. **Future is uncertain:** Forecasting of changes in technological, social, economic, and political conditions cannot be made with accuracy. Human Resource Planning is based on certain assumptions, which may prove to be dangerous. However, it is better to try and plan for human resources, rather than leaving actions to chance.

2. **Conservative attitude of management:** In India there is high rate of unemployment. Conservative managements feel that there is no need for Human Resource Planning as there is abundance of labour in our country. The lack of interest on the part of top management is a vital limitation to the success of Human Resource Planning.

3. **Problem of discarding surplus staff:** In India, management often finds problem in discarding surplus employees due to various labour laws and trade union activities. The voluntary retirement schemes often do not get a favorable response from the surplus staff even when attractive packages are offered.

4. **Time Consuming and Paper Work:** Human Resource Planning requires considerable time and effort on the part of human resource planners. Also, a good deal of reports, and other paper work is required in order to undertake Human Resource Planning process.

5. **Problem of recognizing change:** In India, companies fail to recognize the changes in the environment. This is truer in case of those companies, which are traditionally managed. As a result

of this, they do not give much importance to Human Resource Planning. They consider Human Resource Planning is just a time consuming and non- productive activity. To make Human Resource Planning more effective, there is a need for professional attitude on the part of the management of Indian companies.

6. **Shortages of highly skilled personnel:** Although India is having the second largest pool of scientific and technical personnel in the world, yet there is a shortage of highly skilled personnel of the right type. Thus, Human Resource Planning may be able to recognize the shortages and plan accordingly to get the right type of personnel, yet an organization may find it difficult to identify and recruit the selective personnel.
7. **Expensive:** Human Resource Planning is an expensive process. This is because, Human Resource Planning experts may be required and they do charge a good amount of fees. Again a good amount of money is spent in collection of data relating to future objectives of the organization, listing out of various activities, determining manpower requirements, etc. Again, a lot of money is spent in recruiting and selecting the people and also in providing training (Vaz Michael and Paralikar Vinayak, 2003).

Recruitment Planning

Recruitment is defined as, "a process to discover the sources of manpower to meet the requirements of the staffing schedule. It employs effective measures for attracting the manpower in adequate numbers to facilitate effective selection of efficient personnel" (Rao Subha P., 2000).

According to Edwin Flippo, "Recruitment is a process of searching for prospective employees and stimulating them to apply for jobs" (Vaz Michael and Paralikar Vinayak, 2003).

Recruitment is also defined as, "Searching for and obtaining potential job candidates in sufficient numbers and quality so that the organization can select the most appropriate people to fill its job needs" (Beardwell Ian and Holden Len, 2001).

Recruitment Planning: Recruitment precedes selection and helps in selecting a right candidate.

Recruitment is frequently treated as if it were a one-way process that is, organizations searching for prospective employees. This approach may be viewed as a prospecting theory of recruitment. In practice, however, a prospective employee seeks out organizations just as organizations seek out prospective employees. This view, termed a mating theory of recruitment, appears more realistic. Recruitment success from the organization's perspective and job search success from the applicant's perspective, both depend on timing. If organizations are recruiting at the same time when the applicants are searching for jobs, then conditions are ripe for the two to meet.

In order for organizations and applicants actually to meet, three conditions must be satisfied. These are: (1) There must be a common communication medium, (2) the job seeker must perceive a match between his or her personal characteristics and stated job requirements, (3) the job seeker must be motivated to apply for the job. Recruitment planning must address these issues.

The process of recruitment planning begins with a clear specification of Human Resource needs and the time frame within which such requirements must be met. This is particularly relevant to the setting of workforce diversity goals and timetables.

The next step is to project a timetable for researching this ultimate goal based on expected job vacancies. If Human Resource forecast by job group is available the problem is straightforward. But the basic procedure in all cases is to look at what has occurred in a job group over the past several years. These are in terms of new hires, promotions, and transfers. This provides an index of what to expect in the coming year. Employers also should examine applicant flow and internal availability to determine how many of these expected vacancies can reasonably be filled.

The effective use of "in-house" talent should come first. If an organization undertakes external recruitment efforts without considering the desires, capabilities, and potential of present employees, it may incur both short and long run costs. In the short run, morale may degenerate. In the long run, an organization with a reputation for consistent neglect of in-house talent, may find it difficult to attract new employees and to retain experienced ones. Because of all this, action plans, which incorporate developmental and training needs for each employee, promotability indexes, and replacement charts, are so important.

Recruitment Planning may begin with a comprehensive Human Resource plan. They are for the various segments of work force, e.g., entry-level, managerial, professional and technical. To do this, three key parameters must be estimated. They are: the time, the money, and the staff necessary to achieve a given hiring rate. The basic statistic needed to estimate these parameters is the number of leads needed to generate a given number of hires in a given time. Certainly the easiest way to derive this figure is on the basis of prior recruitment experience. If accurate records exist regarding yield ratio and time-lapse data, there is no problem, since it is possible to determine trends and to generate reliable predictions. Yield ratios are the ratios of leads to invites, invites to interviews, interviews to offers, and offers to hire obtained over some specified time period. Time-lapse data provides the average intervals between events, such as between the extension of an offer to a candidate, acceptance, and addition to the payroll.

If no experience data exists, then it is necessary to establish some "best guesses" or hypotheses and to monitor performance as the operational recruitment program unfolds. Although time frames differ from job to job and industry to industry. Mostly, three months from the receipt of a requisition to the new employee's start date is considered an acceptable time period for recruiting a journey level professional (Lord, 1989). The time period also depends on labour market conditions. A labour market is a geographical area, within which the forces of supply i.e., people looking for work; interact with the forces of demand i.e., employers looking for people; and, thereby, determine the price of labour. However, since the geographical areas over which employers extend their recruiting efforts depend partly on the type of job being filled. It is impossible to define the boundaries of a local labour market in any clear-cut manner (Reynolds et al., 1986). If the supply of suitable workers in a particular lobour market is high relative to available jobs, then the price of labour generally will be cheaper. On the other hand, if the supply is limited, then it must widen the search and investigate additional labour markets in order to realize required yield ratios.

Time-lapse data may have to be revised to account for the change in labour market conditions, and the price of labour generally will also rise. Recruitment is fairly simple for a small manufacturing firm in a well-populated rural area. But in large, high technology firms with global markets face far different recruitment challenges (Cascio Wayne F., 1998).

Source Analysis

Analyses of recruiting sources facilitate effective planning. Three types of analyses are required cost-per-hire, time-lapse from candidate identification to hire, and source yield.

Cost-per-hire studies the most expensive sources. They generally are private employment agencies and executive search firms. The next most expensive sources are field trips, for both advertising expenses and recruiter's travel and living expenses are incurred. Less expensive are advertising responses, write-ins, and company transfers and promotions. Employee referrals and walk-ins are the cheapest sources of candidates.

Time-lapse studies of recruiting sources are especially useful for planning purposes, since the time from initial contact to report on board varies across sources.

The third index of source performance is source yield. This information is especially valuable for determining how effectively time is being spent in a particular market.

At this point, recruitment operations are ready to begin. Recruiting efficiency can be heightened considerably, however, once employment requirements are defined thoroughly in advance. This is an essential step for both technical and non-technical jobs. Recruiters must be familiar with the job description of available jobs. They must understand the work to be performed. Research has shown clearly that, characteristics of organization and jobs have a greater influence on the likelihood of job acceptance by candidates, than do characteristics of the recruiter (Vaz Michael and Paralikar Vinayak, 2003); (Cascio Wayne F., 1998).

Managing Recruitment Operations

The first step in recruiting operations is to examine internal sources for qualified or qualifiable candidates. This is especially true of large, decentralized organizations that are likely to maintain comprehensive talent inventories with detailed information on each employee. It is essential to update the inventory periodically to reflect changes in employee skills, educational and training achievements, job title and so forth.

Regardless of organizational size, however, promotion from within policies must be supported by a managerial philosophy that permits employees to consider available opportunities for transfer or promotion. Candidates may be identified either by talent inventory search or by responding to in-house posting of available jobs. On the other hand, organizations often turn to external sources to fill entry-level jobs, jobs created by expansion, and jobs whose specifications cannot be met by present employee (Cascio Wayne F., 1998).

Objectives of Recruitment

The objectives of Recruitment are:

1. To attract people with multi-dimensional skills and experiences that suits the present and future organizational strategies.
2. To induct outsiders with a new perspective to lead the company.
3. To infuse fresh blood at all levels of the organization.
4. To develop an organizational culture that attracts competent people to the company.
5. To search or head hunt/ head pouch people whose skills fit the company's values.
6. To devise methodologies for assessing psychological traits.
7. To seek out non-conventional development grounds of talent.
8. To search for talent globally and not just within the company.
9. To design entry pay that competes on quality but not on quantum.
10. To anticipate and find people for positions that does not exist yet (Rao Subha P., 2000).

Recruitment Methods

The most effective recruitment method is one that produces the best results in terms of able candidates for the least cost. Organizations can choose from a wide variety of methods, including the use of:

- Informal personal contacts, such as existing employees, informal grapevine (word of mouth), and speculative applications;
- Formal personal contacts, such as careers fairs, open days, and leaflet drops;

- Notice boards, accessible by current staff or the general public;
- Advertising, including local and national press, specialist publications, radio and television, and the Internet;
- External assistance, including job centers, career service, employment agencies, and 'head-hunters'.

Decisions about the most appropriate method or methods are likely to be influenced by the level of the vacancy and its importance within the organization. Other factors to be taken into account when choosing the most appropriate method include the resources available within the organization. They are in terms of personnel and finance, the perceived target groups and the organization's stance on internal versus external recruitment. Human resource management literature, emphasizes the need to have well-developed internal lobour market arrangements. They are for promotion, training and career development, which would suggest that many openings can and should be filled internally. However, a number of organizations, particularly those in the public sector, have policies that require the majority of posts to be advertised externally (Beardwell Ian and Holden Len, 2001).

Internal Sources for Recruiting Applicants

The internal sources refer to sources from within the company. The various internal sources are as follows:

1. **Promotions:** When a vacancy arises at a higher level, qualified and experienced employee from within the company can be promoted at the higher level. For instance, an understudy candidate may be promoted to the post of his superior who has retired or promoted or transferred.
2. **Transfers:** The vacancy can also be filled through internal transfers. An existing executive who is experienced and capable of handling the duties in the new department can be transferred.
3. **Retired Managers:** At times, retired managers may be recalled, especially for a short duration, when it is difficult to find a suitable candidate for the post from which the managers has retired.
4. **Internal Advertisements:** The company may also display on its notice boards or inform the departmental heads of a vacancy at executive levels.

Accordingly, interested candidates may apply for the position.

Advantages of Internal Sources

- It is time saving and economical as there is no need to advertise the 'jobs' in external media and also no need to conduct interviews of several candidates.
- There is no need for induction training, especially in respect of company related information.
- It reduces executive turnovers.
- It develops loyalty and a sense of responsibility.
- The internal candidate is well versed with company's policies, rules and regulations.
- It improves morale of the company personnel.

Demerits of Internal Sources

- It prevents candidates from outside with innovative ideas, fresh thinking and dynamism from entering the company.
- It offers limited scope for selection and there is a possibility of not finding the required executive within the company.
- The position of the person so promoted or transferred falls vacant.
- There may be bias or partiality in promotion or transferring personnel, from within the company.
- It may generate a feeling of discontent among those who are not promoted.
- It requires well-maintained confidential reports of employees so that the right executive is promoted or transferred (Vaz Michael and Paralikar Vinayak, 2003).

External Sources for Recruiting Applicants

A wide variety of external recruiting sources is available, with the choice of source contingent upon specific hiring requirements and source analysis results.

The sources include:

1. **Advertisements:** This is one of the most popular sources of recruitment. Advertisement of the vacancy can be inserted in

newspapers, businessï magazines, technical and professional journals, direct mail, television, the Internet, and outdoor advertising.

2. **Management Consultants**: Some companies take help of management consultants to select executive personnel for their organization.
3. **Employment agencies:** Some companies take help of federal and state agencies, private agencies, executive search firms, management consulting firms, and agencies specializing in temporary help.
4. **Educational institutions:** Some companies also do campus recruitment to select the best students with the cooperation of the institutes. The campus recruitment takes place at technical and trade schools, colleges and universities, co-operative work/ study programs, and alumni placement offices.
5. **Professional organizations:** Technical society meetings and conventions, which might be regional and national, and society placement services, help in recruiting programs.
6. **Military:** Military helps some companies in placement services, administered by regional and national retired officer associations.
7. **Labor unions:**
8. **Career fairs:**
9. **Outplacement firms:**
10. **Walk-ins:**
11. **Write-ins:**
12. **Intracompany transfers and company retirees:**
13. **Employee referrals (Vaz Michael and Paralikar Vinayak, 2003); (Cascio Wayne F., 1998).**

Advantages of External Sources

- It encourages new talent with innovative ideas, fresh thinking, drive and dynamism to enter the company.
- It offers wider scope in selection, as there is a possibility of a large number of candidates with the requisite qualifications and experience, appearing for the selection process.

- There are less chances of partiality, as outsiders have less chance in influencing selection decisions.
- It does not require well-maintained confidential records.

Demerits of External Sources

- There are chances of existing executive turnover, as outsiders are given a chance.
- It may not develop loyalty among the existing executives.
- It is time consuming, as lengthy selection process is required.
- It is also expensive, as advertisements and various tests, need to be conducted.

Every company has a number of alternative sources for recruitment purpose. However, the best source is to tap the internal first and then external one. But in reality, the choice of internal or external source depends upon a number of factors, such as the nature of the job, time available for selection, skills required, cost involved, policy of the company, position of labour market, and so on (Vaz Michael and Paralikar Vinayak, 2003).

These sources may be classified as formal, which includes institutionalized search methods such as employment agencies, advertising and labour unions, or informal, which includes walk-ins, write-ins and employee referrals. These are in terms of the most popular sources, used by employer's evidence, which indicates that:

- Candidates at all occupational levels use informal contacts widely and effectively;
- Use of the employment service declines as required job skills increase;
- The internal market is a major recruitment method except for entry-level, unskilled, and semiskilled workers;
- Larger firms are the most frequent users of walk-ins, write-ins, and the internal market.

Regardless of the recruitment sources used to generate an applicant population, and regardless of the differences in applicants across recruitment sources, once a final applicant pool has been generated, organizations can maximize the payoff from their selection systems by ignoring recruitment sources and using a predictor-based selection strategy (Cascio Wayne F., 1998).

Managing Recruiting Operations

A well-coordinated administrative system for recording and controlling applicant flow is essential to effective recruitment operations and subsequent evaluation. In addition, such controls are essential if the organization is to meet its legal, ethical, and public relations responsibilities.

The records are as follows:

1. Incoming applications and resumes.
2. Activity at important points in the recruiting "pipeline" for each candidate (e.g.; invitations, interviews, offers, acceptances/ rejections, reports onto payroll). Acknowledgements and "no interest" letters for each candidate.
3. Offers and acceptances relative to open staffing requisitions.
4. Records of closed cases.

In order to perform these activities accurately and in timely manner, more and more firms are turning to computers for help. The work is performed in a typical system. The date of receipt and other pertinent information are first extracted from each incoming resume, and assignment is made to a recruiter. Each step in the recruiting pipeline is recorded for each candidate by date of action. Each recruiter then receives a list of his or her assigned files with the current action recorded for each applicant. At the same time, a master active list and pipeline count are generated. Offers and acceptances are recorded against open staffing requisitions. Each recruiter routinely communicates with the system to update the file and keep records current. Time-lapse data and yield ratios, together with analyses of source and recruiter efficiency, can be generated regularly. In addition to cutting recruiting costs in large organizations, such a system permits enhanced control and evaluation of the overall recruitment effort (Cascio Wayne F., 1998).

Impact Recruitment on Productivity

Ensuring the selection of the right people to join the work force is one of the important activities in the life of an organization. The recruitment and selection process is concerned with identifying, attracting and choosing suitable people to meet an organization's human resource requirements. Recruitment can be considered as a process to discover the sources of manpower to meet the requirements of the staffing schedule and to employ effective measures for attracting that manpower in adequate numbers to facilitate effective selection of efficient personnel. Selection is a process of selecting right person for the right job. Recruitment and selection are integrated activities in an organization and where one activity stops and the other begins is difficult to pin point.

The sources of recruitment refer to personnel from amongst which the potential employees can be attracted to apply for the job and accordingly selected. There are two types of sources, namely, internal, i.e., from within the company and external which refers to personnel from outside the company. For proper selection, job description and specification are very important. A proper job analysis allows the right type of candidate to apply for the job. This saves a lot of time and effort during selection. To arrive at personnel specification, depending on the job requirements, the following points should be considered:

1. Physical make-up,
2. Appearance,
3. Speech and manner,
4. Education,
5. Vocational training,
6. Work experience,
7. Quickness of comprehension and aptitude for learning,
8. Individual goals, consistency and determination in following them up,
9. Emotional stability,
10. Ability to stand up to stress and ability to get on with people.

Management has to decide what are the company's requirements and what type of person will suit these requirements. Once such a decision is made, the next thing to look for is the time limit, which the management can afford in trying to find out the suitable person. If the time required is short, necessitating urgent selection, the easiest option will be to look for the most suitable person from amongst those working in the company. However, if there is sufficient time for selection, one should try out the option of selecting somebody from outside. This does not mean that internal candidate should not be considered. However, internal candidates will have to compete with the external candidates to prove their merit.

If recruitment is to be made from internal source, it can be through promotion of a qualified and experienced employee to the higher position; transferring a capable employee from another department; having a retired executive when it is difficult to find a suitable candidate. This way a suitable candidate can be selected in the shortest possible time. This has an added advantage of increased loyalty and sense of responsibility. This improves morale of the company personnel improving the productivity. However, internal source prevents outside candidates with new ideas, fresh thinking and dynamism from entering the company. There may be partiality in promoting or transferring. Also, those who are not promoted may feel discontented. These can affect the productivity adversely.

If an external candidate is to be selected, the scope of selection is wide. This way new ideas, thinking and drive can be brought into the company. Chances of partiality are reduced. This may help in development of new problems or new methods for improved production. The disadvantages of this method are no loyalty from the existing employees. Also, it takes a lot of time, energy and resources to select a proper candidate for a proper job. In effect this may affect the production on time scale. However, if management is trying for diversification of product, it is better to bring in external suitable person already in the field. Also, if the present executives are not able to manage the situation in the company, suitable external person may be brought in to get over the problems and improve production.

One has to weigh pros and cons of the situation and decide the recruitment strategy for the best or improved productivity (Beardwell Ian and Holden Len, 2001); (Cascio Wayne F., 1998).

References and Further Reading

1. Beardwell Ian And Holden Len (2001). Human Resource Management: A Contemporary Approach. England: Pearson Education Ltd., Printice Hall.
2. Cascio Wayne F. (1998). Applied Psychology In Human Resource Management. Printice Hall International, Inc., Mc Graw Hill.
3. Rao P. Subha (2000). Personal And Human Resource Management. Mumbai: Himalaya Publishing House.
4. Vaz Michael And Paralikar Vinayak (2003). Management And Human Resource Development. Mumbai: Manan Prakashan.

3

Recruitment

Definition

Personnel Selection is the methodical placement of individuals into jobs. Its impact on the organization is realized when employees achieve years or decades of service to the employer. The process of selection follows a methodology to collect information about an individual in order to determine if that individual should be employed. The methodology used should not violate any laws regarding personnel selection.

Sources of Recruitment

Internal Source

Merit Promotion Programme: The underlying principle of Merit Promotion Programs is the identification, qualification evaluation, and selection of candidates which will be made without regard to political, religious, labor organization affiliation, marital status, race, color, sex, national origin, non-disqualifying physical or mental handicap, or age and shall be based solely on job- related criteria in accordance with legitimate position requirements. A sound merit promotion program properly administered and fully supported by management officials and employees at all levels is essential to the staffing of an effective and highly motivated civilian work force.

Reassignment

Reassignment is the noncompetitive movement of an employee to another position for which he/she qualifies at the same grade level and with an equivalent target grade if applicable.

A reassignment eligible is considered a noncompetitive candidate, or is a noncompetitive referral, because he/she has already competed for and currently holds, or has held, an equivalent position to the one being filled. However, reassignments to restructured positions (e.g., Upward Mobility Program), which are targeted above the grade level currently held by the employee, must be processed competitively. This means that all in-service placement rules apply and competition must occur between all in-service placement candidates within the area of consideration.

Reassignments can be "management directed." These actions are initiated by management to laterally move an employee to another position within the organization or between organizations. This often occurs when placing employees in order to avoid reduction-in-force actions or for other reasons when an employee's skills can be better utilized in another equivalent position.

A reassignment can also be a "voluntary request." An employee wishing to move to another position who has submitted written requests to be referred noncompetitive for vacancies initiates these actions.

Reassignment candidates may be referred when the selecting official requests to review this recruiting source or at any time along with Merit Promotion candidates. Reassignment candidates would be referred with other noncompetitive candidates such as change to lower grade and repromotion eligible. Order of referral of no competing candidates may be contained in your agency guidelines.

Change to Lower Grade

A change to lower grade is the noncompetitive movement of an employee to another position for which he/she qualifies at a lower grade than currently held. This is not considered an adverse action if it is voluntarily requested by the employee.

A change to lower grade candidate is considered a noncompetitive candidate, or is a noncompetitive referral, because he/she has already competed for and currently holds a position at a higher-grade level than the one being filled. However, changes to lower grade for restructured positions, or upward mobility programme positions, which are targeted above the grade level currently held by the employee, must be processed competitively. This means that all in-service placement rules apply and competition must occur between all in-service placement candidates within the area of consideration.

Change to lower grade candidates may be referred when the selecting official requests to review this recruitment source or at any time along with merit promotion candidates. Change to lower grade candidates would be referred with other noncompetitive candidates such as reassignment and repromotion eligible. Order of referral of noncompetitive candidates may be contained in your agency guidelines.

Detail

A detail is the temporary assignment of an employee to a different position or set of duties for a specified period with the employee returning to his/her original position at the end of the detail. There is no formal position change; officially the employee continues to hold the position from which detailed and keeps the same status and pay. Employees do not need to meet qualification standards in order to be detailed.

Details are intended for meeting temporary needs of the agency's work program when necessary services cannot be provided by other means. Details can be used in situations such as temporary shortage of military or civilian personnel or emergency work situations.

An employee who continues to carry out the duties of the position to which permanently assigned and also performs some of the duties of another position for a limited time generally is not considered to be on detail. Details to higher level positions must be made competitively when the duration of the detail will exceed 120 days and the nature of the assignment are such that an employee can be expected to perform the majority of the grade- controlling duties.

Details are affected in 120-day increments. For employees covered by the bargaining unit, the union contracts should be reviewed prior to affecting a detail.

Details of 30 days or less are documented in the Supervisor's Records. An SF 52 for personal action must be processed for details in excess of 30 days, which results in an official personnel action filed in the employee's Official Personnel Folder.

Temporary Promotion

A temporary promotion is the temporary assignment of an employee to a higher graded position for a specified period of time, with the employee returning to his/her permanent position upon the expiration of the temporary action or the employee being permanently assigned to the higher graded position under competitive procedures. The temporarily promoted employee receives the higher graded salary for the period assigned and gains quality level experience and time-in-grade at the higher-grade level.

Temporary promotions are intended for meeting temporary needs of the agency's work program when necessary services cannot be provided by other means. Temporary promotions can be used in situations such as unanticipated absences, temporary shortage of military or civilian personnel, emergency work situations, or pending permanent action.

The initial 120 days of a temporary promotion may be made noncompetitive, which means the selected employee does not have to compete with other employees for the temporary assignment. However, if it is to be extended beyond that time it must be opened for competition with others. For an employee to be temporarily promoted, all recruitments must be met the same as if the promotion were permanent.

Temporary promotions normally can be extended up to one year, however, it is not intended to fill a long-term need. In some instances it may be necessary to extend for more than one year, especially at installations that are facing closure or reorganizations/realignments.

For employees covered by the bargaining unit, the union contracts should be reviewed prior to effecting this action.

- Contributing to the accomplishment of mission goals by staffing positions with high-quality employees.
- Providing career opportunities for employees and ensuring that promotion opportunity information is made available to all employees.
- Bringing to the attention of management high-quality employees who have the capacity to perform in more responsible assignments.
- Fostering and facilitating the mobility of employees in the interest of broadening their experiences and increasing their qualifications.
- Ensuring the maximum utilization of employees in positions for which they are best qualified.

- Ensuring that the skills, qualifications, achievements, and promotion potential of employees are recognized and fairly considered in the staffing process.
- Encouraging employees to improve their performance to develop their knowledge, skills, and abilities.

External Sources

Careers office: no fee charged. Details mainly with the school leavers, today they are more proactive in the field of offering constructive advice to young people. Important to bear in mind that their work is to assist young people in finding employment rather than acting on behalf of the employer.

Job center: free service. Have made strenuous efforts in recent years to overcome their old 'labors exchange' image, with varying degree of successes. They do offer counseling services to applicants and will do a limited amount of pre-screening before recommending people to apply for the job. Still largely associated with trying to get unemployed people into jobs rather than helping those who wish to change their jobs, although their services are available to all regardless to employment status. Most of the positions they advertise are for clerical, manual and junior position.

Commercial recruitment agencies: vary enormously in the range, quality and price of service offered. Many will specialize by occupation, for instance clerical and secretarial, and some by the industry, for instance insurance and banking. Others will specialize in the recruitment of senior staff ('executive recruitment'), while still others will act as an intermediary and approach potential employees to gauge their interest in changing their current job.

Web Site Recruitment

There is a steady trend among the world's largest companies towards recruiting with a "Careers" section on their corporate Web sites, according to a current survey by recruitsoft.com/iLogos Research. In 2000, more than three-quarters (79 per cent) of the Global 500 companies recruit on their corporate Web sites. By comparison, only 29 per cent of these companies recruited on their Web sites in 1998; 60 per cent did so in 1999.

Research predicts that by 2001, more than 90% of the Global 500 will recruit online and forecasts a complete adoption by 2002. Increased competition for a limited talent pool and the very high level of Internet usage among the general population will compel those slow to embrace online recruiting methods to catch up to the earlier adopters.

Interview Method

Interviews: A selection procedure designed to predict future job performance on the basis of applicants' oral responses to oral inquiries.

Tips for Effective Interview

Minimize Stereotypes: To minimize the influence of racial and sex stereotypes in the interview process, provide interviewers with a job description and specification of the requirements for the position. Interviewers with little information about the job may be more likely to make stereotypical judgments about the suitability of candidates than are interviewers with detailed information about the job and candidate.

Job Related: Try to make the interview questions job related. If the questions are not related to the job, then the validity of the interview procedure may be lower.

Train Interviewers: Improve the interpersonal skills of the interviewer and the interviewer's ability to make decisions without influence from non-job related information. Interviewers should be trained to:

- Avoid asking questions unrelated to the job
- Avoid making quick decisions about an applicant
- Avoid stereotyping applicants
- Avoid giving too much weight to a few characteristics.
- Try to put the applicant at ease during the interview
- Communicate clearly with the applicant
- Maintain consistency in the questions asked

Types of Interviews

1. **Unstructured Interview:** involves a procedure where different questions may be asked of different applicants.

2. **Structured Interview:** In a structured interview, a pre-established set of questions and/or scenarios are presented to the candidate in a face-to-face meeting with one or more interviewer(s). An important requirement of this approach is that all candidates experience the same basic interview experience. If desired, responses to specific questions may be elaborated upon in a non-standardized manner; that is, where the candidate seems weak, the interviewer may decide to further probe the candidate's knowledge. The interview should be about 1 to 1½ hours long. A structured interview is well suited to evaluating knowledge, abilities and communication skills, and can aid in exploring potential problem areas.
3. **Situational Interview:** Candidates are interviewed about what actions they would take in various job-related situations. The job-related situations are usually identified using the job analysis technique by critical incidence. The interviews are then scored using a scoring guide constructed by job experts.
4. **Behavior Description Interviews:** Candidates are asked what actions they have taken in prior job situations that are similar to situations they may encounter on the job. The interviews are then scored using a scoring guide constructed by job experts.
5. **Comprehensive Structured Interviews::** Candidates are asked questions pertaining to how they would handle job-related situations, job knowledge, worker requirements, and how the candidate would perform various job simulations. Interviews tapping job knowledge offer a way to assess a candidate's current level of knowledge related to relevant implicit dimensions of job performance (i.e., "tacit knowledge" or "practical intelligence" related to a specific job position).
6. **Structured Behavioral Interview:** This technique involves asking all interviewees' standardized questions about how they handled past situations that were similar to situations they may encounter on the job. The interviewer may also ask discretionary probing questions for details of the situations, the interviewee's behavior in the situation and the outcome. The interviewee's responses are then scored with behaviorally anchored rating scales.
7. **Oral Interview Boards:** This technique entails the job candidate giving oral responses to job-related questions asked by a panel

of interviewers. Each member of the panel then rates each interviewee on such dimensions as work history, motivation, creative thinking, and presentation. The scoring procedure for oral interview boards has typically been subjective; thus, it would be subject to personal biases of those individuals sitting on the board. This technique may not be feasible for jobs in which there are a large number of applicants that must be interviewed.

Advantages of Interview

- Useful for determining if the applicant has requisite communicative or social skills which may be necessary for the job.
- Interviewer can obtain supplementary information.
- Used to appraise candidates' verbal fluency.
- Can assess the applicant's job knowledge.
- Can be used for selection among equally qualified applicants.
- Enables the supervisor and/or co-workers to determine if there is compatibility between the applicant and the employees.
- Allows the applicant to ask questions that may reveal additional information useful for making a selection decision.
- The interview may be modified as needed to gather important information.

Disadvantages of Interview

- Subjective evaluations are made.
- Decisions tend to be made within the first few minutes of the interview with the remainder of the interview used to validate or justify the original decision.
- Interviewers form stereotypes concerning the characteristics required for success on the job.
- Research has shown disproportionate rates of selection between minority and non-minority members using interviews.
- Negative information seems to be given more weight.

- Not much evidence of validity of the selection procedure.
- Not as reliable as tests.

Exit Interviews

The exit interview is an interview given to a departing employee. This is usually done for employees that voluntarily quit instead of those that are fired or laid off.

Exit interviews offer a fleeting opportunity to find out information that otherwise might be more difficult or impossible to obtain.

The following are some thoughts on the exit interview:

1. Interviews can be conducted orally or written. Most people prefer the oral interview.
2. Think carefully about the information you would like to get before the interview. This greatly increases the success of a interview.
3. Save the hardest questions for the latter part of the interview. Work up to the tough stuff!
4. A good question to break the ice is 'would you like for us to be a reference/recommendation for you'? Do not make this offer if you would not recommend the employee!
5. Be prepared for some bombshells. Expect the unexpected – if it ever is to happen it will happen in an exit interview.
6. Carefully select the interviewer. Look for someone that listens well and is open-minded. It serves no purpose for the interviewer to get into an argument with the departing employee.
7. Throughout the interview stay focused on the employee!
8. Look for open-ended questions that allow for plenty of expression. An example of this might be "how did you feel you were managed during your employment with us?" or "how do you feel the company is run?"
9. Other excellent questions are 'under what conditions would you have stayed?' and 'if you had had a magic wand, what would you have changed?'
10. At some point in the interview ask 'why are you leaving?' if you do not already know.

11. Good general questions are 'what did you like most (least) about your position?'
12. Try to find out if there were things the departing employee would suggest improving conditions, production or morale.
13. Try to get a good feel for how they viewed their compensation and benefits package.
14. Leave room at the end of the interview for general comments.
15. Take notes of the high points. Get the general idea – it is not essential to get exact quotes. It is more important to listen than write.
16. Immediately after the interview determine if you would rehire the employee. Assume they will reapply.
17. Make use of the information gathered. If you do not use this new information then why do an exit interview?

The exit interview provides us with a good mechanism to take a hard look at how your company is perceived. Since the employee is leaving, they will often be more open and frank in their discussions about the company.

Those companies that do not conduct exit interviews miss out on a great opportunity!

Summary of Interviews

In general, interviews have the following weaknesses:

1. Validity of the interview is relatively low.
2. Reliability of the interview is also low.
3. Stereotyping by interviewers, in general, may lead to adverse impact against minorities.
4. The subjective nature of this procedure may allow bias such as favoritism and politics to enter into the selection process.
5. This procedure is not standardized.
6. Not useful when large numbers of applicants must be evaluated and/or selected.

Principle of Assessment

A wide range of assessment methods may be used in licensure, certification, continuing competence, management and personnel selection and prior learning and recognition (PLAR) programs. The following six key factors should be considered when selecting an assessment methodology.

What is to be Assessed? The competencies or standards to be assessed should be considered when selecting the testing methodology. Different assessment methods have particular strengths for assessing some knowledge, skills and abilities but are not ideal for others. Often, it is best to use a combination of several assessment methods within an assessment program. While this may increase costs, it should increase the reliability and validity of the assessment program and candidate satisfaction.

The Assessment Experience of Candidates: Most of the testing that candidates are likely to encounter is in the context of their education programs, employment selection or in training programs provided by their employer. Individuals who have been working for several years probably have not written a formal examination for some time. This can lead to resistance and the possibility that their performance could be contaminated by their lack of familiarity with the assessment methodology. This issue needs to be carefully considered, and if a traditional formal examination is selected, appropriate practice exercises need to be provided to the candidates.

How Many Candidates are Likely to be Assessed: An important issue in determining the most cost effective means of providing an assessment program is the number of candidates to be assessed. The financial viability of each assessment methodology is substantially influenced by the size of the program.

Cost of the Assessment Tool: Each methodology comes with its own price tag, and the range of costs is wide. Assessment methodologies vary in cost and the information they provide about a candidate's level of competence. Although cost is not the only issue, it is clearly a significant factor and must be considered when evaluating the various methodologies.

Psychometric Properties of the Assessment Instrument: All professional assessment programs should be developed on the foundation of accepted testing standards. Attention to psychometric properties typically focuses on the issues of reliability and validity. In more general terms, it is critical to ascertain that an assessment tool produces consistent scores and that it measures what it was intended to measure. In addition, establishing fair procedures that do not unduly bias against an individual or group should be a primary concern in developing an assessment tool. Fairness refers not only to nondiscriminatory language but also to procedures for dealing with those with disabilities, appeals and feedback to candidates. Every attempt should be made to give the candidate full opportunity to demonstrate their competence. This can be impeded by onerous administrative policies or distracting and inappropriate examination content. Problems concerning fairness are one of the most likely areas for litigation.

Some common and professionally accepted assessment instruments are:

Key Features/Case Study: Key features have gained popularity in the past few years as an assessment method that is well suited to assessing critical thinking skills and applying knowledge.

As a case study or short answer type of assessment, a key feature is in many ways a pencil-and-paper version of a work simulation. The primary difference is that the simulation encountered is described on paper and responses are written rather than oral. The case study development process is a structured activity that is as demanding as designing a work simulation and the development of a reliable and comprehensive scoring key can be complex as well. Each case is fully described and the candidate is asked to indicate how they would proceed in dealing with the situation. Each response is either generated in a short answer format or as a choice made from a long list of possible options. Scoring is standardized such that credit is given for providing the correct elements of the ideal response or for selecting the appropriate choices from the list provided.

Portfolio: A portfolio is an assessment technique that is widely used in educational settings, appears well suited to assessing some aspects of occupational and professional practice and is particularly well suited to evaluating professional development. They are essentially an elaborate résumé, with varying degrees of structure depending on the purpose. A portfolio is created by the candidate and must have certain key elements such as work history, education history, evidence of continuing education, evidence of continuing professional practice, evidence of competence in a designated specialty and so on. The evidence may comprise academic transcripts, letters of reference, written essays and completed questionnaires. It is not unusual for a portfolio to be more than 100 pages long and therefore can be time consuming to create. The onus is on the candidate to provide evidence that will clearly demonstrate that they possess the competencies of interest. This information must be verifiable if the program is to be credible.

Self-Assessment: A self-assessment instrument is an efficient means of evaluating occupational skills in that the candidate answers direct questions about their competence and assessment. Typically, the assessment can be completed quickly and at minimal cost. In general, the self-assessment instrument is in the form of a questionnaire where the candidate simply indicates their level of ability in each competency area on a three to five-point rating scale. A self-assessment has benefit of being able to assess all desired competency areas.

Supervisory Evaluation: A supervisor evaluation is essentially the same technique as self-assessment, except that the supervisor rates the performance (and possibly peers). In this evaluation, each of the identified competencies would be rated for each candidate. There would also likely be global ratings of performance in several key competency areas. Supervisor evaluations are particularly well suited to assessing communication and performance-based skills.

Work Simulation: Work simulations have seen substantial use in recent years. When well designed, they can closely imitate actual work experiences and so provide a direct evaluation of ability.

A typical work simulation is divided into 5 to 15 encounters, each of which may require from 5 to 15 minutes to complete and score. Typically, the candidate is presented with a standardized workplace encounter and is required to perform whatever interventions are necessary. In some simulations, actors play the roles of customers, employers, or co-workers. At least one rater evaluates performance on a pre-established set of criteria. This is often followed by a set of questions designed to evaluate more fully the thought processes that went into the performed actions.

Work simulations are well suited to evaluating direct on-the-job performance and communication skills.

Multiple Choices: Multiple-choice examinations are the most popular tool for assessing competence. This methodology has been well researched, and has a long history. Multiple-choice examinations are generally considered to be the most cost efficient means for assessing a large number of candidates on a large number of competencies.

Most people are familiar with the format of a multiple-choice examination. Typically, a question is posed or a statement is made which the candidate is to respond. The candidate is presented with a set of three, four, or five response options, and is asked to choose the option that best answers the question or statement. Variations to this form of assessment involve presenting the candidate with a problem where they select the most appropriate option(s) from a menu. Multiple-choice items can be independent of other examination content or appear as a set linked by a common body of text or graphic such as a workplace situation or engineering schematic. Generally, at least 150 items are needed to achieve sound psychometric properties (e.g., acceptable reliability and content validity) with occupational examinations.

Multiple-choice examinations are considered to be extremely well suited to assessing knowledge and its applications. There is, however, debate surrounding their ability to assess other aspects of competence such as communication and problem solving.

Personality Tests: A selection procedure measures the personality characteristics of applicants that are related to future job performance. Personality tests typically measure one or more of five personality dimensions: extroversion, emotional stability, agreeableness, conscientiousness, and openness to experience.

Advantages

- Can result in lower turnover if applicants are selected for traits that are highly correlated with employees who have high longevity within the organization.
- Can reveal more information about applicant's abilities and interests.
- Can identify interpersonal traits that may be needed for certain jobs.

Disadvantages

- Difficult to measure personality traits that may not be well defined.
- Applicant's training and experience may have greater impact on job performance than applicant's personality.

- Responses by applicant may be altered by applicant's desire to respond in a way they feel would result in their selection.
- Lack of diversity if all selected applicants have similar personality traits.
- Cost may be prohibitive for both the test and interpretation of results.
- Lack of evidence to support validity of use of personality tests.

Types of Personality Tests

1. **Personal Attribute Inventory:** An interpersonal assessment instrument, which consists of 50 positive and 50 negative adjectives from Gough's Adjective Check List. The subject is to select 30, which are most descriptive of the target group or person in question. This instrument was specifically designed to tap affective reactions and may be used in either assessing attitudes toward others or as a self-concept scale.
2. **Personality Adjective Checklist:** A comprehensive, objective measure of eight personality styles (which are closely aligned with DSM-III-R Axis II constructs). These eight personality styles are: introversive, inhibited, cooperative, sociable, confident, forceful, respectful, and sensitive. This instrument is designed for use with no psychiatric patients and normal adults who read minimally at the eighth grade level. Test reports are computer-generated and are intended for use by qualified professionals only. Interpretive statements are based on empirical data and theoretical inference. They are considered probabilistic in nature and cannot be considered definitive.
3. **Cross Cultural Adaptability Inventory:** Self-scoring six-point rating scale is a training instrument designed to provide feedback to individuals about their potential for cross-cultural effectiveness. It is most effective when used as part of a training program. It can also be used as a team-building tool for culturally diverse work groups and as a counseling tool for people in the process of cross-cultural adjustment. The inventory contains 50 items, distributed among 4 subscales: emotional resilience, flexibility/openness, perceptual acuity, and personal autonomy.

Aptitude Test

These tests measure whether an individual has the capacity or talent to learn a given job if given adequate training. Aptitudes can be divided into general and mental ability or intelligence and specific aptitudes such as mechanical, clerical, manipulative etc.

Intelligence Test: these tests generally measure intelligence quotient of a candidate. In detail these test measure the capacity for comprehension, reasoning, word fluency, verbal comprehension, numbers, memory and space.

Mechanical Aptitude test: these tests measure the capacities of spatial visualization, perceptual speed and knowledge of mechanical matter. These test are useful for selecting skilled mechanical employees or technicians.

Psychomotor Test: these tests measure abilities like manual dexterity, motor ability and eye hand coordination of candidates. These tests are useful to select semi-skilled workers for repetitive operations like packing,ÿ watch assembly.

Clerical Aptitude Test: measure specific capacities involved in office work. Items of this test include spelling, computation, comprehension, copying, word measuring etc.

Induction/Orientation

We are all aware of the implications of poor recruitment decisions. They can cost the company time and money, and they can result in low employee morale, and reduced productivity. One basic step to ensuring that new employees get off to a positive start is to conduct an effective induction programme. Employees who are properly trained and introduced to the company early feel better about their choice of employer and usually fit in more quickly.

Employees join a Company/Organization with the honest intentions of contributing to the best of their ability to the success of the Company. It is therefore in the Company's best interests to seize this opportunity in order to maximize the Employee's contribution by providing the best possible programme of Induction/Orientation and Training from the first day of employment.

Each new Employee has a very strong desire to "Belong" and be accepted as a member of the team in their new place of Employment.

The first day of any new employment is usually preceded by days of mixed feelings including trepidation, anxiety, ambition, inadequacy etc., but most of all desire to be accepted in their new work environment. The Company should strive to satisfy this desire by designing/ implementing an Induction/Orientation and Training programme that meets/exceeds the Employee's expectations while satisfying the goals of the Organization.

Below are some best practice factors to take into consideration when preparing an employee induction programme in an organization.

Involve Others: If the new employee is filling an existing position, in an ideal situation, the person leaving the job will still be there when the new employee starts and will be able to conduct a full handover with them. Given the delays often present in the recruitment process though, this often isn't possible. Instead, ask the person leaving the job to write a series of brief handover notes. As long as they're leaving on good terms, this shouldn't present a problem, and it gives the leaver a chance to tie up loose ends before passing on outstanding work. Include peers, administrative staff, front office employees, management, and others who will be working with new staff members in the induction process by making sure that all are introduced to the new employee and spend some time, however short, with them. Ask someone in the department to take the new employee to lunch on the first day, and ask others to instruct on how to use the phone systems, voicemail, locate stationery supplies and so on. Think about including a tour of work areas as part of the process. This could be anything from a walk around the office, to a visit to a number of company sites involving 'mini-lectures' from different employees.

Create a Mentor System: Appoint a mentor for the first week or first few weeks. This could be a line manager, but it's probably more practical to ask someone who'll be working closely with the new member of staff. Use the mentor system to help new employees become familiar with the overall culture and work ethic of the organization. A mentor system gives the newly recruited employee a person to whom he or she can ask basic questions such as what the dress code is, where the good places to get lunch are, and work-based questions such as how client service questions are handled, and so on. It also gives them someone to turn to if there's a problem. Such a scheme also ensures that others in the firm have an active role in the success of the new employee.

Create a Series of Checklists: of items to cover during the induction process - think about one for the HR representative, one for mentors to use and one for colleagues (the last two should be created with help from the new employees department themselves).

The HR checklist should be used to ensure all essential documents and forms have been brought in and completed by the employee. personal details, bank details for payroll processing, pension applications and benefits paperwork.

Look at the Detail: What's important when putting together an induction process is to think about the detail as well as the 'bigger picture'. Ensure the new employee knows the things they need to know to do their job on a daily basis, as well as providing more 'strategic' information about the company. The more detailed you are in this process, the more you will gain from the long-term effects of a well-prepared programme. Use your policy manual (if you have one) to assist you with the preparation of your orientation process. This will help ensure that you cover all areas that will affect you and your employees.

But don't Forget the 'Bigger Picture': Some of the more difficult information to impart relates to company aims, culture and plans for the future. Often, this is difficult for a new employee to understand until they've been with the company for some time, so consider meeting with them again after a couple of months to make sure that the mission statement you gave them hasn't just been filed away and forgotten about.

Create an Extended Programme: It's difficult for most people to take in the huge amount of information they can be presented with during their first few weeks at work. It's best practice to make sure there is a follow up with each new employee regularly, to keep lines of communication open. An extended induction programme also reassures new employees of the company's commitment to the employee. Newcomers are always under pressure to perform and settle in, and this will keep the door open for any problems that may arise in the first few months of employment. An extended programme shows the company is willing to invest time in an individual's development.

Ask for Feedback from New Employees:. Keep records of the types of questions new employees ask and incorporate them into your checklist. Distribute a questionnaire or ask them for their experiences during the first month or so, and establish which items may require additional clarification. This is a great tool to measure the effectiveness of the induction process and to ensure you have covered all areas that need be addressed.

References and Further Reading

1. Barry Cushway (2001). Human Resource Management. Crest Publishing House. New Delhi.
2. Chaudhari K K (1998). Personnel Management for Executives. Himalaya Publishing House. 1st edition.
3. Randal S. Schuler, Vandral L Huber (1999). Personnel and Human Resource Management. 5th edition. West Publishing Company.
4. Sally Harper (Ed.) (1998). Personnel Management Handbook. A Gower Handbook.
5. www.HR.com
6. www.workfamily.com

4
Motivation at Work Place

The Challenge of Motivation

What makes people work? Why some people perform better than others? Why does the same person act different at times? Perhaps one of the biggest question confronting organizations today is the "peoples" question. Human behavior is the result of motivating process. But how do we motivate employees to achieve the goals of an organization and at the same time satisfy the needs of employees? The managers encounter an interesting problem here. The manager is responsible for completing a task. However a manager alone cannot complete the task. The contributed efforts of his/her subordinates are necessary and vital. How do we get people perform at a higher percent than "normal" percent of their physical and mental capacities and also maintain satisfaction? This is the challenge of motivation. Motivation is an inspirational process of the team which impels the members, to pull their weight effectively, to give their loyalty to the group, to carry out properly the task that they have accepted and generally to play an effective part in the job that the group has undertaken (*M.G. Rao and V.S.P. Rao, 1993)*.

The Meaning of Motivation

Motivation has been variously defined by scholars. "Motivation is a Latin word, meaning to move". Brereton and Steiner states: "A motive is an inner state that energizes, activates or moves and directs or channels behavior towards goals". Lillis observes "It is the stimulation of any emotion or desire operating upon one's will and prompting or driving it to action". According to Durbin, "Motivation is the complex of forces starting and keeping a person at work in an organization" (*C.B. Mamoria, 1997)*.

The Encyclopedia of Management observes, "Motivation refers to the degree of readiness of an organism to pursue some designated goal and implies the determination of the nature and locus of the forces, including the degree of readiness".

Psychologist generally agrees that all behavior is motivated and that people have reasons for doing the things they do or for behaving in the manner that they do.

Motivation consists of the three interacting and interdependent elements of needs, drives and goals.

Needs: These are the deficiencies and are created whenever there is a physiological or psychological imbalance.

Drives or Motives: are set to alleviate needs. These are action-oriented and provide an energizing thrust towards goal accomplishment. They are the very heart of motivational ï3Xprocess.

Goals: is anything which will alleviate a need.

The Nature of Motivation in Organisation

Motivation is described as the set of processes that arouse, direct and maintain human behaviour toward attaining a goal .The following diagram explains it:-

Arousal Direction Maintenance

Arousal is a result of the drive/ urge behind actions. A hungry person is aroused to seek food and a lonely person seeks for company. People in organization have various needs like making money, impressing supervisors and coworkers etc. The drive to satisfy these goals leads to motivation. People choose from different options one or more which give direction to their behavior for attaining the goal e.g. a hungry person may go to a hotel or just have a sandwich.

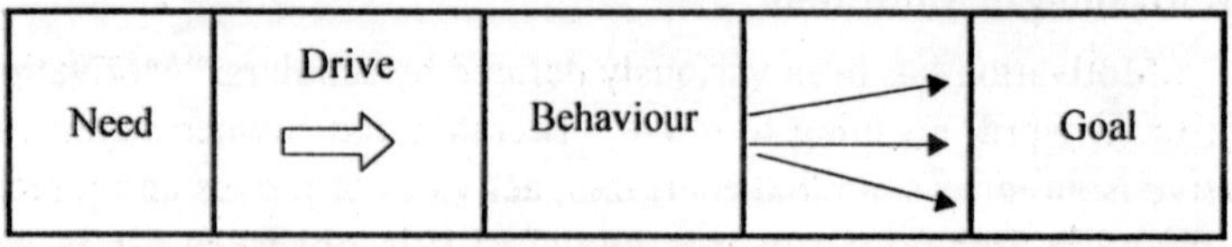

Diagram 1.1

People who are motivated maintain their action towards meeting the goal and don't give up on the way. So motivation requires 3 important components of arousal, direction, and maintenance of goal-directed behavior.

Motivation and job performance are not same. It is one important aspect of job performance. Motivation is also multifaceted i.e. several motives may operate at the same time (Baron *Robert A. and Greenberg. Jerald, 1990)*.

Five Critical Concepts in Motivation

1. **Behavior:** Behavior is the action from which we infer motivation. The behavior in question may be the typing speed, firing a rifle at a target or any of a broad constellation of human activities.
2. **Performance:** Performance is some evaluation of behavior. 60 words per minute might represent adequate performance in some jobs and inadequate performance in others. Most theories tend to be concerned with performance, not just behavior.
3. **Ability:** Ability is one important aspect. It is regarded to be fairly stable within individuals.
4. **Situational Constraints:** There is some things beyond control they are environmental factors and opportunities that facilitate or retard behavior. e.g. tools, production, etc.
5. **Motivation:** Motivation is what you will do. This leads to performance (*Paul M. Muchinsky, 1999)*

Work Motivation Theories

Theories are basic frameworks for explaining a concept. Motivation theories are classifieds as follows –

I. Need Theories.

II. Goal Setting Theory.

III. Equity Theory.

IV. Expectancy Theory.

V. Reinforcement Theory.

Need Theory: The basic theories of motivation emphasise on human needs. Following are the need theories:

Maslow's Need Hierarchy Theory. Maslow a clinical psychologist observed his patients for years and on that basis introduced a theory of personal adjustment. He proposed that healthy, well adjusted individuals grow up in an environment where their needs are met and so can function well. His approach became popular as it could be applied to organizations .It means that people who function effectively have been able to meet their needs on the job. He theorized that people have five types of needs which are activated in a hierarchical manner. The needs are aroused from the lowest to the highest in a specific order. The need order is as follows:

Physiological Needs: These are the lowest order needs which are most basic and biological in nature like for food, air, water and shelter. Proper and adequate salary to afford adequate living conditions (e.g. food and shelter), sufficient rest breaks in job can help people to satisfy their physiological needs. Organizations provide exercise and physical fitness programs for their employees.

Safety Needs: These needs start operating after physiological needs are satisfied. Safety needs are both physiological and psychological. One should be free from threats of physical or psychological harm. Life and health insurance plans, payroll savings, security forces, like police, Fire Protection staffs etc are provided by organization to the employees who help to satisfy safety needs. No-lay off agreement increases psychological safety.

Social Needs: These are the needs of love and belongingness, affiliation, acceptance, and love by others. Participation in social activities like parties, sports, club membership encouraged by organization helps in satisfying such needs.

Esteem Needs: A person needs to develop self-respect, to gain approval from others to achieve success and to have prestige.

Organizations satisfy such needs by recognizing achievements of employees by giving perks, describing success in newsletters etc.

Self-Actualization Needs: They are needs of self-fulfillment – the desire to make the best. Such employees are assets to their organization as they work at their peak and indicate that organization's human resources are most effectively used.

Alderfer's ERG Theory: Clayton Alderfer proposed that there are only three types of needs which need not be necessarily aroused in any specific hierarchical order. Any need can start operating at any time. The three needs are Existence, Relatedness, and Growth. This theory is more flexible than Maslow's. Many theorists don't agree about the exact number of existing needs and their relationship but agree that satisfaction of human needs on jobs can motivate people.

A Comparision

Need Theories: Goal Setting Theory: People are motivated to satisfy their needs on the job and to strive for and attain goals. The process of setting goals can motivate people very strongly in organizations. Locke and Latham in their model of goal setting propose that an assigned goal influences a person's beliefs about being able to perform the task and his/her personal goals. Both the factors then influence performance.

According to the theory the goal serves as a motivator because people compare their capacity to perform with that required to achieve the goal. If they believe that they fall short of a goal, they will feel dissatisfied and will work harder to attain the goal as long as they believe that the goal is possible. Performance increases as goal clarifies the type and level of performance expected and provides information about how well one is performing a task. People accept assigned goals and personal goals. Klein's research supports this. The model also claims that beliefs both about self efficacy and personal goals influence task performance. The belief that one is capable of succeeding leads to willingness to put in more effort and it guides behavior. Several studies support this model.

Equity Theory: J. Stacy Adams proposed this theory; he says that people make social comparisons between themselves and others with respect two variables- outcomes and inputs.

Outcomes: *Things workers believe that they and others get out of their job like pay, fringe benefits and prestige.*

Inputs: *Contribution employees believe they and others make to their jobs like the amount of time worked, the amount of effort put in, the number of units produced and qualification brought on the job.*

It is the perception of the employees of their inputs and outcomes which may not be real. The theory states the comparison made by people of their outcomes and inputs to those of others is the three states of overpayment, underpayment, or equitable payment.

Overpayment inequity*:* occurs when someone's outcome/ input is greater than the corresponding ratio of another person with whom that person compares him/herself. Theory states that overpaid people feel guilty.

Underpayment inequity: Occurs when someone's outcome/ input are less than the corresponding ratio of another person with whom that person compares him / herself. Theory states that underpaid people feel angry.

Equitable Payment: occurs when someone's output/input ratio is equal to the correspondent ratio of another person with whom that person compares him / herself. Theory states that equitability paid people feel satisfied.

The theory states that people are motivated to escape from negative feelings of anger and guilt. Research has generally supported this theory. Practical implications of this theory are that to motivate people under payment should be avoided as it may lead to counter productive behavior. Overpayment should be avoided as the results of improved performance may treat all the employees equitably. So must try to present information about outcomes and inputs in a socially sensitive manner and to be open and honest about it.

Expectancy Theory: It views motivation as part of the overall working environment so it is broadest in its scope. It states that peoples expectations that they will be able to achieve the things they want from the job leads to motivation. Vroom, Porter and Lawler did the pioneering work. The theory specifies that people have three kinds of beliefs that motivate them.

1. **Expectancy**: The belief that one's effort will result in performance.
2. **Instrumentality:** The belief that one's performance will be rewarded.
3. **Valence:** The perceived value of the rewards to the recipient.

Employees may have low expectancy or high expectancy. Low expectancy might lead to not continuing to put more effort. Motivation may be low even with hard work and high level of performance if employees perceive that performance won't be instrumental in getting reward. Motivation may be poor even when employees receive award based on their performance and the reward has a low valence (value) to them. Any reward in cash or kind can increase motivation if it is valued. Motivation will be high when valence, instrumentality and expectancy are all high than when they are low. Research supports the effect of expectancy and instrumentality on motivation but not the contribution of valence.

Reinforcement Theory: This is one of the older approaches to motivation. Also referred to as operant conditioning and behaviorism, this theory has its origins in B.F. Skinner's work of the conditioning of the animals. The theory has three main variables: stimulus, response, and reward. A *stimulus* is any variable that elicits a behavior response. A *response* in industrial setting refers to the job performance like productivity, absenteeism, or accidents. A *reward* is some thing of value given to the employee on the basis of the elicited behavioral response; that is to reinforce the desired response. Most attention should be given to the response-reward connection, the four types of response –reward connections are as follows:

- **Fixed Interval:** the person is rewarded after a fixed time interval, e.g. such as every hour.
- **Fixed Ratio**: the person is rewarded for a fixed number of responses, e.g. a salesman is rewarded after each sale he makes, this is said to be continuous reward schedule.
- **Variable Interval**: the person is rewarded at some time interval that varies.
- **Variable Ratio:** Reward is based on behavior, but the ratio of reward to response is variable, e.g. a salesman might sometimes be paid after each sale and other times after two or three sales.

Advocates of this theory believe that the subject's motivation to respond can be shaped by manipulating these reinforcement schedules. The use of this theory has both supporters and detractors. It has wide applicability for problem solving. Its uses include reducing absence and turnover, enhancing productivity, and improving supervisory training. Unlike other theories its focus is not on the individual but on the environmental factors that shape or modify behavior (Paul M. Muchinsky, 1999).

Techniques for Enhancing Motivation

Creation of jobs that will motivate people is very important. The efforts of the management should be directed at changing the very nature of the job performed. Job design helps to enhance motivation by making the jobs more attractive to employees. Fredrick Taylor in the early part of century tried to increase productivity by discovering the most efficient ways of performing work with the help of analysis of motions involved in the job. This approach of scientific management aimed at making work highly efficient. But resulted in many jobs highly routine and resulting to people remaining absent or quitting.

Some of the approaches which are more human and more effective are as follows-

Job Enlargement: Job Enlargement means expansion of the content of a job by increasing the number of different tasks performed at the same level e.g. the cashier who operates the cash register can be instructed to change prices on sale goods on the shelves when there are no customers checking out. So he would be required to perform a greater number of tasks at the same low level of difficulty required very little responsibility. This is called horizontal job loading. But all the tasks provide an identical level of responsibility.

Job Enrichment: In this employees do more jobs and also at higher level. Employees get the opportunity to have greater responsibility and greater control over how to do their jobs. This process of job enrichment increases the job's greater control over how to do their jobs. This process of job enrichment increases the job's vertical loading. Fredrick Herzberg developed this idea of job enrichment.

Job enlargement and enrichment programs are reported as often effective, but without sufficient scientific evidence. Following are some of the difficulties in establishing them.

(a) **Difficulty of Implementation**: Redesigning jobs require redesigning of existing physical plants which can be quite costly. To perform the jobs differently might be difficult because of the required technology by some jobs.

(b) **Lack of Acceptance**: Job enrichment is not for every one. All employees don't like the added responsibility which goes along with job enrichment. Studies show that people who have a high need for achievement work harder at job enrichment. Other feels frustrated and dissatisfied.

B. The Job Characteristics Model: People want more out of job than pay. They want a feeling of input importance. The model helps to understand as to how jobs can be designed to give that feeling to the employees. The model identifies the following five core job dimensions-

(i) **Skill Variety:** It is the extent to which a job requires a number of activities using several of the employee's skill and talents.

(ii) **Task Identity:** It is the extent to which a job requires to finish a whole piece of work from the start to the end.

(iii) **Task Significance:** It is the degree of job impact the job is believed to have on other people either within the organization or in the world at large.

The above three contribute to task's experienced meaningfulness. A task is considered meaningful if it is experienced as meaningful if it is experienced as important, valuable and worthwhile.

(iv) **Autonomy:** It is the extent to which an employee has the freedom and discretion to plan, schedule and carry out the job as desired. It makes workers feel personally responsible and accountable for the work he/she performs and for the results good or bad.

(v) **Feedback:** It is the extent to which a job allows people to have information about the effective feedback which can improve the effectiveness of job performance.

Job Diagnostic Survey a questionnaire was developed to measure the degrees to which different job characteristics are present in a particular job. Responses help to predict the degree to which a job motivates the people who perform it. So an index MPS- Motivational Potential Score is computed as follows-

MPS = Skill Variety + Task Identity + Task Significance × Autonomy × Feedback 3

The higher MPS for a given job indicates the more chances of experiencing beneficial personal and work outcomes. This index can help identification of jobs to be redesigned to be beneficial. The model specifies following ways to redesign jobs to improve motivation and performance.

Motivation also requires discovering and understanding employee drives and needs, since it originates within an individual. Positive acts performed for the organization-such as creating customer satisfaction through personalized service-need to be reinforced. And employees will be more motivated when they have clear goals to achieve.

A. Model of Motivation

The role of motivation in performance is summarized in the model of motivation. Internal needs and drives create tensions that are affected by one's environment. For example the need for food produces a tension of hunger. The hungry person then examines the surroundings to see which foods (external incentives) are available to satisfy that hunger. Since environment affects one's appetite for particular kinds of food. A South Seas native may want roast fish, while a Colorado rancher may prefer broiled steak. Both persons are ready to achieve their goals, but they will seek different foods to satisfy their needs. This is an example of both individual differences and cultural influences in action.

Potential performance (P) is a ($P=A\times M$) Product of ability (A) and motivation (M). Results occur when motivated employees are provided with the opportunity (such as the proper training) to perform and the resources (such as the proper tools) to do so. The presence of goals and the awareness of incentives to satisfy one's needs are also powerful motivational factors leading to the release of effort. When an employee is productive and the organization takes note of it, rewards will be distributed. If those rewards are appropriate in nature, timing, and distribution, the employee's original needs and drives are satisfied. At that time, new needs may emerge and cycle will begin again.

	Principle of Job Design Core Job Dimensions Incorporated	
1.	Combine jobs, enabling workers to Skill Variety perform the entire job. Task Identity.	
2.	Form natural work units, allowing Task Identity. workers to be identified with their Task Significance work.	
3.	Establish client relationships, Skill Variety allowing providers of a service Autonomy to meet the recipients. Feedback.	
4.	Load job vertically, allowing greater Autonomy responsibility and control over work.	
5.	Open feedback channels, giving Feedback workers knowledge of the results of their work.	

Motivational Drives

People tend to develop certain motivational drives as a product of the cultural environment in which they live, and these drives affect the way people view their jobs and approach their lives. Much of the interests in these patterns of motivation were generated by the research of David C. McClelland of Harvard University. He developed a classification scheme highlighting three of the more dominant drives and pointed out their significance to motivation. McClelland's research focused on the drives for achievement, affiliation, and power. An addition to these three is the competence drive which is an important factor in current attempts to attain high quality products and services.

Achievement Motivation

Achievement Motivation is a drive some people have to pursue and attain goals. An individual with this drive wishes to achieve objectives and advance up the ladder of success. Accomplishment is seen as important primarily for its own sake, not just for the rewards that accompany it.

A number of characteristics define achievement-oriented employees. They work harder when they perceive that they will receive personal credit for their efforts, when there is only moderate risk of failure, and when they receive specific feedback about their past performance. As managers, they tend to expect that their employees will also be oriented toward achievement. These high expectations sometimes make it difficult for achievement-oriented managers to delegate effectively, and for "average" employees to satisfy their manager's demands

Affilation Motivation

Affiliation motivation is a drive to relate to people on a social basis. Comparisons of achievement-motivated employees with affiliation-motivated employees, illustrate how the two patterns influence behavior. Achievement-oriented people work harder when their supervisors provide detailed evaluations of their work behavior. But people with affiliation motives work better when they are complimented for their favorable attitudes and cooperation. Achievement-motivated people select assistants who are technically capable with little regard for personal feelings about them; those who are affiliation motivated tend to select friends to surround them. They receive inner satisfactions from being with friends, and they want the job freedom to develop those relationships.

Managers with strong needs for affiliation may have difficulty being effective managers. Although a high concern for positive social relationships usually results in a cooperative work environment where employees genuinely enjoy working together, managerial overemphasis on the social dimension may interfere with the usual process of getting things done. Affiliation-oriented managers may have difficulty assigning challenging tasks, directing work activities, and monitoring work effectiveness.

Competence Motivation

Competence motivation is a drive to be good at something the individual wishes to perform high-quality work. Competence-motivated employees seek job mastery, take pride in developing and using their problem-solving skills, and strive to be creative when confronted with obstacles to their work most important, they profit from their experiences and continually improve their skills. In general, they tend to perform their jobs capably because of the inner satisfaction they feel from doing a job well and the esteem they gain from others who notice their work.

Competence-motivated people also expect high –quality work from their associates and may become impatient if those working with them or for them do poor work.

Power Motivation

Power motivation is a drive to influence people and change situations. Power-motivated people wish to create an impact on their organizations and are willing to take risks to do so. Once this power is obtained, it may be used either constructively or destructively.

Power-motivated people make excellent managers if their drives are for institutional power instead of personal power. *Institutional power* is the need to influence others' behavior for the good of the whole organization. People with this need seek power through legitimate means, rise to leadership positions through successful performance, and therefore are accepted by others. However, if an employee's drives are toward personal power, that person tends to be an unsuccessful organizational leader.

Managerial Application of the Drives

Knowledge of the difference among the four motivational drives requires managers to understand the work attitudes of each employee. They can then deal with employees differently according to the strongest motivational drive that they identify in each employee. For example, an achievement-motivated employee can be assigned a job accompanied by an explanation of its challenges. A competence-motivated employee could be assigned a similar job with emphasis on its requirements for high –quality work.

Practical Implications of Motivational Models

1. Identify each employee's needs and drives and how they change over time.
2. Reduce the distracting influence of hygiene factors before turning your attentions to providing motivators.
3. Establish strong connections between desired behaviors and rewards given; provide rewards that recognize high achievers

more that other employees; administer rewards on a systematic basis.

4. Set performance oriented goals that are specific, challenging, and acceptable.
5. Seek information regarding employee perception of valence, expectancy, and instrumentality; share key information with employee's to improve their assessment.
6. Discover the referent people or groups and perceived outcome/ input ratios for employees equity; compare your assessment of likely equity with theirs.
7. Monitor your own attributions for employee behaviors; seek to avoid the fundamental attribution bias.

Motivation and Work

People work for various reasons, sometimes for a combination of reasons and sometimes for different reasons at different times. In India, the vast majority of people work for money, for livelihood and maintenance of the family. Those who get beyond the stage of "making the two ends meet", may work for gaining good social status or position, to further professional attainment, freedom, challenge and variety in jobs and even for the interest in the job itself. The reasons for work at various stages of working life may also change.

Money or pay is the means to survival and livelihood. It also serves as a means to social position, prestige, status, power, security and fulfilling individual pursuits like philanthrohy, religious or missionary activities, recreational and outdoor activities and the like. Thus money, in the form of pay or earnings, gets inseparably connected with needs and motives of all sorts.

In "working class" pay is the major concern with people working at all levels in organizations. But the commonly held belief on the part of the employers that money is the only concern or demand of employees is a fallacious one,. It is pertinent to believe that everyone in the hierarchy of organizations, including the workmen does have self-respect, and expect fair and human treatment. When self-respect is violated and all the other human aspects are ignored, it is only natural that pay, even good pay at that can bring about only partial motivation and often a good deal of discontent and/or apathy along with it.

Internal and External Motivation

External incentives such as pay, praise and reprimands (in various forms) are frequently offered to employees by employers. Studies have shown that they are somewhat less successful at least in the long run, than incentives which motivate people internally. External motivation stimulated by pay, praise or punishment can be effective only if it corresponds to the internal needs of the person. Internal motivation starts from the social and psychological or ego needs of the person. The status and prestige attached to the job, self-respect, a sense of accomplishment in doing a job well, sense of belonging with the work group or the organization are instances of internal motivation.

It seems clear that motivation cannot be totally effective merely by the application of external praise or punishment. Whether the incentives offered by industry will be effective or not depends more on the internal state of the employee, his level of aspiration on his role, perception, his nature of interaction with other people and his perception of and relationship with the environment in which he is operating.

Kinds of Incentives

Incentives may be classified "financial" and "non-financial", but it seems more desirable to classify them as "competitive" and "co-operative". In both education and industry, the values of incentives based upon co-operation are beginning to be realized. Organizing people into meaningful groups and having them work together towards a common goal results in more learning at the educational level and greater production at the industrial level.

The term incentive is used for a spurring force that is introduced as a means of achieving a goal. An incentive bolsters activity in the direction of the goal. An individual may introduce his own incentives, in which case they are extremely meaningful. However, in industry, the incentive is often used as a means of spurring on an employee towards someone else's goal. He may not be interested in either reduced costs or increased production, but he may be persuaded to achieve this goal by an incentive. When the incentive results in satisfaction for the employee and the achievement of the goal results in equal satisfaction for the employer, the plant is being successfully operated. The major difficulty with financial incentives has been the fact that the additional money has not meant as much to the employee as the employer assumed it would. The outstanding reason for employee objections to such plans has been the fear of a rate cut. There is also the fear of a layoff, and so the worker does not respond to the magic of a financial incentive to the extent that its proponents would have us believe.

Both competition and co-operation may be regarded as incentives. Competition calls for one individual to do better than the next individual. Co-operation calls for people to contribute equal and maximum efforts towards common goal. Competition and co-operation are not mutually exclusive, especially when individuals co-operate in groups to compete with other groups. Industry in the past has placed too much emphasis upon competition; only recently have the advantages of co-operative behavior as an incentive been recognized. The use of co-operation as an incentive holds considerable promise of success.

The Role of Incentives

One of the inescapable responsibilities of management is the establishment of incentives for employees. Although pay in some form is an important incentive, there are other forms as well that are operative in the industrial setting. The incentives can be either formal or informal, either positive or negative

Formal Incentive Positive: money, bonuses, promotions, awards, formal commendations, special privileges (membership in clubs, officer's dining room privilege, special parking locations etc) choice of work schedule.

Negative: Reprimand, disciplinary actions, demotions, layoffs, discharges, withholding or withdrawal of privileges,

Informal Incentives Positive: Praise, encouragement, friendly attitudes by others, acceptance by group, minimum supervision, respect by management and fellow workers;

Negative: disapproval and rejection by others, criticism, assignment to more onerous job, lack of work co-operation by fellows, being "picked on" by supervisors and fellow workers.

The importance of incentives in industry cannot be overemphasized. It is a well substantiated principle that behavior that is "rewarded" will tend to be repeated and that behavior that is unrewarded (or punished) will tend to be eliminated. Thus, the "reward" system-formal or informal-should be so tuned that good work performance is somehow recognized and rewarded. It is in part through the system of rewards and punishment that intentionally or not management influences the behavior of people in the organization. A research carried out on incentives conducted by Blum and Russ (1942) attempted to determine its importance.

For example: (1) The need that money satisfies; (2) Methods of pay and the values they create, etc. The other important factors concerning motivation are promotion, verbal recognition, competition, praise and punishment and achievement.

Important Incentives

The important motives of Indian workers and supervisors as found by Ganguli are adequate income, job security, opportunity for promotion, recognition, opportunity to learn a job, have further training, and a good and sympathetic superior. These motives are stimulated by the incentives of pay, various ways of assuring security, co-operation, reward and punishment system, training facilities, and congenial working relationship with supervisors.

Limitation to Motivation

While motivation is intended to be a general explanation for behavior, it is not sufficient to explain all behavior. There are a number of variables that do not easily fit within the motivation framework. In certain cases, these factors can affect the relevance.

Motivation and Ability

A common assumption of psychologists is that performance is a function of both motivation and ability. This means that in order to successfully perform a task, one must both be motivated to perform the task and have the skills, knowledge, experience, and so forth to perform. If either factor is lacking, successful performance is unlikely. Let's assume that the interns are all highly motivated to do their jobs well. Their poor performance then might be due to an inability to perform the required tasks. They might be expected, for example, to analyze data from marketing research, yet the college programs from which they are selected may not offer the necessary statistics course.

The students seem to be uninterested in their work, and are not putting much effort into their jobs. Although this may seem to be a clear-cut case of poor motivation, it is possible that once the interns discovered that they lacked the skills to perform the job, they saw further effort as being futile. The solution would, in this case, involve improving selection or training procedures, rather than trying to increase motivation.

Individual Differences In Motives

One important way in which people differ from one another is in terms of the goals they pursue. If everyone was motivated to achieve the same goals, managers would have a much easier time getting workers to do what they wanted them to do. The fact that workers have different goals means that efforts to increase the motivation of one worker may have no effect, or even a negative effect, on another worker's motivation. Further, if management makes incorrect assumptions about the worker's goals, efforts to increase motivation may be useless.

Motivation as An Inferred State

Many of the behaviors that I/O psychologists study are more – or – less objective; they can be measured in fairly (although not absolutely) unambiguous ways. Productivity, turnover and absenteeism are some examples. Other variables, however, are not so clear – cut. Motivation is a psychological state of the individual worker. While it may have an effect on people's observable behavior, it is not the same as that behavior. Since we cannot observe motivation directly, we must infer it from our observation of the behavior that we can see.

The Dynamic Nature of Motives

The factors that motivate workers do change, and when this happens managers can find themselves out of touch which their workers needs, and unable to motivate them with the technique that worked in the past.

Stereotypes

Understanding worker motivation is made more difficult by the fact that everyone holds stereotypical views about what motivates people. McCormick and Ilgen (1980) described general stereotypes about motivation. The first of these they called "trait" stereotype. This is a belief that motivation is a characteristic of individual workers, and that some people have more of it than others. People who hold this stereotype are likely to believe that the only way to improve work motivation is to replace the workers you have with more highly motivated people. Motivation thus becomes a selection problem.

The second stereotype is an "external-state" view of motivation. This approach stresses the working conditions and the nature of the supervision, pay, and other aspects of the job that assumed to have an effect on worker motivation.

Characteristic Features of Motivation

1. **Motivation is Internal to Person:** Motivation is an internal feeling. It is psychologically generated behavior which forces a person to action.
2. **Motivation is An Ongoing Process:** Motivation is a continuous activity that goes on endlessly because needs and desires are many. One need may give rise to the other. They are numerous and motivate person for their satisfaction.
3. **Motivation varies from Person to Person and Time to Time:** Motivation is different for different persons and it also varies according to time and place because wants are different for different people, times and places. Moreover, motivation is a psychological phenomenon and it is difficult to make clear assessment as to what exactly is the cause of motivation.
4. **Motivation May be Positive or Negative:** Positive motivation is based on incentives or reward as pointed out by Edwin B.Flippo that, "positive motivation is a process of attempting to influence others to do your will through the possibility of gain or reward." This incentive may be in the form of monetary or non-monetary. People can be motivated by praising them or giving them respect or by giving them authority and recognizing their contribution and seeking participation from them. Competition is another factor which will motivate them to work more than their fellow employees to show their superiority.

   Negative motivation is based on penalties, calling for explanation threats, fear etc.

Fear of losing job or promotion, pay deduction causes employee to work more. These reasons push him towards work. Negative motivation if used frequently may create disloyalty and non-cooperation which may in turn result in low performance.

A person is also motivated if he is given fringe benefits, medical facilities, facilities for education of employee's children, housing accommodation, holidays and vacation, retirement benefits etc. Training and development is also a cause of motivation.

General Guidelines for Motivation

The following are the guidelines for motivating the human resources of an organization.

1. The organization must consider human resources as the most valuable asset of all the assets and treat them with respect and honor.
2. There should be good and quality working conditions at the plant, factory and office.
3. Safety and health must be given top priority.
4. There should be adequate and fair salary structure enabling the employees to maintain a good standard of living.
5. Provide them with job security and enough opportunities to move forward i.e. career advancement.
6. Superiors should not forget to shower praise on their subordinates as and when they perform well and achieve the target in due course of time.
7. Equip the employees and subordinates with adequate tools and equipment to perform their job effectively.
8. Superiors should let the subordinates know about their own performance through proper feedback system.
9. Try to win the confidence of the employees bestowing upon them that you care for them.
10. The employee should be provided with opportunities to show their skills and creative instincts in work performance through giving them more freedom, encouraging their participation, MBO, maintaining high morale.
11. Nurture the habit of honoring individual liberty of others at the workplace and off the workplace.

12. Follow the principle of natural justice in handling any grievance or problem of employees. Give full liberty to express them.
13. Be soft spoken. Abstain from abusive language. Use of harsh words and abusive language will throw you miles away from their hearts.
14. Provide adequate training to develop skills and creative abilities of the employees and executives. Training and development programmes should form a part of organization's most sought after activities
15 Superior must provide counseling service to their employees and subordinates. It will keep their morale high and increase their efficiency.
16. Management must encourage employee participation because employees are prepared to accept responsibility and show results. It is rather a difficult exercise because no one seems to be interested in participative management in our country
17. The manager must use appropriate techniques to bring about change in behavioral patterns.

Important Function of Motivation

1. Motivation is an important function of human resource management and receives increased attention by managers, academicians and research Scholars. It is because organizational objectives are to be achieved through human resources and therefore they are to be motivated.
2. Motivation is the force which creates will to work among human resources. They can then put their best efforts and get the work done. Will to work and capacity to work are put together through motivation. Productivity of employees increase.
3. Motivation makes an employee quality conscious. A motivated employee works for extra hours to put his better performance and try to give more output than before and that too of a good quality. Organization gains immensely getting recognition as quality conscious organization.
4. Motivated employees work together with zeal and put their best efforts to attain the organizational objectives. They follow all the policies and procedures laid down by the enterprise. Working

together and understanding the policies of the organization better reduce the labour problems such as absenteeism, labour turnover, indiscipline etc.

5. Motivation provides a basis for coordination. People work together, cooperate with each other and this leads to coordination of activities of different sections and departments.

6. Motivated employees try to remain with the organization. They become loyal to it. Others who are outside the organization join it and above all they engage themselves in doing something creative. Motivations change their behavioral pattern. They try to improve their knowledge and skill and put their best contribution to the organization. It helps them satisfying their needs.

7. Motivated employees gladly accept organizational changes which are essential to cope up with the changes taking place in the fields of science and technology, economy and society. They do not resist change and it becomes easier for the organization to implement any change and precede with organizational development programmers. All this helps organization to put a better image.

8. Motivation is a complex phenomenon and manager must understand it along with the typical behavior of the employees and workers at the workplace. He should closely watch the reactions of the employees after providing certain incentives to them as they relate to the performance and job satisfaction.

9. Managers paying attention to motivation also means that increasing importance is given to human resource management. This attention comes from the top management of the organization. (A.M.Sheikh, 1999)

Recent Research

Husain, Akbar and Khan Mohd Ilyas (AMU Aligarh) in the Journal of community guidance and Research, 2001, 18(1), 17-24, focuses on the motivational factors of rural development. Personnel motivation being the driving force is required for the success of any activity. Particularly in a rural setting there is a positive relationship between motivation of personnel's and rural development. Motivational factors include individual needs. Besides these the strengths and capabilities are important components. However it has been argued that teaching them the long-term perspectives of their work can enhance achievement motivation of development personnel. (Indian Psychological Abstracts and Reviews Vol-9 No1 January-June 2002).

A study (Elvira, Marata M. "Pay me now or pay me later", Analyzing the relationship between bonus and promotion incentives, Work and Occupational Journal, 2001(August) Vol- 28 (3), 346-370) addressed the relationship between bonuses and promotions. The author tests whether these incentives are traded off, reflecting a balance between insurance and incentive provisions in employment contracts. Analyses of data for 8,549 employees of a financial firm support no trade off. Individuals who earn bonuses are more likely to be promoted than those paid on a salary basis after controlling for performance. This finding holds across different occupations and is especially strong for managers, because employees in higher levels benefit most from multiple rewards, power explanations best describe the incentives mix observed here.

According to Mael, Fred A.; Waldman, David A. and Mulqueen, Casey, Movement into Management is often difficult for the technical or scientific employee who may lack the motivation needed to succeed in management. The present study identified specific motivational factors that distinguish those individuals who aspire to management from those who do not. An intranet survey study completed by 256 employees with all scientific research institute, showed that those who aspire to enter management tend to have higher motivation for power and influence, desire for upward mobility, motivation for security and respect and need for dominance. The authors discuss how these findings can inform human resource and organization strategies for dealing with technical personnel who wish to enter management position (Journal of Vocational Behavior, 2001, August).

Martin, James E and Sinclair Robert R. in Journal of Organization Behavior 2001 (June) Vol-22(4), 387-40) attempts to study strike propensities which refer to the extent to which union members are willing to engage in strikes. The present paper identifies 4 motivational explanations for individual propensity to strike-social exchange relationship between member and union, and member and company economic circumstances and social status. These 4 models complement each other and together permit substantial integration of previous literature. While the economic model explained the most variance in the strike propensity, each model accounted for a significant account of unique variation in the members strike propensities. The authors present organizational frame work of the motivational explanations of strike propensity into 4 distinct but complementary motivational models (Psychological Abstracts -88-No7-8, 2001).

Allen, David G. and Griffith, Rodger W. tested a mediated performance- turnover relationship highlighting the moderating roles of visibility and reward contingency. Despite the importance of understanding the conditions under which high performing employees are more likely or less likely to voluntarily leave an organization. The nature of relationship between job performance and voluntary turnover has proven to be elusive. A model of performance-turnover relationship that highlights important moderators and mediators is proposed and tested. Data consisted of organization performance and turnover records and survey responses for 130 employees of a medical services organization results indicate the visibility and reward contingencies, moderate performance relationship with alternatives and job satisfaction respectively and that performance may influence turnover through multiple mechanisms (Journal of Applied Psychology, 2001 (Oct) Vol-86(3) 1041-1021).

A Study on Motivation

The Objectives of the study was to identify the level of motivation among the women telephone operators of M.T.N.L. Company.

Sample: 50 women telephone operators engaged in providing help to the subscribers. A random sampling method was used, before which a stress management programme was conducted to build a rapport and the subjects could feel comfortable in the rest of the process and cooperate.The sample was requested to give honest answers. The jobs performed by the operators are providing directory service, giving alarm, updating and providing information about the changed telephone numbers. The age range is between 35-60 years. These operators are supervised by their supervisors.

The test used is the MAO – B to identify the motivation level among the operators.

Motivational Analysis of Organization–Behavior was developed by Pareek (1987). It was developed to study the behavior in an organization. MAO-B contains of 60 items, 5 for each dimension (approach and avoidance), and for each of the 6 motives: Achievement, Affiliation, Extension, Influence, Control and Dependency.

1. **Achievement (A):** The need to excel, to take up challenges and to do unique things. Excess of this may lead to over- competitive tendency and even go to the extent to put down the person.
2. **Influence (I):**The need to use power to have an impact on people or events. People may use this for self recognition.
3. **Control (C):** The need to direct and control the events and people. The person tends to be very suspicious of people and events that are not in control. They may not give may give freedom to act on their own will.
4. **Extention (E):** The need to relate to others, helps and serves others. They may tend to be over-sympathetic to others and make people depend on them.
5. **Affiliation (A):** The need to establish close and personal relationships. This might tend to a need to belong and the person will do anything to belong to the group. Need for acceptance is high and they constantly need support. Such people however can work in teams.

The behavior of an employee or a manager can be explained in terms of the six motives but it can be analyzed more accurately from the perspective of (positive) approach or (negative) avoidance, reflected by hope for success or fear of failure.

According to Pareek, achievement, expert power and extension motives promote effective performance. On the other hand, control, dependence and affiliation reduce chances of effectiveness.

The organization must use effective and advance techniques to develop the motives which are for the growth and development of the employees and for the organization at large.

Conclusion And Implications

"Achievement" having been found at the first place should be an eye opener for M.T.N.L. It indicates that majority of the telephone operators are concerned to bring excellence in their work behavior. They are concerned to bring excellence in their work behavior by

M.T.N.L. This is a positive aspect for the growth and development of M.T.N.L. The management should encourage the operators to maintain this motive and if possible try and increase this motive.

The fact that "dependence" is the second highest motive for the group of telephone operators gives a hint towards the readiness, eagerness and desire of the telephone operators to receive help of others in their own work. This would imply that other counterparts of the organization are to be monitored and counseled to perform their role effectively in order that the telephone operators perform their role effectively and the productivity of M.T.N.L increases. This factor to a very large extent can have negative aspects also. So the management must spot this quickly because it can affect the effectiveness of the organization.

"Extension" motive having been as the third highest motive, the organization must put forth strategies to enhance interest to meet super-ordinate goals. The management should stress on developing a sense of extension in the organization.

"Control" having been found at the fourth place. They are little concerned with orderliness and have little urge to monitor and take corrective action in relation to their work, when needed. This can be increased by developing strategies to give importance to the ideas given by the telephone operators in regard to bringing improvements in their work.

"Affiliation" has been found on the fifth place, the telephone operators have less concern to build personal relationship. So M.T.N.L must plan strategies and provide them opportunities for establishing and maintaining close personal relationship in their peer groups and with their assistants. Lack of such relationship between the telephone operators and their assistants may result to inefficiency.

"Influence" having been found at the sixth place or the lowest motive, indicates urge and concern in the telephone operators for making an impact on their co-workers. This can easily be done by the organization by listening to the telephone operators and actions to be taken on their ideas.

The research gives an insight into the area of modification for the telephone operators of M.T.N.L.

Recommendations

How to Motivate Your Subordinates: Below are 18 positive suggestions for improving your own capacity to motivate their subordinates; each one should be integrated into your day-to-day behavior.

1. Know Your Standards, Communicate Them, and be Consistent: When an individual knows he is being evaluated according to single, fair standard, he has a target to shoot for. He can modify his performance accordingly and try to meet that standard. If your standards are multiple, unfair, or erratic, then employees will try to beat the game. The very least that fair standards will do is minimize misdirected efforts. However, standards usually also tell your people just what is expected of them. No one wants to work without an objective.

Part of a standard's effectiveness comes in its consistency. For example, say a company's board of directors looks at an embarrassing profit and loss statement and directs that 10 percent of all employees be laid off in order to cut expenses. Then six months later, the board demands to know why the company doesn't have any promo table people. The reason is because the board has switched signals. Where do the company's officers stand? The standard against which they were being measured has been changed. People who could have been trained for positions of responsibility were laid off!

Of course, there is nothing wrong with being flexible in your standards. To be consistent to the point of inflexibility is poor management. As Ralph Waldo Emerson has said, complete consistency is the hobgoblin of small minds. But if you are going to modify your standards, at least communicate this in advance so that your people can expect a measure of flexibility and remain flexible themselves.

2. Be Aware of Your Own Biases and Prejudices towards People So That They Do Not Interfere With Your Evaluation of Performances: All of us have biases and prejudices; no one is completely devoid of them. The question is, are you aware of your prejudices? If, for example, an executive is very unhappy with his plant manager because the manager is always five minutes late to meetings, this annoyance may develop into a prejudice. The executive is likely to grade the manager on the bases of his ability to get to a meeting on time, rather than on his ability to manage a plant. A matter of little consequence is interfering with the executive's ability to appraise performance fairly.

How do you become aware of your prejudices? Keep records of your predictions about peoples' perfoþrmances. If you predict a man's performance, and it doesn't measure up to what you predicted, ask yourself if you aren't responding to some irrelevant variable, such as his religion, his wife, his dirty fingernails, or his untidy desk. If you do have prejudices, your people will perceive them and know you as a supervisor who is not really fair-a man who is responding to his own opinions rather than fact.

3. Let People Know Where They Stand: Do this consistently, by means of performance review or other methods. The positives and negatives that are nestling in the back of your head do your people no service unless they know what you are thinking. Give each man sufficient attention; let him be aware that you are looking for ways to help him improve himself. Manifest your concern.

One executive says, "The only guy here who really knows that I'm doing and how well I'm doing it, is too busy to tell me" Hence, that executive is demotivated. Anyone else can pat him on the back, but no one else is knowledgeable enough to be sincere about it.

4. Praise When It Is Appropriate: You should avoid praising every little thing your employees do, for it will quickly lose meaning and may even demotivate them. Moreover, try not to exaggerate in your praise. Praise is like seasoning-a little bit is better than a lot.

Properly handled, praise is one of the best motivating factors. It's especially helpful when you praise someone in the area of his anxiety- where he is trying to do a good job and where you know he feels he ought to be making some progress. It's also a good idea to save your praise for a particularly difficult job, handled well.

It is not, contrary to what you may have been told, a good idea to always give your praise in public. This has pitfalls. If you over-praise a man by just a little, this man may be embarrassed in front of his colleagues and work-fellows. If you under praise in the same situation, it may create doubts in the minds of his work-fellows. So, as a general rule, praise a man in public only if, it is important that others know you have a high opinion of him. This, too, might be embarrassing, but it would be even more embarrassing if you didn't praise him at all.

5. Keep Your Employees Informed Of Changes Which May Affect Them: You don't have to tell every company secret, but it is an evidence of your regard to inform employees of matters in which they have direct interest. It's another way of showing your concern.

For example, if changes in the corporate structure create a position for which one of your men qualifies, tell him about it. Even though he may not get the job, at least you have given him a crack at it. Avoid the indictment of ignoring your employee's promotional opportunities.

6. Care about Your Employees: You must be sufficiently attuned to the fact that each one of your people is individually concerned about his own future and his own self, and everyone must feel that you, too, are concerned about them as individuals.

Lack of communicating with employees about themselves, lack of caring about them as individuals, is summed up nearly in this poem by Phyllis McGinley: "Sticks and stones can break the bones, when thrown with accurate art. Words can sting like anything, but silence breaks the heart".

The man who best motivates others recognizes that others have purposes of their own that do not necessarily coincide with those of the supervisor or the company. The best supervisors generally help their key employees set their own goals. Many executives think they "care" about employees because they help people do better jobs. Yet, the real test is not merely helping a man carry out your purpose' are you willing to help him achieve his purpose too?

7. Perceive People as Ends, Not Means: The object here is to avoid the charge that you are "using" people for your own selfish purposes. The conductor of an orchestra regards his players as individual goals, but all working toward a common purpose.

When the explorer Thomas Cook discovered a new island, he named the discovery after the first man who spotted it. He regarded every man in his crew, even the ship's boy, as partner in the adventure. Cook apparently was a modest man, but his crew loved him for the feeling of usefulness that he gave them as individuals

8. Go Out Of Your Way to Help: If you are a good manager, you will go out of your way to help others-especially when it calls for only a little extra effort on your part. You really help your personnel when you are willing to take pain for them, when you are ready to sacrifice some of your own comfort for them, when you are ready to inconvenience yourself for them.

This means more than merely doing favors for your people. Frequently, it may mean criticizing the person you care about and want to help. Remember, however, that in (a) correcting, where there is an error, (b) improving, where there is deficiency and(c) strengthening, where there is weakness, you must first know the individual. You must know what gives him joy and what brings him sorrow. And this may take long hours of hard thought to discover.

9. Take Responsibility For Others: If you wish to motivate people, then you must assume some responsibility for what happens to them. This is all a part of caring for your personnel. The supervisor who is concerned has a personal involvement in the success of the subordinate. If the worker fails, then a part of the supervisor also fails. Caring usually creates a bond of responsibility between superior and subordinate.

Famed Frank Stanton of the Columbia Broadcasting System is known to his men as a leader who cares. When working with a subordinate, he frequently challenges the man with this question: "Is this the best job you and I can do together?" The way the question is phrased shows the subordinate that, first, Stanton assumes partial responsibility for the success of the project, and, second, that Stanton cares.

10. Build Independence: Again, this is closely allied to caring for your employees. A superior who cares seeks to loosen and ultimately drop the reins of supervision. He would prefer that his subordinates learn to think and act properly, independent of supervision. He encourages them to show initiative, to think critically, to ask penetrating questions about their own work.

In short, one of the best ways to motivate people is to help them achieve their own fullest potential through independence.

11. Exhibit Personal Diligence: It is difficult to see a successful supervisor or executive- a man who could motivate the people beneath him-who himself was not highly motivated. The best motivators of men are those who themselves are hard working, almost to the point of total commitment to their work.

You motivate by example. In spite of the hostility behind statements that employees make about hardworking. Dedicated superiors, there is always a feeling of pride as well. Employees like to feel that they are living up to an image of their boss, particularly when the boss is devoted to the job of making his company successful. And, conversely, the best way to demotivate an employee is to stop working yourself.

12. Be Tactful with Your Employees: Tact covers many things: consideration, courtesy, a sense of balance, an appreciation of the views and feelings of others. It's important in dealing with any employee to be critical. One of the best ways to learn how to be tactful is to observe those whom you yourself consider tactful, polite, and diplomatic. Listen to their conversations with other, observe their behavior, and try to find out how they handle themselves in arguments and uncomfortable situations.

It has been said to Thomas Jefferson, who always made other feel as ease, "He never sought to over shadow or overawe. Inferior men were never embarrassed or depressed in his presence. He was amazingly thoughtful and considerate.

13. Be Willing to Learn From others: As a manager, it must be assumed that you know a great deal about the work of your department and personnel. But be honest with yourself. Acknowledge that you may not have all the information and new knowledge that could be helpful to you and your people. When others come to you with an idea, a suggestion, a proposed change, give them an honest audience. At least, listen to what they have to say.

You may not like the idea; you may have positive proof that the idea absolutely will not work. But, by lending an ear, you will motivate employees into thinking for themselves-and you may learn a thing or two yourself, which, when applied for practical purpose, will further motivate the originator.

This is one of the basic reasons for the regular success of "beneficial suggestion plans" used in industrial plants and factories. Employees like to show off their insight and intelligence to their bosses and the best bosses like to learn from their employees.

14. Stay Flexible: Don't have hard and fast regulations and policies, or procedures and plans that never sway even under the most extreme pressures. Stay loose. Be sensitive to the possibility of change, especially when the ideas or pressures rise from below.

Winston Churchill appreciated that it was not a sign of weakness to modify an opinion or a position. "There is nothing wrong in change", he said, "if it is in the right direction. To improve is to change, so to be perfect is to have changed often."

15. Demonstrate Confidence: If you have any doubts about your department, your staff, your projects, or your company, review them alone and in private. Exhibiting doubt to subordinates disheartens them and completely destroys any motivation. If the leader is afraid, what is there left to inspire in followers?

Conversely, the demonstration of a leader's confidence builds up confidence among others. Show by your behavior and speech that you are confident that the work can be done; that you are confident of your own responsibility and confident of your employees' ability to handle the job.

A successful company president said the following; He pointed out at the water and said:

See that school of fish out there? There's one in front, big and strong, and all the others are following calmly and peacefully. If I am that leader, all the others will either scatter individually or try to devour the wounded one. I'm like the lead fish. As an executive, I must be big and strong, demonstrating confidence and satisfaction. In this way, all my executives will be motivated to Follow me. But if I lose my confidence and exhibit doubt, then all my executives will similarly lose confidence.

16. Allow Freedom of Expression: Assuming that your subordinates are reasonably competent, it never hurts to relax your vigil and allow them to do things their way once in a while. Every employee ought to have the right to make his own job more interesting by doing it his own way. All you have to do is be sure that the results are what you seek and that the employee is working within the framework of company policy.

Countless experiments have shown that, even on assembly line operations, this technique works. Girls, who are given some discretion and choice as to what time to take their coffee breaks, are more highly motivated and when to take their coffee break times is simply posted. A salesman who schedules his road trips himself is likely to work harder, see more customers in less time, than when he receives a schedule from the home office. The psychologist sees in this phenomenon the individual's urge for independent action and the need to demonstrate his competence.

17. Delegate: Assuming that the people who work for you are competent individuals who want to get ahead, delegate to them as much of your burden as possible. Pressure often motivates employees. Let them bite off as much as they can chew; then, let them ride with their own decisions (insofar as possible), let them learn through their own mistakes, and let them revel in their own successes.

By so doing, you not only motivate competent men, you also build people you can rely upon when going gets tough. Paul Meyer, president of the success Motivation Institute, was quoted on this subject in Business Management magazine: "Give your man a project and the freedom to do with it as he wants. Make sure he can either break it or make it on his own. Meanwhile, protect yourself by making sure the project is in an area of his interest. Changes are the man will work like the devil to make the project 'go'.

Joe Crail, president of Coast Federal Savings and Loan, strives to delegate responsibility to his executives. And to make sure that they bear the responsibility well, he makes them share the risks. Like all good executives, Crail knows that the higher a man climbs in management, the more he must be held responsible for his own decisions.

Crail, for example, has set up a strict policy on when not to grant loans to applicants. If one of his staff recommends an exception to policy. Crail says, "O.K. But you will have to share the risk. I don't want you to play games with my marbles alone. If the loan is forfeited, you pay half and I'll pay half. If the loan is repaid, you collect all the interest." Crail reposts that only two men have taken him up on this proposition. One man is now Crail's chief assistant, and the other is now president of a rival bank.

18. Encourage·Ingenuity: This technique works with anyone. When discuss creativity, you will learn that anyone-even the lowest paid clerk-can be creative. You would encourage this creativity and ingenuity by challenging your subordinates to beat your system of doing things. If, for example, your filing system is not satisfactory, don't change it yourself; have you clerks and office manager recommend changes.

Paul Meyer of the success Motivation Institute knows the value of this technique and suggests it to his clients. He tells a story to illustrate how he challenges his own office staff in this manner: A typist questioned a tax report that Meyer had prepared. He challenged her to prove her point. That evening, she asked an accountant to look it over. He gave her an idea that she carried to Meyer, who used it the next day to save nearly $3,000 (Mortimer R Feinberg, 1968).

Build Intrinsic Motivation Into Your Incentive Programs

A criticism leveled at many incentives and incentive programs is that they tend to diminish intrinsic (internal) motivation since the nature of any reward is extrinsic (external) to the individual being rewarded. As the argument goes, over time the external rewards will erode any intrinsic motivation that existed (such as a filling of fulfillment) and the employee will come to resent the activity. This does not have to be the case, especially if you follow the following three guidelines:

1. Set goals that have mutual benefit. The best goals have something in it for the employee as well as the organization. And that something is rarely just money. In almost every incentive program, for example, there is a chance for employees to learn and develop new skills that can be used in the future. Find out what career goals each employee has and you can use that information to help tailor a general program to also be a specific development program. For example, if you have an employee who is interested in learning cross-selling skills, those skills can be taught and practiced as part of an incentive program focused on obtaining a higher level of sales. Such customized goal- setting is best when mutually determined with each employee, encouraging their ideas and initiative as much as possible.
2. Partner in the achievement of goals. Increasingly, a every manager's job is changing from controlling to coaching. Demonstrate that you are on each employee's side in reaching incentive program goals by offering ongoing personal praise, encouragement and assistance however possible. Fact of the matter is, most employees indicate they are more highly motivated by direct thanks and recognition from their managers in person or writing than more formal incentives. Use this fact to urge employees on in their quest to achieve incentive program goals.
3. Allow for individual choice in rewards. Ideally, this means asking employees what they would consider motivating if they achieved certain milestones in their performance. For example, Kirk Malcki,

president of Pegasus Personal Fitness Centers in Dallas, asks new physical- fitness trainers to make a list of rewards, ranging in value from $25 to $200, they would like to receive for reaching weekly and monthly goals. Instead of commonplace prizes, his fifteen employees have opted for tickets to rock- concerts, limousine rentals and half days off. Thanks in part to the more personalized incentives; sales have more than doubled in six years.

If you do decide to have a fixed class of reward, say merchandise, give employees flexibility within that choice. This can be done through the use of gift certificates, for example, or by allowing a selection within a certain range of value from a gift catalog.

By paying attention to individual employee interests and desires, a manager can help customize almost any incentive program to produce more lasting, personal results with each and every employee.

References and Further Reading

1. A.M.Sheikh, (1999) H.R.D and Management, S.Chand and Company Ltd, New Delhi. India.
2. Baron Robert A. and Greenberg Jerald,(1990) Behavior In Organization Understanding and Managing the Human Side of Work.
3. Frank.E.Saal and Patrick A. Knight, (1988) Industrial/ Organization Psychology Science and Practice, Brooks/Cole Publishing Company Pacific Grove, California.
4. John W.Newstrom and Keith Davis, (2001) Organization Behavior Human Behavior at Work.
5. Journal of Applied Psychology, Oct (2001), Vol-86(3).
6. Journal of Vocational Behavior, August (2001).
7. Indian Psychological Abstracts and Reviews, Jan- June (2002), Vol-9 No1.
8. Mortimer R.Feinberg, (1968) Effective Psychology for Managers, Eagle Wood Cliff, N. J, U.S.A, New York.
9. Paul M.Muchinsky, (2000) Psychology Applied to Work, Sixth Edition, Wadsworth Thomas Learning.
10. Pravin G. Deosthalee, (1982) Industrial Psychology, Vipul Prakashan, Mumbai, India.
11. Psychological Abstracts, (2001) Vol-88 No-7-8.
12. Work and Occupational Journal, Aug (2001), Vol-28(3), 346-370.

5

Training in Organizations

Training

Organisations select employees on the basis of their predicted likelihood of succeeding on the job. Although some employees are expected to perform their jobs immediately upon hire, the vast majority are granted time to grow into their new jobs. This growth process is expedited by formal organizational training processes designed for that purpose. **Goldstein (1991)** referred to training processes as "*the systematic acquisition of attitudes, concepts, knowledge, roles or skills that result in improved performance at work*".

The relative importance of training to enhance job performance is increasing. A major reason for this emphasis is increasing reliance on computers in the conduct of work, and its repercussions on the human requirements of work. Such talents can be acquired only through additional preparations for work. There is a growing emphasis in all areas of work to operate more efficiently and to enhance the overall quality of goods and services. Such advances are the basis for enhancing organizational performance in increasingly competitive markets. Training, therefore, is a process to enhance the fit between job demands and human attributes.

The Strategic Value of Training

Organisations do not train their employees for the sheer sake of doing so. Rather, it is because employees represent a competitive advantage that enhances organizational performance when managed wisely. The competitive strategy an organization uses is the means by which it competes for business in the marketplace. There is a linkage between the type of competitive strategy an organization uses and its training practices (Jackson & Schuler, 1990).

(a) A **speed strategy** is designed to offer the customers a competitive value in terms of reduced time for products and services. A training practice that serves this function emphasizes teamwork among employees and methods of streamlined production.

(b) An **innovative strategy** is used to develop products or services that differ from the competition. The focus of training in this context is on developing new products, services or technologies.

(c) A **quality-enhancement strategy** is designed to provide value by offering a product or service of higher quality than that offered by the competitors. Here the employees are trained to provide a consistently high level of service quality with no defects.

(d) A **cost-reduction strategy** is designed to gain a competitive advantage by being a low-cost provider of services. Here relatively little emphasis is placed on enhancing employee skills through training.

Training, a Cost or An Investment?

There is no clear answer to this question. Looking at the above strategic values, it can be concluded that training is definitely an investment. But, a word of caution-training can be called an investment only if it is utilized properly and for the purpose for which it was undertaken otherwise training is counted as a cost if it is not used after the training process.

The Pretraining Environment

Tannenbaum and Yukl (1992) reviewed evidence suggesting that events that take place prior to training can influence the effectiveness of training. Management actions and decisions provide cues that signal employee motivation for training. Cohen (1990) found that trainees with more supportive supervisors entered training with stronger beliefs that training would be useful. Baldwin and Magjuka (1991) found that trainees who entered training expecting some form of follow-up activity or assessment afterward, reported stronger intention to transfer what they had learned back on the job.

Salas (1990) found that trainees who reported many limitations in their job entered training with lower motivation to learn. These trainees had little incentive to learn new skills in an environment where the skills could not be applied. Another factor that defines the pretraining environment is trainee input and choice in training. Baldwin, Magjuka and Loher (1991) found that allowing trainees to specify what training they wanted increased their motivation to learn provided they were given the training of their choice.

As Tannenbaum and Yukl (1992) articulated, several factors representative of the organization environment in which training occurs bear directly on its effectiveness. Training does not occur in a vacuum; it is but a means to an end. Factors that strengthen the linkage between training and relevant outcomes can be as critical as the training itself.

Identification of Training Needs

A first step in establishing a viable training program is needs assessment, which determines the training needs of the organizations. While very few companies actually conduct formal needs assessment, its importance cannot be emphasized enough. Without determining the need for training, there is no guarantee that the right training will be provided for the right trainee. The following types of needs assessments should be done-

1. **Organizational Needs Analysis:**Conducting an organizational needs analysis is the first step in effective needs assessment. It begins with the short and long term objectives of the organization and the trends that are likely to affect these objectives. This can include a human resource analysis, analyses of efficiency indices and assessment of the organizational climate. This analysis should translate the organisation's objectives into an accurate estimate of the demand for human resource.

2. **Job Needs Analysis:** The content of present or anticipated jobs should be examined through job needs analysis. For existing jobs, information on the tasks to be performed in each job, the skills necessary to perform those tasks and the minimum acceptable standards are gathered. This information can then be used to ensure that training programs are job-specific and useful.

3. **Demographic Needs Analysis:** Organizations should conduct demographic studies to determine the training needs of specific populations of workers. Research indicates different groups have different training needs. For example, first-line supervisors need more technical training, while mid-level managers rate HRM courses as most important for their needs and upper-level managers rate conceptual courses as critical to their development. These should also be taken into account before deciding the type of training.

Setting Up Training Programs

Successful implementation of training programs depends on selecting the right programs for the right people under the right circumstances.

Who Participates In The Training?

Once a training need has been established, decision must be made regarding who will be trained. This is because, for most programs, only one target audience is in attendance and the training program is designed to address only one topic. Also important here is how many employees are to be trained since the program must be cost-effective.

Who Conducts The Training?

Training programs may be taught by one of several people including:

- The supervisor
- A co-worker
- An internal or external subject area expert
- The employee (self-paced instruction)

Which of these people is selected often depends on where the program is being held and which skills are being taught. For example, the immediate supervisor or a co-worker usually teaches basic skills, whereas a member of the HRM staff usually handles a basic organizational orientation. Professors or consultants usually teach interpersonal skills and conceptual, integrative skills for management. However, technical skills maybe taught by either internal or external subject matter experts.

What Type Of Skills Are To Be Acquired?

The training program must have content congruence with the types of skills being taught. In general, skills fall into three broad areas-

Basic Skills

Training that expands or maintains the technical expertise of employees falls under basic jobs skills training. Due to rapid changes in technology and the implementation of automated office, industrial and managerial systems, technological updating and skill building have become a major thrust in training to keep technical skills current.

Interpersonal Skills

Skills in communications, human relationships, performance appraisal and leadership and negotiations are increasingly in demand. This type of training tops the list of training needs for first and middle-level managers. The development of interpersonal skills is also important for those employees who interface with the public.

Conceptual integrative Skills

Strategic and operational planning, organization design and policy skills are needed by organizational planners as well as by top management. Adapting to complex and changing environments is often a part of top and middle-management responsibilities and conceptual training helps such employees to make new associations.

Choosing The Right Method of Training

Imparting Knowledge and Changing Attitudes

The trainer must choose which method of instruction he is going to adopt as soon as he knows the instructional objective. The trainer needs to have a good overall picture of the range of strategies open to him. To further this, there follows a discussion on the major ways in which a trainer can impart knowledge and change attitudes with comments on the usefulness of each method.

The Lecture

This is traditionally the most formal method of instruction and usually consists of verbal explanation or description of the subject matter. Usually, the trainee is passive, listening and watching in silence without interruption in the form of questions or discussion. It is often lengthy with a separate question session later. It has been in use for centuries and is the preferred style to this day in many organizations.

As a strategy, it has many advantages for the trainer and several purposes, including –

- It can be used to give an overall view of the subject matter as an introduction, the detail being filled in later.
- The presentation of new techniques and procedures, of which the trainees can have no previous knowledge.
- The stimulation of interest in a new direction, line of thought or development.
- Teaching complex information, which can be precisely worked out beforehand even to the exact word.

The most obvious application is where there are large numbers of trainees needing information, where participation is not possible because of the sheer volume of people. The timing can be worked out exactly and entered in the lesson plan with sure knowledge that the trainer will in fact cover the ground he intended to. This is rarely so in any other method of instruction.

Some of the disadvantages of the lecture as a learning experience are obvious. The lack of involvement of the trainee leaves the trainer without feedback on the trainee's rate of assimilation of the material. Unless the whole of the presentation from beginning to end is fully understood and assimilated, the sequence and sense will be lost, since only questioning at the end will provide enlightenment and that may be too late. The problem is of course that not enough of the senses are employed in this method of instruction and thus perception is affected.

To counter this problem, seminars are sometimes arranged after a lecture. In a seminar one member has prepared an opening paper based upon the previous lecture, and a group discussion ensues. This gives an opportunity for clarification, development of concepts and exchange of views and ideas on the subject matter. Seminars need not, of course, follow a lecture but be based upon an agreed subject, known in advance to all the members, who can acquaint themselves with it and come prepared to make an informed contribution. The opening statement should not occupy more than 1/4-1/5 th of the time available, and the trainer should stay in the background so that the trainees can learn to express themselves, discuss and classify their own ideas on the topic. The maximum number of participants should not exceed twenty in any one group, and a seminar can be followed by tutorials.

Tutorials are usually one-to-one or one-to-two-or-three at the maximum in trainer/trainee ratio. Tutorials are the final link in the lecture, seminar chain when individual problems are ironed out or the student prepares some work for the trainer to criticize constructively. It is an almost essential feature of the lecture system, since it provides the evaluation phase in this rather remote form of tuition, both for lecturer and student.

Although lectures are becoming less popular as a form of learning design, they still have great relevance, particularly in large companies, on topics like new research, product development or new legislation (especially in health, safety and hygiene areas) and are also much used in the induction process where large numbers of trainees are taken on simultaneously.

Talks/Lessons

Talks and lessons incorporate a variety of techniques, but their chief difference from a lecture is in the amount of participation allowed by the trainer. This format is suitable for knowledge type sessions to groups of not more than twenty trainees and preferably twelve to eighteen, since participation is difficult to handle above such numbers. The lesson is classically planned in the commencement, core, conclusion style, with the trainee involvement generally in the core and conclusion phases. The trainer will encourage participation by questioning, being questioned and discussion in the core phase and by some form of testing in the conclusion phase. There will also be visual aids to help to display summaries, some form of note taking and a little direction from the trainer who will allow interruptions for clarification and other points. It is more of a two-way dialogue than a lecture with 50:50 or 60:40 ratio of trainer/trainee input. The student uses more senses in his learning process and the trainer has more awareness of student needs, so it should be a more efficient learning vehicle than the lecture.

However there are, needless to say, some snags. The timing of a lesson is more difficult to gauge, since the amount of trainee participation is impossible to assess first time around and, indeed, differs from group to group.

In some groups, nothing may come back in the form of questioning or reaction from the trainees, whilst other groups will argue and furiously debate every teaching point. Also the trainer must have good interactive skills to handle a participative group successfully, unlike the straight lecturer, being able to draw out the shy and control the talkative, but, in return, he will have a much more accurate idea of the trainee's ability. Whether it is lesson or lecture, a general rule of thumb guide to input for the trainer is to limit his concepts to not more than four per hour.

This is difficult to achieve, but is the key to successful knowledge-type instruction. If nothing much comes back from the trainees, the instructor will tend to rush through his material until it becomes rather like a lecture, and he will fail to achieve his instructional objective. If his groups are over talkative, he again may fail since he cannot introduce sufficient concepts in his allotted time span. Careful planning, experience and the ability to handle his group with empathy and with sensitive 'antennae' are the only ways to overcome the dangers of the participative talk or lesson. It is important to test objectively the amount of learning that has taken place during the core phase by some means before terminating the session, since this will provide the information for future talks or lessons on the receptivity of the individual student, on the success of the lesson and on the amount of remedial teaching that may be necessary in the future.

Discussion Groups

One of the most effective means of inducing attitudes and developing social skills is the group discussion. The trainer acts in a limited way as a scene setter, referee or catalyst, getting his students to put into words their feelings, ideas and opinions on the topic in question. There are several different kinds of discussion groups depending upon the instructional objective. The controlled discussion group has a set topic and the trainer exercises control so that the group ends with a set conclusion. This teaches by exchange of information where prior knowledge of core facts is assumed but where interpretation may be a matter of opinion. The associative group discussion uses a specific topic, but the trainees arrive at their own conclusions, although the trainer does not allow too much deviation and would probably summarize at the end. The free discussion has no set topic and teaches discussion methods mainly (debate, argument, development of logic, confidence in expression etc.) as an end in itself, the conclusion not being paramount.

Trainees are influenced by one another in peer groups and are much more likely to change attitudes during group discussion than if they were told that their attitude should be changed by their boss. It is also a valuable means of obtaining feedback for the instructor, particularly when the practical applications of some new knowledge are being discussed, since he can gather information about the way in which the group has grasped important concepts. Finally it helps the trainer to assess the verbal skills, the level of motivation and some aspects of personality in his group. Needless to say, there are some disadvantages in running group discussions. The balance of the group needs careful analysis if the dynamics are to be correct, with the right proportions of strong contributors, shy introverts, logical thinkers and happy followers.

Numbers too are important in group discussion, with maximum interaction occurring between five and eight people; certainly anything over twelve should be split into two groups, although this does present chairmanship difficulties. The role of the trainer is important in controlled group discussions where trainees may stray from the subject or fail to discuss it fully, or may display entrenched attitudes and futile personality conflicts. Suffice it to say here that the instructional objective must be carefully worked out to include one or more of the following applications:

- Influencing colleagues' attitudes.
- Inducing attitudes to the organization and its customers.
- Relating practice to principles.
- Problem solving.
- Analysis of existing procedures and practices and 'brainstorming' solutions.

Role-play

This is a primary means of teaching social skills and inducing preferred attitudes. The trainees are asked to enact a role which will be the same, or as near to, their working role, but in the protected environment of the training scene. It is often linked to some prior input such as lectures, talks or conferences and is used as an opportunity for the trainees to put into practice some of the skills, especially the communication and human relations skills, which have been discussed. It is valuable as a means of giving the trainee an insight into his own behavior and its effect upon other people, and is especially valuable when linked to some objective feedback system like CCTV video recordings.

Typically, two or more trainees will role-play a situation in front of the rest of the group. The scenario is usually unscripted, but the trainer, usually without rehearsal, gives full briefing of the role and the setting. The trainees are allowed to plan their actions, prior to a spontaneous performance before the group. Typical situations where role play can be used effectively are instructor training, interviewing (grievance, selection, disciplinary), counseling, appraisal, sales training and customer relations. It is especially recommended for service industries, where such a lot depends upon social skill and yet where little effort seems to be made in some concerns to develop natural abilities in this field.

The advantages of role-play are:

- It has high interest and involvement for the trainees.
- There is almost immediate knowledge of results from the objective appraisal of the spectators and tutor.
- It increases sensitivity to other people's points of view since it is relatively easy in most role-play situations to reverse roles (i.e. the interviewer becomes the interviewee).
- The trainer can appraise fairly accurately (by the success or otherwise of the role playing) how well his instruction has been absorbed, and give a fair assessment of his trainees' likely work performance after some practice at this interactive technique.
- The trainees get the feel of the real-life pressures of the working situation and yet are protected. This results almost invariably in an increase in self-confidence on the part of the trainee.

Of course, it is a technique not without its dangers. Trainees may become embarrassed, especially those of a shy, introvert nature, unused to such situations. Most will suffer from initial nervousness, which will have to be counteracted by empathetic help and encouragement from the instructor. On the other hand, the extrovert can 'overact' and regard the session as a 'bit of a lark' not to be taken too seriously. (From experience the best way of dealing with the latter situation is to allow the group to exercise its own discipline upon the deviant member.) However, in spite of these drawbacks, it remains one of the most effective teaching media for face-to-face situations, i.e. where people interact socially in the work situation, and with a practiced trainer, can really help with self analysis and improvement in attitudes.

Case Study

Another excellent means of promoting self-awareness, developing empathy towards other people's points of view and gaining knowledge by doing is the case study. Widely used in teaching supervisory and management techniques (such as personnel, industrial relations, marketing, business law and production policy), it consists of a historical report of a set of circumstances or an event, with all the relevant material and background for the trainees to be able to examine the case, solve problems maybe or to derive useful generalizations and principles. Like role play and discussion groups, it is a highly active method of training, with maximum involvement of all the senses and student interest is usually high, especially if the case history is based upon a series of actual events.

The real advantages of this approach are in attitude formation and change. It is extremely useful for illustrating important principles about business life, e.g. the possibility of several solutions to a problem and the consequent reduction of narrow-mindedness, the frustration of situations in which no-one tells people what to do, and the advantages of integrating knowledge obtained from a number of foundation disciplines, etc. Again it is free from the actual working pressures and helps to form the ability to take a long, cool look at situations that have occurred in real life. Needless to say, the studies must be realistic, the briefing and concluding plenary sessions properly conducted by the trainer and careful selection for balance be made in the groups working together upon the case, or trainees may get the wrong impression of the real work situation. Bonuses from the case study come when students have to learn to defend their proposals, often in the face of keen criticism from other groups. They also learn to weld dissimilar disciplines such as engineering and salesmanship and soon appreciate that there is no single answer to a problem and no progress without compromise in many areas.

The foregoing methods of instruction offer a choice in imparting knowledge and changing attitudes. They are just some of the major techniques used in this area; the trainer must take into account the advantages and disadvantages of each approach when examining his instructional objective.

Demonstration and Practice

The usual way of imparting skill is by an experienced trainer performing the working activity, at pre-determined speeds, telling the trainee how to do the task, showing the trainee the movements involved and coaching the trainee whilst he practices. This we tend to call demonstration, though in fact each of these parts could be a complete session in itself. Often the task is broken down into distinct stages, each one being practiced separately. The whole skill is thus built up from step-by-step instruction. It will be noted that this technique merely teaches psychomotor dexterity and any resultant principles or theory must be taught by one of the methods outlined above.

It is successful because it uses all of the learner's senses, if properly planned and organized. Visual material, discussion, question and answer techniques will all provide important learning stimuli to back up the demonstration. Needless to say, an essential aspect of this technique from the trainer's point of view is the need for prior rehearsal of the skill, often to a pre-determined speed and quality standard. Failure to achieve this sort of target often results in lack of credibility since the trainee does not believe the targets are really possible. A smooth performance during demonstration increases confidence on both sides of the learning relationship, so it is well worthwhile to get in some practice prior to the event! The dictionary definition of 'to demonstrate' is 'to make manifest', therefore it is essential that demonstrations as far as possible use the actual equipment in the real workplace, i.e. on-the job training, if skills are being taught.

Simulation

Equipment or techniques that duplicate actual conditions as closely as possible, yet in an off-job situation, are known as simulators. The classic examples of simulation are the Link trainers used to train pilots during World War Two and the modern mock-ups of the flight deck which are used to train commercial airline pilots. Simulation is most necessary where on job practice would result in serious injury, or expensive error, if the trainee were to make his normal quota of mistakes. Usually trainee interest is extremely high in simulation exercises, since it most closely follows actual job conditions, and consequently the trainer has few motivational problems. However the cost of simulators is high as a rule, since much research and development is necessary to produce the often-complex equipment. It is obviously most important that the simulation closely follows normal practice and is constantly updated by operational data as actual working conditions change, and also that the standard of instruction is high.

Business and Management Games

Not all simulation is to do with psychomotor skills, since it is the core of Business and Management Games, essential in developing supervisory and managerial skills. In this simulated environment, trainees are presented with information about a concern - its markets, products, work force, financial position etc. - and the trainees assume given management roles usually in groups. These groups then run the company; making decisions, dealing with people and taking action. Often the results of the game are computerized, comparing the groups' actions to a pre-determined model of the likely outcome. Feedback is prompt, so that analysis of the trainee's actions and their likely effects is quickly forthcoming. The simulation of the real-life situation aids the transfer of learning from classroom to boardroom, and again is necessary since managers applying theoretical principles to actual situations without practice could end up in severe financial straits or cause endless labor relations problems. The main difficulty, of course, is in assessing the probable results of a trainee's actions, since the learning outcome for the trainee will be affected if he feels the assessment is not realistic, but if credibility in this crucial aspect is achieved, business games can help in developing many facets of a manager's role. Simulation is a valuable tool in assessing trainees' likely performance on the job and providing the trainer with a good idea of the potential of individual trainees.

In-tray Exercises

Another form of simulation, used in the skill training of desk workers at all levels in the company hierarchy, is the In-tray. Trainees are given a series of letters, papers, memos and files similar to the assortment they would get in a normal day's work. They are then asked to take action on each piece of material, giving their reasoning for each decision, and the results are given as feedback to the trainer. Not only does this method teach skills of organization, communication, paper handling and recognition, it also helps with attitude formation on such things as judgment of priorities, panic decisions, attitudes to superiors and juniors, complaint procedures etc. It has the usual pros and cons of simulations, i.e. the need to follow closely real-life practices and pressures to be credible and the need for empathetic feedback by the trainer, which should build confidence rather than sap it. However, clerical and desk skills in general seem to develop quickly by this method, especially where real bits of material from a real in-tray have been incorporated into the session.

Exercises

These are really means of developing skills rather than imparting them, but are included here because they often follow closely on a demonstration, or may occur as a test of existing skill prior to training. In this method of instruction, trainees are asked to undertake a task leading to a specific result, following well-defined lines. The trainer briefs the individual or group, determining the line of activity the trainee will take and marks or assesses the results of their actions.

To some extent, during exercises, the trainees are on their own; more so than when being supervised during initial practice of the skills concerned. The trainer often acts only as observer during exercises, not as coach, since it is a 'half way house' to the real thing. A highly active form of learning, exercises are suitable for any situation where the trainees have to put into practice skills which are partially developed, and relate them to their future jobs, following a pattern or formula laid down by the trainer. Best results are gained from graded exercises, which allow trainees to feel the result is reasonably attainable, not too easy nor too difficult, or the trainees will experience frustration and lose confidence. A splendid form of assessment, exercises are often used nowadays instead of formal tests, to gauge students' progress.

Do-It-Yourself Learning - Programmed and Experiential Instruction

Certain training techniques require very little didactic input from the instructor. The learning situation is devised so that the trainee can control his own instructional process, with the majority of the trainer's effort being expended in the design phase. This has some advantages for the trainee in that (a) he can learn at his own pace, (b) there is a great deal of participation by the trainee in his own learning process, therefore he is using all the senses, and (c) the motivational aspect is high as a result.

Programmed Instruction

This is a fairly recent development in the field, dating back to the fifties. It is based on Skinner's work on operant conditioning and concentrates on changes in behavior, and so is therefore a true learning experience. However the programme is the critical factor, in which the instructional objective is expressed as initial behavior and terminal behavior, bridged by four or five logical steps between key points. The basic unit of a programme is called a frame since it represents material that is exposed at one time, either in a book, manual or so called 'teaching machine'. The frame contains a statement, a question or a problem, to which the trainee makes a response. Sometimes the frames review old material or consolidate, but mostly they introduce new material a little at a time. The student may be required to answer a question, to write a solution or to make a choice from multiple answers, and is given immediate feedback.

The two major formats used in programming are the linear programme and the branching programme. The linear programme, as its name suggests, proceeds in a straight line from initial behavior to terminal behavior, with the student moving on from frame to frame regardless of whether his response was correct or not. In the branching programme, the learner is given alternatives from which to select and depending upon his answer, travels down one branch or another. If he chooses incorrectly, his error will be pointed out to him and he is referred to an earlier step to avoid making the error again. If he chooses correctly, he moves ahead and may be given the opportunity to jump a few frames if he shows real insight.

From the foregoing, it will be appreciated that linear programmes can be presented in an unsophisticated format such as a book. The branching programme on the other hand needs an automated device if it is complex, and these are often termed 'teaching machines'. These devices display the frame on a small screen and choices are made by means of buttons or some other mechanism. In some cases computers may assist the mechanism to decide from moment to moment what should be done in instructional sequence.

Algorithms

These are similar to programmed instructions in that they represent a logically ordered sequence of rules, questions or instructions, 'branched' to allow a variety of possible responses, but exhibited as a complete diagram rather than frame by Do-it-Yourself Learning frame. They have an extremely wide instructional application since any context involving choice or decision can be described as an algorithm. Widely used for faultfinding charts, identification keys and basic calculations, the use of an algorithm avoids the need for instruction altogether, or can be used as post-instructional training material. In this form trainees for permanent aides-memoire and reference, and as a testing implement can retain them. If the student can design one, they demonstrate a complete grasp of the subject.

Projects/Assignments

These are methods of discovery or 'experiential' learning which give the trainee great opportunity to display initiative and creativity. The trainer lays down the task or end product and resources may be listed for the trainee to research if desired, but the lines to be followed in reaching the objective are left completely to the trainee. Another highly active learning situation, it is ideal for the busy trainer, who has trainees with some intelligence and motivation, for whom knowledge acquisition is the expected learning outcome. From experience, it seems that the knowledge assignment is insufficiently exploited by trainers, who sometimes see learning situations purely in formal terms when, quite often, a trainee has the capacity and the desire to follow lines of his own in arriving at the training goal. Again, importantly, it is a good method of assessing trainee's performance, providing feedback on a range of personal qualities, such as attitudes and range of interests. It can be used in place of formal tests, but be wary of criticism of project work; trainees are not objective when experiential work is criticized, tending to take it as personal devaluation.

Another important factor is in gaining the commitment of the trainee prior to project/assignment work. Since many hours may be spent in this activity it must therefore be seen to be directly relevant to the trainee's needs. Thus the briefing for this form of learning must be very carefully done, concentrating on mutual objectives and methods of achievement, planning co-operation and coaching where necessary. Didactic instructors will see it from the example that there is a considerable saving in tutorial explanation of routines and in planning training sessions. The preparation is restricted to filling in the objective and listing the basic resources; the trainee writing in his action plan and agreeing the completion date during the initial briefing interview.

Group Dynamics

For the trainer who is skilled in interactive techniques, or has access to trained psychologists/sociologists in the work team, a valuable experiential learning situation exists in 'group dynamics'. This technique examines the behavior of the individual in a group (and the group as a whole) and helps the trainee to learn the effects of his own behavior upon others and his reactions to their behavior towards him. By simply experiencing the situation, trainees become more enlightened about how and why people at work behave as they do, increase their communication skills and hopefully increase their self awareness and powers of observation.

A group task may be set, or the group allowed to decide its own way of structuring their time, and the process of what goes on is observed by the trained tutor. A plenary 'wash-up' session at the end allows discussion on how the group felt, and feedback to individual members is given by the tutor/observer. It is important that problems arising during the session are cleared up before the group breaks up. The advantages of this technique for management and supervisory training are obvious. Points to watch are (a) that the observer records objectively, with some method of quantitative chart or score sheet, the interactions that occur (many systems of interactive analysis technique exist to aid this), (b) that concrete examples of behavior patterns are illustrable and (c) that examinations of motives and private behavior are used in a constructive rather than a destructive way and always at the discretion of the trainee. It is obvious that difficulties can arise if the trainee discovers something about himself that is distasteful. This may be necessary for his future growth. This is one reason why this method of training should be undertaken by trained people and the formation of the groups planned extremely carefully to give a correct mix. In the right hands however, it a valuable means of self discovery and bears further study in the 'training of attitudes towards people' in the working situation.

Laboratory Training

This is a development of the above and has a variety of names (sensitivity training, T-groups, D-groups, action-centred groups, etc.) but essentially similar procedures. Groups of trainees, usually of managerial or supervisory grade, spend a period of time together participating in group activities designed to promote understanding of themselves and each other. Personal problems and counseling may occur, role play or simulation exercises carried out and other interactive situations take place in a social vacuum, away from work with the participants stripped of rank. The success of the group depends upon the way that the members interact away from the organizational umbrella replacing dictated goals by their own. Essentially, by its very nature, laboratory training is outside the scope of the in-plant trainer, but for selected employees consultant trainers can be bought in (though the location would have to be different and the group mix preferably a vertical slice from differing disciplines). Usually however employees are sent away for specialist training on an external course.

Training Evaluation

Barely lagging behind the massive increases in training efforts and expenditures have been the efforts and expenditures involved in their evaluation. By the early 1970s evaluation had generated its own literature of journals, books and, above all, manuals; a field for specialized research; and doctoral dissertations; and a growing body of experts. By now any time gap between training and its evaluation has vanished in many places; policy-makers and funders of training, disillusioned by past performance, press for assurance of better results in the next budget period. Even in advance of the events to be approved and funded: we know of current programs that send the evaluation form out as part of their application package and require applicants to send it back completed before they are even admitted!

Yet, there is evidence that for actually improving training-resolving issues of training strategy, staffing, organization and management, choices of methods and materials, follow-up, participant selection, and pre- and post-training work with client organizations-evaluation has so far been of little help. References here and there to exceptions to the rule serve to emphasize this sad but true generalization.

Ritual elements still predominate in the evaluation of training, with their own logic and rich elaborations. They seek to propitiate the powerful providers of training funds with reassurances that higher training budgets can indeed be justified, that controls on expenditures are in place, and that weeding out of worthless training does occur. Since training's lifeline depends on these assurances, questions regarding how and on what bases they are offered, and how evaluation actually affects training plans remain obtuse. In many places the administrators of training programs and institutions have arrogated primary responsibility for evaluation to themselves. Or, to ensure that the data, its interpretation and the funding recommendations carry the extra weight associated with independent study, they call on specialist staff and outside experts to do the evaluation. These outsiders then intrude with their agenda while trainers try also to cope with on-going programs. Distant at best, adversarial and potentially destructive at worst, they report on participant numbers, curricula, and program duration on the one hand, and relate them to allotted staff and funding on the other-the type of data that policy-makers and administrators routinely look over for proper housekeeping. No insightful pointers to training effectiveness or to improving programs or policies are usually offered or expected.

Evaluation by trainers themselves and also by academic researchers has likewise been largely ineffective, but for other reasons. Much of it is really in-program monitoring in that it takes program structures, participant composition and other key components as given. This is appropriate for adjusting a program while it is going on but inadequate for evaluation, for it avoids the very dimensions to assess at the end, such as how far the program actually met the learning objectives, which trainers and methods were more effective than others and how far the new capabilities area built in to the system as planned.

Still other evaluations focus on fine points of conceptual or methodological interest not directly related to program objectives, resources, and contexts. In this confusion of purposes and interests, all labeled evaluation, the actual partners in training hold back. Instead of helping each other see and understand what the training did and did not achieve, they jockey for immediate safety and even become openly adversarial.

The essential first step through the confusion is to recognize that policy-makers and managers, trainers and participants do approach evaluation with different points of view and different purposes, and to disentangle and sort these out. Policy-makers and managers scrutinize training for its overall effectiveness for the change(s) on which they have set out and for staying within budget; this is essentially evaluating from outside the program. Trainers, in focus here, approach evaluation essentially from the inside, assessing a program's success in terms of the strategy and objectives set for it in advance together with the policymakers and managers and funded by them. How well did the strategy and the program 'work,' overall and part-by-part, and how right were the resources allocated to it (so it can be done again if needed).

Evaluation by participants-the third party-is from a different angle again. Where they are independent agents, in choosing to go to a program or not to go and what of the training to put to use afterwards they are like customers and clients. If satisfied that their time, efforts and fees had been well spent, the program was "good" and can be recommended to others, if not, not. Where their options were limited in the first place because the training was a required step to a job they wanted or a condition for rehabilitation at home or advancement in their organization, these consequences will reflect the value of the training most directly; and that evaluation is ordinarily and practically their home organization's business. Least significant to true evaluation, though immediately most heartwarming for trainers as well as participants, is end-of-program euphoria: participants praise the program and the trainers, shed tears at parting and promise each other to stay in touch; they even set up solid-sounding arrangements for professional as well as social contact to continue. All this is quite common. But the emotions expressed there have many sources and shed little light to go by on the quality of the program or its management and economy and none on its effectiveness back home.

With three parties involved, each with its distinctive perspectives and responsibilities, trainers make a strategic error when they evaluate beyond what they can. It would be well if the who-does-what part had been clarified in the scope of work they agreed upon before working out the program itself. If they exceed it now they only add confusion. Though present on the scene and immersed in training more than the others, trainers can still only have the first cut at evaluation; others have theirs to do too. And just as the strength of a chain is determined by its weakest link, so a weak contribution from any one partner limits program evaluation overall. By no means can every weakness or failure in training be attributed to the trainers, the program or the institution, nor assessed and rectified by improvement there. Many a participant was simply not up to the challenge or her organization at home is too weak to use well-trained participants. Possible causes of shortfalls in training are numerous.

Why Evaluate?

Evaluation is a systematic process to determine the value, or meaning of an activity or process. In a broad sense, evaluation is undertaken to improve HRD processes, or to decide the future of a program. These broad purposes can be divided into ten evaluation purposes, identified and described below –

1. To determine success in accomplishing program objectives.
2. To identify the strengths and weaknesses in the HRD processes.
3. To compare the costs to the benefits of an HRD program.
4. To decide who should participate in future programs.
5. To test the clarity and validity of tests, cases and exercises.
6. To identify which participants were the most successful with the program.
7. To reinforce major points made to the participant.
8. To gather data to assist in marketing future programs.
9. To determine if the program was the appropriate solution for the specific need.
10. To establish a database that can assist management in making decisions.

Different Models of Evaluation

The question of what to evaluate is crucial to evaluation strategy. The answer depends on the type of HRD program, the organization and the purposes of evaluation. The following section presents five models.

1. The Kirkpatrick Four – Level Approach

Donald Kirkpatrick has developed a very popular evaluation model that has been used since the late 1950s by the training community. The focus is on measuring four kinds of outcomes that should result from a highly effective training program. Kirkpatrick's model includes four levels or steps of outcome evaluation:

Level 1—Reaction

Here the goal is to measure participants' reactions to the training program. HR personnel should measure their reactions immediately after the program. Level one evaluation should not just include reactions toward the overall program (e.g., Did you like the program?); it should also include measurement of participants' reactions or attitudes toward specific components of the program, such as the instructor, the topics, the presentation style, the schedule, audiovisuals, etc. Furthermore, each of these components can be further broken down into sub-components for evaluation (e.g., you can ask participants to evaluate specific characteristics of the instructor, the presentation, etc.). In short, level one evaluation is far more than just the measurement of overall customer satisfaction.

Learning (Level two outcomes) and transfer of learning (Level three outcomes) are unlikely to occur unless participants have positive attitudes toward the training program. Therefore, it is important to determine participants' reactions to the training program. Also, positive reactions are important because managers are more likely to eliminate unpopular training programs. Finally, the measurement of specific aspects of the training program can provide important information about what aspects of the training program can be improved in the future.

Level 2—Learning

Here the goal is to determine what the training program participants learned during the training event. Because the training instructor should have specific learning objectives, one hopes to find clear learning outcomes. Learning outcomes can include changes in knowledge (e.g., What are the key differences between Windows 95 and Windows ME?), skills (Can the participant upload a new operating system to a computer), or attitudes (Have participants' attitudes toward computers improved?). Some training events will emphasize knowledge, some will emphasize skills, some will emphasize attitudes, and some will emphasize multiple learning outcomes. The evaluation should focus on measuring what was covered in the training event (i.e., the learning objectives).

Level two evaluation should be done immediately after the training event to determine if participants gained the knowledge, skills, or attitudes. A couple of issues here are (a) how shall one measure knowledge, skills, and attitudes, and (b) what research design should be used to demonstrate improvement in level two outcomes?

First, let's talk about the measurement of level two outcomes. Knowledge is typically measured using already available or instructor constructed **achievement tests** (i.e., tests designed to measure the degree of learning that has taken place). In the training environment, these tests are usually criterion-referenced. Note that **norm-referenced tests** are traditional standardized tests that are constructed to maximize individual differences and to allow comparison of individuals to an external norming group. A normal curve often characterizes the performance distribution of the norming group. In contrast, **criterion-referenced tests** are constructed to determine whether learners have mastered one or more learning objectives and these tests include a cutoff point (pass/fail). The results of criterion-referenced tests often take the form of a negatively skewed curve, where the vast majority of the learners have reached or surpassed the criterion or cut-off point (i.e., the point at which one must reach in order to pass the test) and only a few learners have lower scores.

Skills typically require some kind of motor or manual response on the examinee's part, or some kind of manipulation; therefore, a **performance test** is used. A performance test is just a test that requires the test taker to create a product or demonstrate a process. Obviously the goal is to determine whether each person can perform the skills they have been taught in the training event.

Attitudes are measured with questionnaires similar to the questionnaires described for level one evaluation. You will typically have the participants give their ratings for various items (responding with Strongly Agree, Agree, Neutral, Disagree, or Strongly Disagree or with other rating scales), and you should include some open-ended items to allow participants to respond in their own words (e.g., How do you feel about diversity in the workplace?).

Second, Kirkpartick also briefly discusses the issue of research design. He suggests that you include a control group in your design when possible, and he briefly mentions using a pretest measure when possible.

Level 3—Behaviour

Here the goal is to find out if training program participants change their on-the-job-behaviour (OJB) as a result of their having attended and participated in the training program. If the behavior change does not occur, you also want to find out why the change did not occur. The level three question is, Did the training have a positive effect on job performance? Level three evaluation specifically involves measuring the **transfer** of knowledge, skills, and attitudes from the training context to the workplace.

Learning is likely to transfer only if the conditions in the work setting are favorable for transfer. In addition, there are obviously many things that trainers can do to increase the likelihood of transfer. In other words, transfer is affected by "training factors" before trainees go back to their workplace as well as "workplace factors" that operate in their workplace when they return. Here are two sets of factors that make transfer more likely to occur:

Level 4—Results

Here the goal is to find out if the training program led to final results, especially business results that contribute to the "bottom line" (i.e., business profits). Level four outcomes are not limited return on training investment (ROI). Level four outcomes can include other major results that contribute to the well functioning of an organization. Level four includes any outcome that most people would agree is "good for the business." Level four outcomes are either changes in financial outcomes (such as positive ROI or increased profits) or changes in variables that should have a relatively direct effect on financial outcomes at some point in the future.

Here are some examples of different kinds of level four outcomes:

- Improved quality of work.
- Higher productivity.
- Reduction in turnover.
- Reduction in scrap rate (i.e., less wasted resources)
- Improved quality of work life.
- Increased sales.
- Fewer grievances.
- Lower absenteeism.
- Higher worker morale.
- Fewer accidents.
- Greater job satisfaction.
- Increased profits.

2. Kaufman's Five Levels of Evaluation

Some researchers, recognizing shortcomings of the previous model have attempted to modify and add to this basic framework. Kaufman has expanded the definition of level 1 and added a fifth level addressing societal issues. The 5 levels are as follows –

1. **(a) Enabling:** Availability and quality of human, financial and physical resources input.

   (b) Reaction: Methods, means and processes, acceptability and efficiency.
2. **Acquisition:** Individual and small group mastery and competency.
3. **Application:** Individual and small group (products) utilization within the organization.
4. **Organizational output:** Organizational contributions and payoffs.
5. **Societal outcomes:** Societal and client responsiveness, consequences and payoffs.

3. The CIRO Approach

Another 4 level approach, originally developed by Warr, Bird and Rackham is a unique way to classify evaluation processes. The 4 general categories of evaluations are described below –

1. **Context evaluation:** This involves collecting information about a performance deficiency, assessing the information to establish HRD needs and on the basis of those findings, setting objectives at 3 levels.
2. **Input evaluation:** This involves obtaining and using information about possible training resources to choose between alternative inputs to HRD. This type of evaluation involves analyzing the resources available and determining how they can be developed so that there is a maximum chance of achieving the desired objectives.
3. **Reaction evaluation:** This involves obtaining and using information about participants' reactions to improve the HRD processes. The distinguishing feature of this type of evaluation is that it relies on the subjective input of the participants.
4. **Outcome evaluation:** This involves obtaining and using information about the results or outcomes of HRD and is usually regarded as the most important part of the evaluation. If outcome evaluation is to be successful, it requires careful preparation before the program begins.

4. CIPP Model

This evaluation model is similar to the CIRO model. It was developed by educators and claimed to be practical, effective, comprehensive and balanced. The first 2 levels are the same as the CIRO model. The next two levels are –

Process Evaluation

This provides feedback to the individuals responsible for implementation. It is accomplished by monitoring potential sources for failure, providing information for preplanned decisions during implementation and describing what actually occurs. Both formal and informal approaches are used in data collection. These include reaction sheets, rating scales and analysis of existing records.

Product Evaluation

This measures and interprets the results of objectives, including both Intended and unintended outcomes. Evaluation at this level can take place both before and after the program. Any traditional evaluation procedure may be used at this level, provided it is a good fit for the situation.

5. The Phillips Five-Level ROI Framework

The ROI process adds a fifth level to the 4 levels of evaluation developed by Kirkpatrick. The first four steps are the same as the Kirkpatrick model with slightly altered names. The last and fifth stage, the Return on Investment, measures the monetary value of the results and costs for the program, usually expressed as a percentage.

Which Model is the Most Effective and Why?

The most strongly recommended model is 'the Kirkpatrick model' since it is one of the oldest and many other models are based on its basic concepts. It is very easy to understand since its concepts are very clear. All the explanations are worded in easily understandable language. It is the most well known and widely used models even today.

Another reason it is very practical is that other organizational factors are also taken into account. There are many advantages at each level. Even if only 1 or 2 levels are conducted, some useful data will be gathered. The only thing missing is the calculation of ROI at the end but that is not done by most organizations since it makes the process longer and complicated. But for a quick and thorough evaluation it is the best choice.

Summary of The Training and Evaluation Methods of Some Organisations

A form was prepared with the help of a training manager and used to interview the training heads of the following organizations –

- Larsen and Toubro- finance
- Hotel Marine Plaza
- Shoppers Stop
- Hotel Taj Mahal Palace

The following are summaries of the responses got from the above organizations on individual questions. The form consisted of 14 questions related to different aspects of training and evaluation.

When asked about the identification of training needs and whether self or supervisor nominations have worked best, there have been varied responses where two organisations felt that supervisor nominations worked better, one organisation felt self nominations worked best since the employee does not feel forced to take part and one organisation felt that both type of nominations worked well. **Shopper's stop** uses their appraisal, mystery shoppers and customer satisfaction forms as the basis for identifying the training needs. **L and T – finance** uses the annual review for this purpose while **Hotel Marine Plaza** used a standardized form according to their standard operating procedures (SOPs). Another form used mostly in their restaurants for identifying the needs of waiters is a checklist of positive, negative and neutral behaviours.

When asked what is the first step after identification of training needs

Shoppers Stop says they prepare a training calendar for the entire year. **L and T- Finance** and **Hotel Marine Plaza** respond that they organize workshops as needed while **Hotel Taj** says they analyze the needs that have been identified.

The next question inquired about how the training briefs like objectives were got and whether the HR personnel sat with the supervisors for this. Two organizations said they sit with the entire team to discuss this while one organisation discussed this with only the supervisors while in another organisation, once the needs are identified the training workshop is organized by the department on their own.

The next question is related to how many days in advance the training is announced. **Shoppers Stop** releases its training calendar in April every year. The other three companies announce their programs and workshops 2 – 30 days in advance. Two organizations just tell their participants. **Hotel Taj Mahal Palace** informs employees by mail while **Hotel Marine Plaza** also just informs people but sometimes there is a choice and sometimes it is compulsory.

When asked how the feedback is collected, **Hotel Marine Plaza** say that a form is collected after every session. **Shoppers Stop** use the feedback from the mystery shoppers. **L and T- Finance** say that a 'formal' form exists but mostly oral feedback is taken since employees are more frank when verbal feedback is taken.

The next question refers to the qualities and types of trainers used. All the organizations focus on the presentation skills and knowledge of the material to be presented but all admit that these change according to the program. **Shoppers Stop** has about 60 in-house trainers and they also have a program to 'train the trainers'. The 2 hotels also have some trainers but they also outsource for some types of training while **L and T- Finance** hires all the trainers from either their headquarters or from other institutes. All organizations have an annual budget for training programs which they are expected to adhere to strictly.

The next question asked about all aspects of evaluation. Only **The Taj Palace Hotel** said they used the Kirkpatrick model of evaluation. **Shoppers Stop** said they evaluate actual behaviors immediately by supervisors. **Hotel Marine Plaza** said they do not have any formal evaluation. **L and T-Finance** also do not evaluate since the changes are subtle which will be reflected in the annual review.

Most of the organizations say that the employees are receptive of the evaluation since the culture of the organisation is such and they see it as a fair and unbiased evaluation. None of the organizations except **Shoppers Stop** conduct pre and post rating of skills before and after the training.

All the organizations internally train for technical skills and for lower and middle level managers and employees. External training is preferred for soft skills and senior management. Most organizations have negative consequences if the evaluation is lacking. It can be as subtle as no growth in the organisation to formal meetings with superiors, warnings and counseling.

Thus, from the above it can be seen that hardly any organizations use a proper system and objective measures for their training and its evaluation. There are cases where evaluation is not done at all. So, we can conclude that though evaluation is not yet a completely established concept, organizations are aware of it and starting to implement it in their programs as much as possible.

Suggestions

Conducting a Training Needs Assessment

A review of literature indicates that training programs are often prescribed as the drug of choice to problem situations in organizations.

How often have you heard, "We've got a training problem..." or "They're not doing it the way they're supposed to..."? Often these statements are only *symptoms* of a problem. Until the problem is understood in greater detail, proposing a solution or an intervention can be a costly and fruitless endeavor. Often overlooked, as the first step in the performance improvement process is the training needs assessment. A *need* is not a want or desire. It is a gap between "what is" and "what ought to be". The needs assessment serves to identify the gaps, and considers if training can solve the problem. The assessment is part of a planning process focusing on identifying and solving performance problems.

Why Conduct a Training Needs Assessment?

- To determine what training is relevant to your employees' jobs,
- To determine what training will improve performance,
- To determine if training will make a difference,
- To distinguish training needs from organizational problems, and
- To link improved job performance with the organization's goals and bottom line.

In reading different articles and books, you will come across the words *need assessment* and *need analysis*. The terms are interchangeable, but they have the same meaning and purpose, to assess and analyze. The primary purpose of the training needs assessment - analysis process is to ensure that there is a need for training and to identify the nature of the content of the training program. Conducting an assessment is a way to collect information that can be used to decide what type of development will be perceived as relevant and useful. An assessment enables a conversation to take place that questions what skills and knowledge is required to be more effective. It is important that we view training or performance improvement efforts as a "system". Our efforts to improve one part of the organizational system will affect other jobs in the workplace environment. The needs assessment process is an important first step in the development of a training program or performance improvement initiatives.

A needs assessment provides an opportunity to consult with a variety of people in the organization. The information collected, ideas generated, and the conversations that take place when people discuss their work lives and lend enthusiasm to the process. The data collected - whether obtained throuӯh interviews, observations, focus groups, performance data, questionnaires or tests - can clarify issues and provide a focus on performance.

Needs Assessment Methods: Scenarios

The format a needs assessment can take can vary. Generally, an assessment is conducted as a survey. However, you may develop questions and conduct individual interviews or focus groups. Or, you can collect and analyze performance data to determine common needs. We will explore these areas through the use of personal observations; additional assessments may include on-site observation, testing and assessment centers. Individuals who are experienced and knowledgeable with regard to performing a task analysis of the work processes, procedures, methods, and practices being observed should conduct on-site observations. These individuals are referred to as subject matter experts (SME's) and they can be found both inside and outside the organization. Typically, SME's are individuals who once worked in the position and have the in-depth knowledge of the concepts, and processes. Subject matter experts offer the troubleshooting information you may need to determine whether additional training is needed, whether the situation is indicative of a needed intervention. If you plan to use testing and assessment centers, or both, you will want to check into validation and reliability studies to ensure compliance with legal requirements.

Scenario One-Surveying Needs

Let's say you work for a small to mid-size company and the president calls you into the office and says, "The organization has identified projected business goals, and we need be certain that (1) our management team understands the implications on an operational level, and (2) we get feedback to ascertain what types of assistance we need to give to our managers to support their needs."

A survey provides both qualitative and quantitative data for planning purposes. It also says to the members of the management team that the organization wants them to succeed. If the survey, results and subsequent feedback are used to determine training content, or operational level changes, managers will feel their input helped human resources facilitate the change effort.

Scenario Two - Interviewing Methods

What do you do when a department manager wants a training program to solve what they think is a problem? Is training the answer? If training is the answer, what content should be covered?

Is the problem centering on an individual performer level or a joint work-in-progress level? This situation may best be served by conducting a problem analysis interview. First, set up a time to meet with the department manager. Prepare for that meeting by developing open-ended questions to determine more completely what the manager believes should be happening, as well as to understand the current situation. *Here are some examples:*

1. Describe the situation you have encountered?
2. What do you observe that indicates there is a problem?
3. What specifically is the performer doing wrong? Doing right?
4. Probe frequency: **How often** does it occur?
5. Probe location: **Where** does it occur?
6. Probe timing: **When** is it a problem?
7. Probe longevity: **How long** has it been a problem?
8. Probe identity: **Who** is the performer in question?
9. Probe desired performance: **What** is the desired performance?
10. Probe who else is affected: **What** or **who else** is affected by the performer?
11. Probe cost value of discrepancy: **How much** is the problem costing the organization?
12. What are some of the reasons you think training is needed?
13. What is the end result you are seeking from a training intervention?
14. If I were to go out and talk to the employee(s) involved, what would they say?

Keep in mind that we are conditioned to ask questions about things that aren't working well - the problems, so that we can fix them. Try to find out about the successes - what has worked? Also, consider the on-site observation as a secondary data-gathering method. Remember, the SME can be of great assistance in regard to work processes, procedures, methods, and practices being observed. For example, you might bring in an SME to perform a safety assessment of the plant operations and a task analysis of the work being performed on the line.

Scenario Three - Data Gathering

With the continuing emphasis on competency development, companies are seeking individuals who consistently meet or exceed performance requirements and organizational goals. In turn, more and more companies are turning to 360-degree feedback, also referred to as multi-rater assessments (MRA), and to testing or assessment centers. These tools play a key part in a training needs assessment from the standpoint of a continuous improvement process!

The first source of acquiring assessment information is to define the abilities desired of managers - competencies, knowledge, skills, tasks, behaviors and actions. This has been the function of job analysis, and the resulting job descriptions.

A second source of assessment information has been performance evaluation data. The purpose of evaluation was to help individuals to enhance those areas needing improvement.

A third source of information may be for the company to use a managerial evaluation or assessment center to develop individuals in career pathing or a succession planning process

A fourth source of information is the identification of exemplary performers who are meeting and exceeding performance criteria. The information gained through the use of interviews can be utilized to evaluate career pathing and succession planning and to improve the development of the workforce

Obviously, when you consider implementing a training program, assessment work is mandatory. A great deal of information is required before you can move forward with a performance improvement effort designed for organizational impact. The HR professional plays a key role in contributing to performance effectiveness within the organization.

Setting up of A Training Evaluation System

The following 7 step model is suggested –

1. Identification of training needs and developing the purpose and objectives of training (determine baseline data)

2. Select an evaluation design and method and estimate the cost/ benefit ratio (present proposal to management)
3. Determine the contents and instruments and method of delivery (test program)
4. Implement the program
5. Collect and analyze data to evaluate program (with time intervals to get data for all 4 levels of the Kirkpatrick model)
6. Calculate the Return on investment (ROI)
7. Communicate the program results.

Step: 1— Identification of Training Needs and Developing The Purpose and Objectives of Training (Determine Baseline Data)

This is the first step where the first thing that is done is the identification of training needs. 3 different methods for this are given below.

1. **Nomination by superiors:** In this method, generally the immediate superior of the employee observes some deficiencies in the employees performance which can be reduced or eliminated by appropriate training. The training needed might be technical or process training. A separate form can be designed for this, which is filled by the superior and submitted either physically or by mail to the HR employee in charge of it.
2. **Self–nomination:** In this method, the employee himself feels that she/he can improve performance if some training is got. Like the above method, a form can be designed which the employee himself fills and submits to the HR personnel.
3. **Performance appraisal:** Another way of identifying the training needs is by checking for low performance areas in the half-yearly or annual performance appraisal and having training for those particular areas.
4. **Checklist (positive, negative and neutral):** Based on the job description, a list of the behaviors needed for the job is made. 'Positive' signifies the behaviors which the employee has learnt and uses on the job. 'Negative' signifies those behaviors which the employee has learnt but does not use on the job. ' Neutral' refers to those behaviors that the employee has not learnt and thus does not use on the job. The HR employee (or superior) can observe the employee on the job and mark on the checklist

whether the employee falls under positive, negative or neutral on each job behavior.

The next thing to do in this step is that once the needs have been identified the HR personnel as well as the management to get together and decide the exact purpose and objectives of the training to be held depending upon the number of members and the type of members. Lastly, the baseline data are decided so that we know where the employees are before the training (pretraining) and what differences can be seen in their behavior after the training (post-training). Thus this is an objective measure. Also, other baseline data like standardized scores (if available) for more concretely measurable data (e.g. – errors in the past year, average monthly sales etc.)

Step: 2— Selection of The Evaluation Design And Estimate The Program Cost/Benefit (Present Proposal)

In the second step the design of the training is decided depending upon the purpose and participants. There are a few characteristics that are necessary for a good and reliable evaluation design. They are –

- Apart from the group receiving the training, there should be a control group also to show that the changes in the training group are due to training and not by chance or coincidental.
- For both the groups, there should be pre as well as post-training evaluation which shows that firstly, there are changes and secondly, these can be attributed to the training.
- The training environment should be as similar to the normal office environment so that transfer of training (putting what is learnt in the training to use in real situations) is easy for the employee.

Also important in this step is to determine the cost and benefits of such a training program. After this step the specific details of the program are decided thus it is necessary to know whether the program is cost effective for the company and should be carried out or cancelled. Once this is done a proposal is prepared and presented to the management for approval.

Step: 3—Determine The Content, Instruments and Delivery Method (Test Program)

The Instrument: An instrument is a data-gathering tool that collects data to describe changes in attitudes, learning, behavior or other results achieved from the program. Instruments may include record-keeping systems, questionnaires, examinations, attitude surveys, interviews, focus groups, observations or job simulations. The instruments should be statistically reliable and easy to use.

The Content: This is probably the most time consuming step. Subject matter experts who decide what the participants need to know to meet the program objectives may determine the content. This step requires careful review by appropriate management and this should continue throughout the design process. Program material that is nice to know but not related to objectives should be excluded.

Delivery Methods: Selecting a delivery method to meet the program's objective is the next step. Instructional systems and audiovisual tools are frequently used because they are readily available and encourage participant interaction. The following are the different methods used for training delivery.

- Presentation – discussion (including lectures, listening and questioning)
- Conference (including seminars)
- Case study
- Role play
- Workshop
- Computer-based instruction (including computer – assisted instruction and computer – managed instruction)
- Simulations and games
- On the job training
- Peer training
- Programmed instruction
- Team teaching / training
- Demonstration
- Field trips
- Preparatory (short course) format

The effectiveness of theses methods varies. Lectures are considered to be the least effective while methods requiring extensive participation interaction are the most effective. The selection of a method (or methods) depends on such factors as –

- Budget
- Available resources
- Program objectives
- Time frame
- Ability of participants
- Ability of program developers
- Ability of instructors
- Location of training

Test the Program

After the program is developed, a run-through may be appropriate. This is often overlooked. There is no need to test a one-time program but will be particularly useful when it is to be repeated with many participants. A well-planned pilot program can help make the months of analysis, interviews and program development pay off. Taking appropriate steps before, during and after the program provides an opportunity to analyze the program's strengths and weaknesses, and improves the chances of a flawless, fail-safe program.

If it is a one-time program, which is not possible to test, it is advisable to at least have a standard checklist or a list of preparations to be done. It shows what needs to be done and what has already been done so that nothing is left pending till the last minute.

Step: 4— Implement the Program

This is an integral part of any evaluation process. It involves conducting the entire training program as planned in the previous steps. A few things should be kept in mind –

- The environment of the training session should be as similar to the post-training environment as possible since this facilitates transfer of learning.
- A pretest according to the design of the program should be conducted.
- The other groups (control groups) according to the design should also be kept in mind and any required test for them should also be conducted.

- The content should be clear and according to the qualifications and level of the participants. A very easy program, where the content is already known to them will be boring while a very difficult program will confuse the participants and not have the desired results. Thus the program should be slightly challenging.
- The trainer should be chosen according to the personalities of the participants.
- The method of delivery and method of training should be chosen keeping in mind the learning styles of the participants. A questionnaire for the same can be conducted prior to the program.
- The trainers should provide real world examples and actual experience performing and practicing the behaviors.
- The importance and applicability of the future on-the-job behaviors must be explained.

Step: 5— collect and analyze data to evaluate the program (with time intervals to get data for all 4 levels of the kirkpatrick model)

Collection of Data

Another logical and critical step of evaluation is the collection of data. A system to accomplish data collection must be implemented at the appropriate time and the predetermined schedule for data collection must be closely followed. Here it is important to remember that some time must be allowed before data collection for the results to be achieved. In other words, many level four outcomes will take some time to occur. As far as possible, data must be collected both before and after the program to see the changes due to the training.

Analysis And Interpretation of Data

Data analysis involves a sometimes-difficult challenge. Responses to questionnaires should be tabulated and prepared for presentation. Tables and graphs can be used for this. Variances need to be analyzed. Statistics are usually needed. There are three general groups of statistics that are particularly useful when analyzing evaluation data – measures of central tendency (mean, median and mode), measures of dispersion and measures of association.

If appropriate for the analysis, the monetary value of the results is calculated at this step. Judgmental factors may be involved in arriving at these values. Also, the analysis and interpretation of results may be done in different stages. For example, data collected during the program will usually be evaluated at that time to provide information for possible program adjustments. On-the-job performance data or follow up data will be collected later and combined with the initial data analysis for a complete program evaluation.

Step: 6—Calculate The Return On Investment (Roi)

Although, the ROI should be calculated whenever possible, it may be unnecessary in some instances, or it may be too unreliable to be useful. The basic ROI formula is –

ROI (%) = Net program benefits / Program costs * 100

When ROI's are calculated, they should be compared to targets for HRD programs. Sometimes these targets are determined based on company standards for capital expenditures. Others are based on what management expects from an HRD program, or what level they would require to approve implementation of a program. The calculation of the ROI deserves much attention, because it represents the ultimate approach to evaluation and is becoming an increasingly important part of the HRD function as business, industry and the government become more bottom-line oriented. It provides a sound base for calculating the efficient use of financial resources allocated to HRD activities.

Step: 7—Communicate Program Results

The final step in developing a model involves communicating the results of the program. While there is a large audience that should receive the evaluation results, four groups are imperative. One of the most important group is the HRD staff, which needs this information to make improvements in the program. Only through refinement, based on feedback, will programs be improved.

Management is another group because it includes key decision makers who determine the future of the program. A fundamental purpose of evaluation is to provide the basis for sound decisions. Should funds be expended to continue this effort? Was the program worthwhile? Answers to these questions should be communicated to the management group.

The third major group is the participants, who need to know how well they have done in the program and compare their performance to others. This feedback can enhance their efforts, as well as the efforts of others who will be involved in future programs.

A fourth group is participants' immediate managers. This group must make adjustments when participants attend programs, and is accordingly very interested in their success.

Communicating results is an often-overlooked step in HRD. Although evaluation data that has been analyzed and interpreted will usually be given to someone, problems occur when others who need the information do not receive it. Care must be taken to present information in an unbiased, effective manner.

The Benefits of Employee Training

How Training Benefits the Organization

- Leads to improved profitability and/or more positive attitudes towards profit orientation.
- Improves the job knowledge and skills at all levels of the organization.
- Improves the morale of the workforce.
- Helps people identify with organization goals.
- Helps create a better corporate image.
- Fosters authencity, openness and trust.
- Improves relationship between boss and subordinate.
- Aids in organizational development.
- Learns from the trainee.
- Helps prepare guidelines for work.
- Aids in understanding and carrying out organizational policies.
- Provides information for future needs in all areas of the organization.
- Organization gets more effective decision making and problem-solving skills.
- Aids in development for promotion from within.
- Aids in develping leadership skills, motivation, loyalty, better attitudes and other aspects that successful workers usually display.

- Aids in increasing productivity and/or quality of work.
- Helps keep costs down in many areas. e.g. Production, personnel, administration, etc.
- Develops a sense of responsibility to the organization for being competent and knowledgable. Improves labour management relations.
- Reduces outside consulting costs by utilizing competent internal consultation.
- Stimulates preventive management as opposed to putting out fires.
- Eliminates suboptimal behavior (such as hiding tools).
- Creates an appropiate climate for growth, communication.
- Aids in improving organizational communication.
- Helps employees adjust to change.
- Avoids in handling conflicts, thereby to prevent stress and tension.

Benefits to the Individual which in Turn Ultimately Should Benefit the Organization

- Helps the individual in making better decisions and effective problem solving.
- Through training and development, motivational variables of recognition, achievement, growth, responsibility and advancement are internalized and operationalised.
- Aids in encouraging and achieving self-development and self-confidence.
- Helps a person handle stress, tension, frustration and conflict.
- Provides information for improving leadership, knowledge, communication skills and attitudes.
- Increases job satisfaction.
- Moves a person towards personal goals while improving interactive skills.
- Satisfies personal needs of the trainer (and trainee).
- Provides the trainee an avenue for growth and a say in his/her future.

- Develops a sense of growth in learning.
- Helps a person develop speaking and listening skills; also writing skills when exercises are required.
- Helps eliminate fear in attempting new tasks.

Though no single training programme yields all the benefits presented, the organization that devotes itself to training and development enhances its HR capabilities and strengthens its competitive edge. At the same time, the employees personal and career goals are furthered, generally adding to his or her abilities and values to the employer.

Summary and Conclusion

In simple terms, training and development refer to the imparting of specific skills, abilities and knowledge to an employee. A formal definition of training and development is: it is any attempt to improve current or future employee performance by increasing an employee's ability to perform through learning, usually by changing the employee's attitude or increasing his or her skills and knowledge. The need for training and development is determined by the employee's performance deficiency, computed as follows:

Training and development need = Standard performance - Actual performance.

A distinction is made among training, education and development. Such distinction helps to acquire a better perspective about the meaning of the terms. Training refers to the process of imparting specific skills. Education is confined to theoretical learning in classrooms.

Though training and education differ in nature and orientation, they are complimentary. An employee who undergoes training is presumed to have had some formal education. No training programme is complete without an element of education. As more and more employees are called upon to exercise judgment and to choose alternative solutions to the job problem, training programmes seek to broaden and develop the individual through education. Organizations must consider elements of both education and training while planning their training programmes.

Development refers to those learning opportunities designed to help employees grow. Development is not primarily skill-oriented.

Instead, it provides general knowledge and attitudes which will be helpful to employees in higher positions. Efforts towards development often depend on personal drive and ambition. Development activities, such as those supplied by management development programmes, are generally voluntary.

Training and development programmes help remove performance deficiencies in employees. This is particularly true when - (i) the deficiency is caused by a lack of ability rather than a lack of motivation to perform, (ii) the individual(s) involved have the aptitude and motivation to learn to do the job better, and (iii) supervisors and peers are supportive of the desired behaviors.

There is greater stability, flexibility, and capacity for growth in an organization. Training contributes to employee stability in at least two ways. Employees become efficient after undergoing training. Efficient employees contribute to the growth of the organization. Growth renders stability to the workforce further, trained employees tend to stay with the organization. They seldom leave the company. Training makes the employees versatile in operations. All rounders can be transferred to any job. Flexibility is therefore ensured.

Accidents, scrap and damage to machinery and equipment can be avoided or minimized through training. Even dissatisfaction, complaints, absenteeism, and turnover can be reduced if employees are well trained.

Future needs of employees will be met through training and development programmes. Organisations take fresh diploma holders or graduates as apprentices. They are absorbed after course completion. Training serves as an effective source of recruitment. Training is an investment in HR with a promise of better returns in future.

Training is one of the most well-known and important activities in any organisation. Since training evaluation is as important as the training itself and a very upcoming concept which most organizations would like to implement (if not already done).

Firstly, a lot of literature review is necessary to get a clear picture of the concept and to use while formulating a system. Secondly, it is necessary to visit some organizations to interview their training heads to see how it is done in their companies. Lastly, based on both the above, a system, which would work for you can be formulated.

References and Further Reading

1. Alliger, G.M. & Janak, E.A. (1989). Kirkpatrick's levels of training criteria: Thirty years later. *Personnel Psychology*, 42, 331-342.
2. Dixon, N.M.(1990). *Evaluation: A Tool for Improving HRD Quality.* University Associates inc., San Diego.
3. Kirkpatrick, D. L., (1994). *Evaluating Training Programs.* Berrett-Koehler Publishers, San Francisco.
4. Lewis, T. "A Model for Thinking About the Evaluation of Training," *Performance Improvement Quarterly*, Vol. 9, No. 1, 1996, pp. 3-22.
5. Mayo, G. and Dubois,P.H.(1989). *The Complete Book of Training: Theory, Principles and Techniques.* University Associates Incorporation, San Diego.
6. Phillips, J.J., (1991). *Handbook of Training Evaluation and Measurement Methods* (3rd ed.). Gulf Publishing Company, Houston, Texas.
7. Warr, P., Bird, M., and Rackham, N. (1970). *Evaluation of Management Training.* Gower Press, London.

6

Job Satisfaction and Quality of Working Life

Introduction

The current economic environment in India has posed increased challenges for business and industry to be competitive, both nationally and internationally, which in turn require these organizations to perform better in terms of productivity, quality, time and service. Forward looking organisations in such a climate, are taking steps to undergo massive cultural change so as to bring about reciprocal changes in their performance. Among various factors, people's attitudes and feelings regarding their jobs and/or job experiences have been found to significantly affect both their personal as well as job behaviour. This pleasurable emotional state arising from the appraisal of one's job or job experiences is called Job Satisfaction(Locke 1976).

The concept of Job Satisfaction is central to many aspects of industrial and organizational behavior. This could perhaps account for this topic being one of the most Researched topics. The extent to which employees are satisfied with their jobs has, therefore been of considerable interest to both scholars and practitioners. The **term Job Satisfaction** is viewed as a "positive attitude towards one's work, which is global in nature and which results from many specific job-related experiences (Sharma and Bhaskar 1991).

Job Satisfaction- Concept and Meaning

Motivation to work well is usually related to Job Satisfaction. However, Satisfaction is not the same as motivation. Job Satisfaction is more of an attitude, an internal state. It could, for example, be associated with a personal feeling of achievement, either quantitative/

qualitative. Job Satisfaction thus, refers to a set of attitudes that employees have about their jobs. It is the psychological disposition of people towards their jobs- how they feel about the work- and this involves numerous attitudes and feelings.

Additional factors can also influence Job Satisfaction, personal factors that are not directly part of the job or work climate. For example job satisfaction varies as a function of age, health, number of years worked, emotional stability, social status, leisure and recreational activities, family relationship and other social outlets and affiliations.

Recent research also suggests that for some employees, job satisfaction may be a stable, enduring, individual characteristics, independent of the factors of the job. For these workers, changes in job status, pay, or working conditions may have little or no effect on their level of job satisfaction. Job satisfaction appears to vary with one's level or type of work. A survey of 209 women in non-managerial position in a food processing factory found that those on the assembly line were significantly less satisfied with their jobs than those not on the assembly lines(Clergy, Wall and Kemp).

Various Dimensions Associated with Job Satisfaction

Characteristics of the work itself and the context or the situation in which the work is performed, strongly influence job satisfaction. Satisfaction in work can be affected by age, level of intelligence, use of skills and length of job experience. Although these factors cannot be changed by the employing organization, they can be used to predict the relative levels of satisfaction to be expected among different groups of workers. The relationship between job satisfaction and number of years on the job is complex. A study of 124 sales persons from 7 companies showed that those with greater time on the job, were less satisfied . In addition, those with more experience did not believe that job performance led to rewards. They were not as challenged or involved with their jobs or as committed to their company as those with less experience (Stout, Sclum and Cron). However, job satisfaction increases after a number of years of experience and improves steadily thereafter. The relationship between job satisfaction and length of experience are closely parallel with age. The higher the occupation or status level of a job, the higher is the job satisfaction. Executives express more satisfaction with their jobs than do firstline supervisors, who, in turn are more satisfied than their subordinates In general, higher the level of the jobs, the greater is the opportunity to satisfy the motivational needs and the greater is the autonomy, challenge and responsibility.

Job satisfaction has also been found to vary with different kinds of occupations. For example, those with the highest satisfaction scores are either in business for themselves or, in construction industry. Chances of dissatisfaction in these two areas are only 1 in 20. Persons in technical, professional and managerial jobs report a 1 in 10 chance of being dissatisfied. The last satisfying occupations are manufacturing service occupations and wholesale or retail businesses (Shepperd and Herrick).

Baron has Listed Certain Factors which Influence Job Satisfaction

1. **Challenging Work:** Work should be challenging but not fatiguing.
2. **Rewards for good performance:** Clear contingencies between rewards and performance are desirable.
3. **Verbal Recognition:** Appreciations, praises and feedback.
4. **Good working conditions:** Physical working conditions should be comfortable.
5. **Concerned Supervision:** supervisors should demonstrate their concern for helping employees.
6. **Positive Interpersonal relations:** Satisfaction is strongly enhanced by friendly relations with co-workers and supervisors.
7. **Effective company policies:** These should help employees attain goals.
8. **Job Security:** Belief that benefits are fairly distributed.
9. **Participation in decision making:** Employees generally feel that they know much about their jobs and should be consulted.

9\. **Pay**: The greater these are, the higher the satisfaction tends to be.

10\. **Degree of autonomy and responsibility:** this has a great effect on satisfaction on the job.

11\. **Role ambiguity:** Individuals wish to know what is expected of them, ambiguity should be avoided.

Job Satisfaction and Work Behavior

Generally the level of job satisfaction seems to have some relation with various aspects of work behaviour like absenteeism, adjustments, accidents, productivity and union affiliation. We thus need to look at various aspects of work behavior that could lead to satisfaction or diss-atisfaction on the job.

Job Satisfaction and Accidents

Studies have shown a variety of variables that seem to explain at least to some extent, the reasons why accidents take place at the work place. These could be reasons in one's personal life, work itself, and the environment in which one is working. Research on the relationship between job satisfaction and accidents shows that the higher the satisfaction with ones job, the lower is the rate of accidents. Though it is difficult to explain such a relationship but generally a satisfied employee would not be careless or negligent and would encounter less possibilities of running into an accident situation. The more favourable the attitude towards the job, the more he will be positively inclined to his job and there would be a lesser chance of him getting into an expected or an unexpected event in which either his action or the reaction of an object or a person may result in personal injury.

Job Satisfaction and Absenteeism

In everyday life certain contingencies require a little extra effort on the part of the workers. Although a number of definitions are available in literature, almost all of them indicate absenteeism as an absence from work when one is expected to work. Absence from work could be attributed to the unwillingness on the part of the employees to work. If however a worker takes his earned leave with prior approval, it is not included as absenteeism, if not, then it falls under the definition of absenteeism. Most Researches on absenteeism and job satisfaction show that the higher the rate of absenteeism, the lower is the job satisfaction.

Job Satisfaction and Adjustment

If the employee is facing problems in general adjustment, it is likely to affect his work life. Adjustment problems usually show themselves in the level of job satisfaction. For long, both the theorists and practitioners have been concerned with employees' adjustment and have provided vocational guidance and training to them to minimise its impact on work behavior. Most literature in this area, generally suggests a positive relationship between adjustment and job satisfaction. People with lower levels of anxiety have been found to be more satisfied with their jobs.

Job Satisfaction and Unionism

In the Indian context, unions are strong and persuasive, to think of job satisfaction without unionism would be very unrealistic. In large cities and industrial belts, unions are a part of life. In the organisational climate, sometimes personnel policies and practises of the management are seen as dissatisfying. Most workers tend to look up at the union official to settle their grievances. Not only this, the dissatisfaction of the employees with the work and work environment is often exploited by union leaders to gain membership and support of the work force. Sharma (1980) studied the relationship between job satisfaction and union involvement. He found out union involve ment correlating significantly with job satisfaction. Union involvement turned out to be the best predictor of variations in job satisfaction.

Job Satisfaction and Personal Characteristics

When a person comes to work he brings with him his total personality, his likes, dislikes, his personal characteristics and these in turn influence the satisfaction he derives from his work. As work is one of the necessary aspects of the total life experience of an individual, it becomes important to examine how his personal characteristics influence his job satisfaction. Personal characteristics here refer to such bio-social variables such as age, marital status, education, income, length of service etc.

Job Satisfaction and Organisational Objectives

Much of job satisfaction research has centred around the correlative studies examining the association of the personality or job factors with job satisfaction. In these studies, respondents have evaluated their understanding of how satisfied/dissatisfied they have felt with various aspects of their job and whether they had anything to do with such factors as age, years of experience, income etc.In the other set of studies, the respondents have been divided into groups based on their biographic variables and the effect of such variables on job satisfaction. Not much is known about how the overall goals of the organization contribute to the degree of satisfaction/ dissatisfaction on the job. Such a study is very pivotal since it may help the organisation to develop organisational level plans to induce greater satisfaction, help the employees to develop an identity with the organisation or just improve their commitment to work and loyalty to the organisation.

What Satisfies Indian Employees

Most Indian studies on job satisfaction have concerned themselves with specific aspects of work .These studies on managers/ supervisors/workers have essentially put forth important findings in the area of job satisfaction. A study looked into a representative sample of 15 studies on managers and supervisors from different organisations in India. On the question of what satisfies the Indian supervisor or managers, the following results were obtained: responsibility ranks as the top most factor contributing to the job satisfaction of the Indian manager or supervisor. This is followed by work Itself. Next aspects related to job satisfaction was achievement and recognition. The general trend of what satisfies Indian managers/supervisors seems to highlight the motivators or content factors as stipulated by Herzberg and others.

What satisfies the Indian Workers: the results of a representative sample of 14 studies dealing with different samples of Indian workers from different organisations was used. The most important factor that contributed to the Job satisfaction of the Indian workers is Money. Undoubtedly economic factors play a significant role in job satisfaction of the Indian workers. This is followed by job security.

Thus in the final analysis, it can be seen that job satisfaction plays a very important role in the life of an employee. Looking into job satisfaction levels of the employees is an important benefit for the organization. It can then try to reduce or try and tackle those areas that lead to a great degree of dissatisfaction among the employees. Because highly satisfied employees will ultimately increase the effectiveness of an organisation on the whole. Some important techniques like Job Rotation, Job Enlargement and Job Enrichment can be used in jobs where such techniques to reduce job dissatisfaction are practical and applicable.

A Research Study

The present study seeks to measure JOB SATISFACTION and QUALITY OF WORKING LIFE among Telephone operators working in the Mahanagar Telephone Nigam Ltd (MTNL), Prabhadevi, Dadar Branch. This study mainly tries to ascertain the Level of Job Satisfation and Quality of Working Life among this section of employees in MTNL. Before we look at the methodology and the findings of this study, it is important to look at the various important aspects and focal dimensions of MTNL as an organization. First and foremost are the historical development or the key achievements of MTNL:

Landmarks in the Growth of the System

Year	*Details*
28.01.1882	First Telephone exchange in Mumbai using Law's call wire equipment commissioned by Mumbai Telephone company at fort
1892-1893	All Exchanges converted into Magneto Exchanges.
1896	Introduction of phonogram at Bombay
1906-1910	Underground cables introduced.
24.05.1924	Auto Exchanges opened for the first time in India.
1932	Automatic time announcing machine with disc records installed.
1941	Charging by meter introduced.
April, 1943	Bombay Telephone Company is taken by Government with 21000 lines.
1950-55	Steps by step stronger exchanges commissioned.
1956-60	Central Disk tape recorder type announcement introduced.
1966-70	Penta Conta cross Bar Exchange installed for the first time in Mumbai.
1971-75	One Max -2 exchange commissioned with STD to Mumbai on 6.9.1975 at vashi, Navi Mumbai . Vashi demand trunk service introduced. Demand trunk to BG, CA and BRD introduced. Telephone accounting computerised. Telephone directory (English) compiled for the first time. Time announcement (175) in Marathi and Hindi introduced.

(Contd.)

Contd.

	STD to madras, Nagpur and Gandhi Nagar introduced. Demank trunk at home street and prabhadevi commissioned. INTELEX commissioned.
1975	First PCM system between city and Andheri commissioned
1976-78	STD to various stations, ISD to London introduced.
1978-79	C-400 Hitachi Crossbar Commissioned on 26.5.78 at Malabar Hill
1983-84	SPC analog exchange commissioned at Cooperage.
1985-86	E10B exchange commissioned at Worli-3 South Colaba, Walada-2, Central and Ghatkopar-2. Navi Mumbai Telecom District formed on 1.4.85 ISD to USA and some of other European countries introduced. Panvel, Taloja, Nhava and Uran taken over from Maharashtra Circle.
1986-87	Formation of MTNL on 1.4. 86
1987-88	Large scale introduction of Push Button instruments.
1988-89	Phone Plus services introduced for subscriber numbers connected with Electronic exchanges.
1991	I-net system commissioned.
1992-93	Fetex –150 commissioned at Fountain -3 and Thane RLC-1 Voice Mail service commissioned at Prabhadevi. Radio paging commissioned at Prabhadevi 197 special services made non- metered.
1993-94	First OCB switch in the network introduced at Kandivali.
1994-95	First EWSD exchanges introduced in network at Vileparle and Borivali.
1995-96	Usage of automatic number announcement services introduced. Interactive fault repair service introduced.
1996-97	ISDN services introduced commercially. Autocom service introduced.
1997-98	Waiting list for new connection brought to NIL. Total

(Contd.)

Contd.	
	of 213475 connections added to the system.
1998-99	IN(Intelligent Network) service introduced. Internet service commenced and MTNL became an ISP.
1999-2000	MTNL Mumbai crossed the 2 million mark in subscriber base. MTNL became 100% electronic.

The Mission of MTNL

To remain mark leader in providing world class Tele- com and IT related services to become a Global player.

The present study aimed at ascertaining Job Satifaction and Perceptions of quality of Working Life among Telephone Operators at MTNL, Prabhadevi office.

Methodology

This study carried out at MTNL, consisted a Sample of 50 Telephone Operators. This sample was drawn from the various Departments in MTNL, consisted of various Grades of Telephone Operators Namely: SRTOAP(Grade 1 to 3),HGTO's,JSR-junior supervisors, Senior Supervisors, And HGTSR's. The Mean age in this sample (N=50) was 46 years .The mean number of years in service/ number of years that subjects in this sample had worked for in this organization was found to be 25 years.

The Measures Used

Job Satisfaction

In this study, a Job Satisfaction Scale was used to measure the level of job satisfaction for the subjects included in this sample(N=50). The **details of the job satisfaction scale** are listed below:

Title of the instrument: A Job Satisfaction Scale.

Purpose: To measure job satisfaction in an organizational set up.

Levels: Individuals / Groups.

Main Features: A 25 item scale on a five point scale.

Scoring: Strongly agree=5,Agree= 4, Undecided =3, Disagree=2, Stongly Disagree=1. Item 24 and 25 are reverse scored.(negative statements)

Reliability: Test Retest = 0.64, Split- Half Reliability Coefficient = 072.

Validity: Independent of Age, education and salary. Moderately and Negatively correlated with unstability (-.50) and extraversion (-0.42) but not with other personality variables like Psychoticism, social desirability, quality of life, depression etc.

Time Limit: 20- 25 minutes

Quality of Working Life (QWL)

QDL was the Second aspect that was included in this study. The method used to assess perceptions of Quality of Working Life was a specially designed Questionnaire. This questionnaire consisted of a total number of 8 statements that had to be answered in YES/NO responses. This questionnaire also had an important area which served as a SUGGESTION BOX that reveals the various suggestions of the employees included in the sample (N=50). This states their views, concerns, opinions as employees of MTNL, as to how MTNL can increase its overall effectiveness and productivity as an organization and this aspect forms an important dimension of improving the QWL in the organization.

This Quality of Working Life Questionnaire that was specially designed focused on 8 dimensions/areas based on the criteria put forward by Professor Walton which make up the Quality of Working Life (QWL) framework. These 8 dimensions are as follows:

1. Adequate and Fair compensation.
2. Safe and Healthy Working conditions.
3. Future Opportunity for Continued Growth and Security.
4. Social Integration in the Work Organisation.
5. Constitutionalism in the Work Organisation.
6. Work and Total life space
7. Grievances and Problem handling
8. Social Relevance of Work Life

Thus these were the Measures used for Assessing Job Satisfaction and Perceptions of QWL among the Telephone Operators at MTNL.

The Findings

The findings or results from both the Job Satisaction Scale and The Quality of Working Life Questionnaire are discussed below respectively.

The data revealed that a greater proportion of the employees in the sample had low levels of Satisfaction on the job. There are various factors that can cause low level of satisfaction on ones job, some of the factors are **monotony** on the job.

Many jobs are characterized by monotony and are repetitive in nature. This could be a source of dissatisfaction, where the employee dosen't feel he has new challenges to meet or new areas on the job in which he can grow and develop. Other aspects that can lead to dissatisfaction are **Uncertainty** about the future in ones job, an environment in which there is a possibility of **Mergers** or **Acquisitions** etc to name a few.

In the final analysis on the issue of Job Satisfaction, **Intrinsic contents** of the Job including Hygienic and Motivating factors are important or pivotal for the employees Job Satisfaction. The proper Job Satisfaction also depends on the employees attitude towards the job and how he/she decides to make the best use of the opportunities etc encountered on the job. Thus it takes both an effort from the Organization as well as the individual employees to experience high levels of Job Satisfaction.

The Second Part of this study attempts to assess the Perceptions of Quality of Working Life (QWL).

1. **Adequate and fair compensation:** (First dimension of QWL Questionnaire): Motivation experts believe that money is still an Important motive which makes people work on the job. However, people also want to see fairness and adequacy in their pay rewards. Equal pay for equal work that is linked to responsibility, skill, performance and individual accomplishment are viewed with great importance. Pay must be also competitive with the external labour market and should be responsive to prevailing practices and changing economic conditions. The data show that 84 per cent of subjects in this sample expressed that they don't think that the organization follows the policy of equal pay for equal work. While only 16 per cent of the employees in this sample felt that the organization adopts the same.

2. **Safe and Healthy Working Conditions:** was the second dimension that the QWL Questionnaire focussed on. An organisation must create working conditions that are physically and psychologically safe for its workers. The emergence of ergonomics in the 1950's has significantly improved equipment design and plant layout to enhance the physical as well as psychological comfort and safety of the employees. The data reveals that 88 per cent of the employees agreed that the working conditions in the organization are safe and healthy. While 12 per cent of the employees in the sample felt that the working conditions aren't safe and healthy.
3. **Immediate Opportunity to use and develop human capacities:** this is the third dimenion of QWL. An Organisation must be responsible for the growth and development of its employees. This involves the training, skill developments, recognition, and promotion. Work assignments should be made challenging enough to expand skills, abilities, and knowledge. They should have a positive effect on self-esteem, autonomy, involvement and motivation. 86% of the employees in the sample agreed that they were getting enough opportunity for growing and developing in their jobs, while 14% of the employees didn't agree to this dimension.
4. **Social Integration in the Work Organisation:** This was the 4th dimension that the QWL questionnaire assessed. The work environment should provide opportunities for preserving an employee's personal identity and self-esteem through freedom from prejudice, a sense of community, and interpersonal openness. The data obtained reveal that 96 per cent of the subjects in the sample felt that they are happy with the social interaction that they have at the workplace, whereas only 4 per cent of the subjects didn't agree to this statement.
5. **Constitutionalism in the Work Organisation:** There should be right to personal privacy, free speech and equitable treatment, in the workplace. The data shows that 88 per cent of the telephone operators felt that they did have the right to freedom of speech and equal treatment in this organization, while 12 per cent of the subjects didn't agree to this statement.
6. **Work and the Total Life Space:** Is the sixth dimension that forms an important part of QWL. A person should not overbalance his

life. Ideally, work schedules, career demands and travel requirements should not take too much of his leisure and family life. Here, 34 per cent of the employees felt that their work load affected their family roles while 66 per cent of the subjects felt that work pressures didn't affect their family roles.

7. **Employee Grievances and Problems:** Is the next important dimension of QWL. This aspect looks at whether employee problems and issues are handled effectively in the work organisation. 86 per cent of the employees in this sample agreed that their grievances are handled effectively by the organisation, while 14% of the employees did not agree to this statement.
8. **Social Relevance and Work Life:** Is the 8th and final dimension included in the frame work of QWL. The standing of an organisation in society can influence an employees value of his work and career. Does the employee take pride in being part of the organization?. Here all the Employees in the sample agreed that they were proud of being a part of MTNL. Thus quality of working life is a broad concept and it embraces such activities as work restructuring enrichment, work humanisation, labour-management co-operation, flextime, job rotation among many others. QWL essentially involves continual commitment from all levels of the organization.

The next aspect of the QWL Questionnaire consisted of an Employee Suggestion Box- what they as employees feel as to how MTNL an Organization can Increase its overall effectiveness. The following statements gives a summary of the key areas/issues/concerns/opinions expressed by all the employees in the sample.

Suggestions

1. All the employees need to put in better work to face competition in the current scenario. Improve work performance to get the best results.
2. The job location given should be the closest to the residence of the employee.
3. MTNL is a good organisation. It should be our motto to give all good services to our customers as (a)good facility for VCC cards, trump cards (b)full range to Dolphin mobile and Garuda.

4. We need to give importance to Customer's demands.
5. Give the Best Services to the Customers.
6. MTNL should go on united as an Organisation, we want it to progress further.
7. All the departments and all the levels of employees should perform effectively.
8. Number of free calls should be increased.
9. The organisation should follow the public demands and bring more improvements by giving more facilities to the customers.
10. Customer Service-subscribers should be given total customer care.
11. Only staff cooperation for better customer service will help MTNL.
12. Directory Service 197 should be available to the subscribers.
13. Emergency Service....the customer service here should be 24 hours.
14. Test room- 24 hours.
15. Forms (for mobile etc) should be processed faster. Free forms should be made available and less documents for these forms should be implemented.
16. Good performance is the most important criteria to improve MTNL on the whole.
17. There should be more peaceful working conditions (less noise)especially during the peak work hours.
18. Improve the Quality of service-Directories should be updated, STD codes, latest information on various MTNL services should be made available.
19. New technologies must be adopted to stay on par and progress further.
20. Favour the Subscribers- Rent is affecting the middle class section, so increase in Rental charges should be averted.
21. Ergonomics, seating facilities should be comfortable for the staff, for them to Perform effectively (Updation Dept.).
22. MTNL landline, TNF-these facilities should be put in remote areas too where it is needed.
23. 197 directories need to be updated.
24. Facilities given to staff should be verified before giving.

25. All technical faults must be removed, 197 subscribers aren't getting signals- sometime the computers don't work- so staff can't perform effectively.
26. New schemes and services of the organization should be informed to Employees, so staff in 197 are up to date and can answer customer queries effectively.
27. 197 Dept-the work environment can be improved-separate cabins are needed so that the noise is reduced and customers can be handled more efficiently.
28. Mobile services should be improved to increase customers. Should not give customer any reason to complain.
29. Cheque collection machines at more places to improve customer services.
30. Work should be done completely with dedication. Supervision should be done to see that staff works to the optimum level.
31. Duplicate bill counter should be there at all exchanges.
32. Late Bill: If the customer is paying the bill at Naigaum, then the other exchanges should get the details through the computer.
33. Work pressure is more here. Due to card punching system we have become more punctual in coming to office. We are more confident of the system now. We are trying our level best to do justice to this organization.
34. If an employee leaves the job, their children should get the job(at least 1 child).
35. When new facilities /services are introduced, then training on these should be imparted to the staff, so they know about various services-at least the operators.
36. Provide more facilities (Transport-i.e. station to office).
37. Reduce night shifts.
38. Rent should not be increased since telephone is a necessity, not a luxury.
39. 197-night duties aren't necessary. Traffic is less, so SSX night duties should decrease.
40. Supervisors must be given more power to take action against employees who don't do their work properly.

41. There should be measures adopted to check the output of the staff apart from just having the punch card system.
42. If competitors reduce prices, we should follow similar policies to deal with competition effectively.
43. Maintenance of technical head gear sets(197) should be improved.

Conclusion

Thus, these were the various aspects that the employees put forth. Quality of Working life is therefore an important aspect to an employee in an organization. Having surveys like these on the same issue can help an organization look into the areas of concern or areas that can be improved upon further. Quality of Working life hence can help an organization to increase its overall effectiveness in the long run. Thus Job Satisfaction and Quality of Working Life are extremely pivotal aspects of organizational life, and care should be taken by organizations to look into these areas. Employee satisfaction and perceptions of quality of work life have an impact on the organization as a whole.

References and Further Reading

1. Beach S Dale, Personnel, Management of People at Work, 5th edition, Macmillan Ltd.
2. Bhatia S. K., Management of Personnel/ HRM, 2nd edition, Deep and Deep Publication Pvt. Ltd.
3. IJIR, Indian Journal of Industrial Relations,Vol. 33, July 1997.
4. IJIR, Vol. 18, Correlated QWL.
5. IJIT, Vol. 31, Employee Satisfaction and Organizational Predictors.
6. Mullins, Management of Organizational Behavior, 2nd edition, Wheeler Publishing.
7. Pestonjee D. M. 3rd handbook of Psychological and Social instruments, Volume 2.
8. Saiyadain- HRM- Tata Mc Graw Hill Publishing House.
9. Reitzn–Behavior in Organizations, Richard D Irwin.
10. www.mtnl.net.in/index.htm.
11. www.mtnl.net.in/vision.htm.
12. www.prodomain.com.

7

Employee Counselling

"Counselling is a process by which a troubled person (client / subject / counsellee) is helped to feel and behave in a more personally satisfying manner through interaction with an uninvolved person (the counsellor) who provides information and reactions which stimulates the client to develop behaviours which enable him to deal more effectively with himself and his environment." – **ROGERS.**

Counselling is discussion of a problem with an employee that usually has emotional content in order to help the employee cope with it better. Counselling seeks to improve employee mental health. Good mental health means that people feel comfortable about themselves, right about other people, and able to meet the demands of life.

The definition of counselling implies a number of characteristics. It is an exchange of ideas and feelings between two people, a counsellor and a counsellee, so it is an act of communication. Since it helps employees cope with problems, it should improve organizational performance, because the employee becomes more cooperative, worries less about personal problems, or improves in other ways. Counselling also helps the organization become more human and considerate of people's problems.

Counselling may be performed by both professionals and nonprofessionals. Counselling is usually confidential so that employees will feel free to talk openly about their problems. It also involves both job and personal problems, since both types of problems may affect an employee's performance on the job. For example one employee may be experiencing the stress of new job expectations, while another may be distraught with grief following the death of a family member. Both employees are potential candidates for receiving the benefits of counselling at work.

Scope of Employee Counselling

The need for counselling arises from a variety of employee problems including stress, absenteeism, burnout, low job satisfaction, family problems, too much of work load etc. When these problems exist, employees benefit from the understanding and guidance that counselling can provide. For example, one employee feels insecure about retirement. Another employee is hesitant to take the risk required by a promotion and thus ceases growing on the job. A third employee may become unstable in the job. In all cases, counselling is a necessity.

More problems that require counselling have some emotional content. Emotions are a normal part of life. Emotions and feelings make people human. On the other hand, emotions can get out of control and cause workers to do things that are harmful to their own best interests and those of the firm. They may leave their jobs because of trifling conflicts that seem large to them, or they may undermine morale in their departments. Managers want their employees to maintain good mental health and to channel their emotions along constructive lines so that they will work together effectively.

Any work related or family related issues that cause mental health problems, employees fall under the scope of employee counselling. The objective of employee counselling is to bring up the emotional health of the employees. Any factors that hinder the emotional growth of employees deal with counsellors.

Aims of Counselling

- To provide psychological assistance to the person who needs it.
- To promote growth of a clear sense of ego identity.
- To enable the individual to examine his own problems and find out healthy solutions.
- To change the attitude of the counsellee in a positive direction.
- To develop insight into his own problems and to gain intergration with his own personality.
- To bring positive change in personality and behaviour.
- To enable the individual to enjoy life in a more satisfying way.
- To enable the individual to be more effective, better adjusted and more productive (Davis, 1999).

The Stages of Counselling

Counseling is often described as a "process"(Hansen, Stevic, &Warner, 1982). The implicit meaning of this process is a progressive movement toward an ultimate conclusion, that conclusion being the resolution of whatever precipitated the need for help. This progressive movement is often described as a series of "stages" through which the counselor and client move. These stages include: (1) rapport or relationship building; (2) assesment or definition of the problem; (3) goal setting; (4) initiating interventions; and (5) termination and followup. The stages overlap in such a way that assessment begins while the relationship is still developing, or early goal setting begins even while assessment is continuing.

Establishing The Relationship

The term relationship has many inferential meanings, including the tics between two people in love, kinship within family etc. In the counseling setting, relationship takes on a more specific meaning. When the counselor establishes rapport with a client, the relationship includes such factors as respect, trust, and a sense of relative psychological comfort. Rapport refers to the psychological climate that emerges from the interpersonal contact between counselor and client. Consequently good rapport sets the stage for positive psychological growth.

This climate will be affected by a number of factors, including the counsselor's personal and professional qualities and the client's interpersonal history and anxiety state. Even the best trained, best adjusted counselor still faces a variety of challenges when meeting a new client. The sensitive client will note the counselor's nonverbal and verbal messages and make inferences about these qualities. The resulting first impressions influence rapport building and may need to be reexamined later when the counselor and client have reached a more comfortable level with one another.

The process begins with adequate social skills. Introduce yourself. Ask the client's name and remember it. The client should be invited to sit down and be made comfortable. Client should be addressed by name. If the client appears highly anxious, engage him or her in some initial social conversation and watch to see if the anxiety begins to dissipate. His nonverbal behaviour should be noticed and that information should be used to try and understand his emotional state. Invite the client to describe his or her reason for coming to talk to the counselor. Allow the client time to respond. Don't finish the client's sentences or interrupt the train of thought. This behaviour is often described as attending or active listening. It communicates to the client that the counselor is intersted in him, what he or she has to say.

Several sessions may be required before the client becomes comfortable with the counselor and begins to admit the counselor into his or her inner world. During these sessions consistency is an important quality. The counselor's behaviour, attitudes, opinions, promptness, and attention to detail will all be observed by the client. If the counselor varies from session to session the client will find him less predictable and will find it more difficult to become comfortable with the counselor.

Assessing the Problem

As the rapport is being built up the second process is beginning. This process involves the information related to the client's reason for seeking counselling. This is called the assessment stage. Assessment can be thought of in two ways. First, assessment depends on the counselor's theoretical and philosophical view of human problems. Second, assessment depends on the conditions present in the client's situation and the counselor's understanding of those conditions.

The assessment stage is, first, a data collecting time. One has to open all communications channels to receive information that the client is communicating. At first one may not see any patterns, or meaning to the information. But as one continue to work with the client, however, patterns will emerge, and one will begin to undestand how the client perceives reality. One will also begin to see the client in the larger context of his or her environment, social setting, or world of relationships.

Goal Setting

Setting goals is very important to the success of counselling. Some client's and even some counsellor's resist setting goals. The act of setting a goal involves making a commitment to a set of conditions, a course of action, or an outcome. Sometimes the highly stressed client or the disoriented client may find goal setting difficult to do.

Goals are set inorder to know how well the counselling is working and when the counselling should be concluded. The client is an important source of information and reaction to counselling. Counselling can generate dependent relationships. When that happens, the immediate desire to hold on to a rewarding relationship may overshadow the more appropriate objectives of counselling. Futhermore the kinds of things that are done in counselling, the interventions, are often detemined by counselling goal.

The process of setting goals is mutually defined by the counsellor and client. The counsellor has the advantages of greater objectivity, training in normal and abnormal behaviour, and experience in the process. The client has the advantages of intensive experience in the problem and its history, potential insights, and awareness of personal investment in change.

Goals can be altered when new information or new insights into the problem call for change. Sometimes a goal is identified inappropriate and must be dropped. The major function of goals is to provide direction to the counsellor and the client.

Initiation of Interventions

The real issue in talking about interventions is change and how it occurs. The whole object of counselling is to initiate and facilitate desirable change. Thus, when the counsellor and client are able to identify desirable goals and outcomes, the next question is how to accomplish these goals.

The first thing a counsellor should do is ask clients what solutions or remedies they have already tried. Most of the time, clients will be able to describe one or more things they have done which were minimally successful in alleviating the problem. This information not only saves the counsellor from suggesting alternatives that will be rejected; it also gives the counsellor some sense of the clients's past efforts to remedy difficulties and the client's resoursefulness as a problem solver. Assuming all client-induced interventions were ineffective, the counsellor's next step is to relate problems to interventions, depending on the character of the problem.

Choosing the right intervention is often a process of adaptation. Not all interventions work with all clients, or as well as on might predict. Sometimes the "perfect" intervention turns out to be perfectly awful.

It is important that the counsellor approach selection of interventions tentatively.

The counsellor also needs to know how clients normally react to a specific intervention. Usually this is expressed in terms of a range of typical reactions. The object is to recognize the abnormal reaction, the unpredictable response, the result of which might intensify the problem rather than alleviate it. These three characteristics— skill with a specific intervention, knowledge of its effects, and ability to "read" client reactions – constitute the skills inherent in effective counselling interventions (ibid, 1982)s.

Termination and Follow-Up

Counselling, and especially good counselling, becomes a very significant event for most clients. The relationship to the counsellor may well be the most important relationship in the client's life at that moment. Thus, it is imperative that the counsellors acknowledge how important he or she is to most clients and how much his or her actions affect them.

Occasionally, clients need a bit of security to take with them, even though they feel ready to terminate. This can be accomplished by making a follow-up appointment six weeks or six months in advance. It may be a good idea to ask clients to decide whether they feel the need to keep the appointments as the date approaches. If they do not, they can call and cancel and let the counsellor know that they are doing well. On the other hand, it is also important to communicate to clients that if new counselling needs arise, they should feel free to call before the appointment date (Sherilyn, 1999).

Skills of Counselling

1. **Receiving:** Receiving a troubled employee to the counseling situation would mean to welcome him and building a psychological rapport in order to get him ready to release his emotional blockages. A warm reception in the beginning with a cup of tea or dialouge to establish relationship with the present situation of counselling is very important for opening up his troubling experiencies.
2. **Listening:** Intelligent listening with eyes and to tap the real problem area is very helpful in the counselling process. While

listening, the counsellor is not only listening to the feeling of a counsellee but he is also framing his responses to interact effectively. Any thing which disturbes the effective listening can be prevented such as telephone call or visitors. Listening to the counsellee with the absense of mind on part of the counsellor may have deteriorating effect on the counselling process.

3. **Responding**: Responding would mean to mirrorize and paraphrase the feeling and emotions of the counsellee and communicating the same to him for clarification of his mind. Responses of the counsellor can also be revealed through non-verbal expressions to convey acceptance or being with the counsellee on what he is narrating.

4. **Questioning:**Questioning is a very important skill of the counsellor to give lead to the counsellee by asking him direct, directive or non-directive questions. Non-directive questions are very helpful in the counselling process that usually starts with "how" and the counsellee begins to narrate his expressions. Directive questions would normally need the desired response and direct questions are asked to confirm the doubtful information from the counsellee. (Pai, 1999).

Functions of Counselling

The general objective of counselling is to help employees develop better mental health so that they will grow in self-confidence, understanding, self control, and ability to work effectively. The counselling objective is achieved through one or more of the following counselling functions.

1. **Advice:** Many people view counselling as primarily an advice giving activity, but in reality this is only one of the several functions that counselling can perform. The giving of advice requires a counsellor to make judgements about a counsellee's problems and to lay out a course of action. Advice giving may breed a new relationship in which the counsellee feels inferior and dependent on the counsellor. Inspite of its ills, advice occurs in routine counselling because workers expect it and managers tend to provide it.

2. **Reassurance:** Counselling can provide employees with reassurance, which is a way of giving them courage to face a

problem or a feeling of confidence that they are pursuing a suitable course of action. One trouble with reassurance is that the counsellees do not always accept it. They are smart enough to know that the counsellor cannot know that the problem will come out all right. Though reassurance has its weakness, it is useful in some situations and is impossible to prohibit.

3. **Communication:** Counselling can improve both upward and dounward communicaton. In an upward direction, it is a way for employees to express their feelings to the management. The art of counselling initiates an upward signal, and if the channels are open, some of these signals will travel higher. Individual names must be kept confidential, but statements of feeling can be grouped and interpreted to management. An important part of any counsellor's job is to discover emotioal problems related to compay policies and to interpret those types of problems to top management. Counselling also achieves downward communication because counsellors help interpret company activities to employees as they discuss problems related to them.

4. **Release of emotional tension:** An important function of nearly all counselling is release of emotional tension; this release is sometimes called emotional catharsis. People tend to get an emotional release from their frustrations and other problems whenever they have an opportunity to tell someone about them. This release of tension does not necessarily solve people's problems, but it does remove mental blocks in the way of solution, enabling to face their problems again and think constructively. In some cases emotional release accomplishes the whole job, dispelling an employee's problems as if they were mental ghosts.

5. **Clarified thinking:** Clarified thinking tends to a normal result of emotinal release, but a skilled counsellor can aid this process. In order to clarify the counsellee's thinking, the counsellor serves as an aid only and refrains from telling the counsellee what is "right". Further the clarified thinking may not take place while the counsellee and counsellor are talking. Part of it may take place later as a result of developments during the counselling relationship.

6. **Reorientation**: This is more than mere emotional release or clear thinking about a problem. Reorientation involves a change in the

employee's psychic self through a change in basic goals and values. It is largely a job for professional counsellors who know its uses and limitaions and who have the necessary training. The manager's job is to recognize those in need of reorientation before their need becomes severe, so that they can be referred to professional help in time for successful treatment.

Approaches to Employee Counselling

In terms of the amount of direction that a counsellor gives a counsellee, counselling can be viewed as a continuum from full direction (directive counselling) to no direction (nondirective counselling). Between the two extremes is participative counselling.

Directive Counselling

Directive counselling is the process of listening to an employee's problem, deciding with the employcc what should be done, and then telling and motivating the employee to do it. Directive counselling mostly achieves the function of advice, but it also may reassure, communicate, give emotional release, and to a minor extent clarify thinking. Reorientation is seldom achieved in directive counselling. Though advice is of questionable value, some of the other functions are worthwhile. If the directive counsellor is a good listener, then the employee should feel some emotional release. As a result of emotional release coupled with ideas that the counsellor imparts, the employee also may clarify thinking. Futhermore, useful communication probably takes place. Both advice and reassurance can be worthwhile if they give the employee more courage to take a helpful course of action that the employee supports.

Nondirective Counselling

Nondirective or client-centered, counselling is at the opposite end of the continuum. It is the process of skillfully listening to and encouraging a counsellee to explain troublesome problems, understand them, and determine appropriate solutions. It focuses on the counsellee rather than on the counsellor as judge and advisor; thus it is client-centered. Managers can use the nondirective approach; however care should be taken to make sure that managers are not oversold on it that they neglect their normal directive leadership responsibilities. Throughout the counselling relationship, it is important for the counsellor to accept feelings rather than judge them, because judgement and evaluation may discourage an employee from stating true feelings. The basic idea is to get the employee to discuss feelings, to explore solutions, and to make wise decisions. In directive counselling the counsellor is the key person, while the counsellee is the key person in a nondirective approach.

Professional counsellors usually practice some form of nondirective counselling and often accomplish four of the six counselling functions. Communication occurs both upward and downward through the counsellor. Emotional release takes place even more effectively than with directive counselling and clarified thinking tends to follow. The unique advantage of nondirective counselling is its ability to cause the employee's reorientation. It emphasizes changing the person instead of dealing only with the immediate problem, in the usual manner of directive counselling.

In some cases counselling itself is a weak solution because it returns the employe to the same environment that caused the problem. What is needed is a better environment for employee psychological support. In this situation the counsellor may step beyond the usual counselling role and give advice to the management to take corrective action.

Participative Counselling

Nondirective counselling of employees is limitted because it requires professional counsellors and is costly. Directive counselling often is not accepted by modern, independent employees. The type of counselling typically used in organizations is between the two extremes of directive and nondirective counselling. This middle ground is called participative counselling.

Participative counselling (also called as cooperative counselling) is a mutual counsellor-counsellee relationship that estasblishes a cooperative exchange of ideas to help solve a counsellee's problems. It is neither wholly counsellor centered nor wholly counsellee centered. Rather, the counsellor and counsellee mutually apply their different knowledge, perspectives, and values to problems. Participative counselling intergrates the ideas of both participants in a counselling relationship. It is, therefore, a balanced compromise that combines many advantages of both directive and nondirective counselling while avoiding most of their disadvantages.

Participative counselling starts by using the listening techniques of nondirective counselling; but as the interview progresses, participative counsellors may play a more active role than nondirective counsellors would. They offer bits of knowledge and insight; they may discuss the situation from their broader knowledge of the organization, thus giving an employee a different view of the problem. In general, participative counsellors apply the four counselling functions of reassurance, communication, emotional release, and clarified thinking. (Davis, 1998)

Conclusion

Counselling basically is an interaction between two people but it can be done in a group also. The counsellee usually has a problem which causes emotional upheavals in him which might induce him to seek help. The problem that is troubling may be a minor one or a major one. The matter might seem trivial to others, which in actuality it might be, but for the counsellee it might be big enough to cause him to be anxious. An employee working in an organizatioon can have work related or family related problems, which hinders his work progress. Any problem which causes him mental anguish, stress, tension, or which causes him to work ineffectively needs counselling.

The counsellor can either be a professional or a non-professional. It can be the person's friend, sister, manager, colleague anybody. The main task of the counsellor is to listen patiently to what is being said by the counsellee without interrupting him/her. The counsellor should most importantly keep in mind not to judge the counsellee but to accept him and make him feel comfortable and put him at ease. The counsellor should have an open mind without any preconceived notions about the counsellee.

The basic aim of counselling is to help the counsellee to deal with life more effectively. Also to bring up his mental health by reducing tension, stress, anxiety etc.

Counselling can be of 3 types-directive, nondirective, and participative counselling. In directive counselling, the counsellor plays the key role. He gives advices, solutions, and directs the counsellee. In non-directive counselling the counsellee plays the key role. He is the one who comes up with solutions, ideas, about how to deal with his problem. In participative counselling both the counsellor and the counsellee decide on ideas and solutions together and decide on a best course of action.

References and Further Reading

1. Counselling Phychology Quarterly (2005), Vol. 18, No. 1, March, 2005, 19-30.
2. Davis Keith, Newstrom John W. (1998). "Organizational Behaviour: Human Behaviour at work". New Delhi: Tata McGraw-Hill Publishing House.
3. Kaila HL et al (2002). Counselling For Growth. Himalaya Publishing House, Mumbai.
4. Pai Satish (1999). "HRD Skills for Organizational Excellence". Himalaya Publication House.
5. Sherilyn, Harold. (1999). The professional counsellor.

8

Managing and Coping with Stress

What is a Stress?

Stress and anxiety have become pervading features of people's life in modern world despite tremendous advancements in science and technology and remarkable growth of economy and sources of luxury, majority of people all over the world seem to be experiencing moderate to high degree of psychological stress in various spheres of their lives. Consistently increasing rate of psychosomatic and psychological disorders and feeling of frustration and dissatisfaction with life in general reflect the high stress being experienced by the people in societies in the present day world.

The term stress has been derived from the Latin word string ere which means to draw tight. The term was used to refer to hardship, strain, adversity or affliction.

Stress is a dynamic condition in which an individual is confronted with an opportunity, constraint, or demand related to what he or she desires and for which the outcome is perceived to be both uncertain and important (Shrivastava, 1999).

Managing and Coping with Stress

Though stress has become an inevitable part of people's life in present day world, it is not entirely uncontrollable and unmanageable. The individual cannot constantly remain in the state of stress he certainly makes some sort of adaptive behavior to cope with or get rid of the stressful situations. It might be fight or flee. Since their origin, the human beings have been encountering the situations of stress and using some remedies or strategies to cope with these situations. The stress researchers and practitioners have concentrated on evolving systematic techniques for the management of the stresses of life in general and of job life in particular. It has become a legitimate field of endeavor and is evolving quickly. The field of stress management has progressed substantially after Lehrer and Woolfolk published first edition of principles and practice of stress management in 1984. Like the term 'psychotherapy' the term 'stress management' is a global concept and involves quite a mix of techniques . The term can be broken into a number of operational steps or phases (Shrivastava, 1999).

Prevention of Occupational Stress

1. At individual level

(a) Cognitive intervention strategies

(b) Behavioral intervention strategies

(c) Physiological intervention strategies

2. Organizational Role Stress

3. Coping with Role Stress

At individual level

Since stress is a very subjective experience it can be most effectively and conveniently prevented or dealt with through individual efforts. Most of the recent studies on stress management have proved the merits of individual oriented techniques in preventing or reducing workers' distress (Murphy, 1984). The individual oriented interventions are more popular than organizational change approaches due to both logistic and conceptual factors. For example, individual oriented programmes:

1. are less or inexpensive and can be established and evaluated quickly without major disruption of work routines;
2. focus on the workers, not the workplace as targets for change;
3. address the issue of individual differences in perceptions of and reaction to stress; and
4. can readily be incorporated into existing employee assistance and other company training programmes.

Self Management

At individual level stresses of job life can be prevented by making necessary restructuring and modifications in employees' cognitive and behavior patterns and by lowering their physiological arousal and stress reactions. Having friends, family, or work colleagues to talk to provides an outlet when stress levels become excessive. Expanding your social support network therefore can be a means for tension reduction. It provides you someone to hear your problems and to offer a more objective perspective on the situation.

Self-Awareness

Stress can also be reduced through increased self-understanding and self-awareness of cognitive and affective reactions to interpersonal events. These skills may be developed through insight therapy, cognitive affective therapy, stress management and interpersonal process recall. Kagan et al. (1994) examined the effectiveness of their intervention model in a sample of the employees of emergency medical services. The study established the effectiveness of the psycho-educational programme in reducing job stress its consequences.

Behavioral Intervention Stretegies

Developing Coping Skills and Resources

The preventive intervention helps in developing coping resources to some extent. Time management has been found one of the useful methods for helping workers in developing coping responses. Many people manage their time poorly. The things they have to accomplish in any given day or week are not necessarily beyond completion if they manage their time properly. The well-organized employee like the well-organized student can often accomplish twice as much as the person who is poorly organized. So an understanding and utilization of basic time management principles can help individual better cope with tension created by job demands.

Few of the more well-known time management principles are:

- Making daily lists of activities to be accomplished.
- Prioritizing activities by importance and urgency.
- Scheduling activities according to the priorities.

- Knowing your daily cycle and handling the most demanding part of your job during the high part of your cycle when you are most alert and productive.

The employee can prevent as well as combat with the stresses of role overload and conflict through effective management of his time and prioritization of job activities or duties. The time management strategies are often focused on two areas: knowledge or information acquisition and skill development. For effective time management the employee should have adequate knowledge of job responsibilities, duties and authorities.

Developing Personal Resources

Another preventive strategy, suggested by Mathney et al., (1986), involves the development of certain behavioral skills which prepare the employees to cope with stressful situation when they occur. The specific strategies, which are included in this category, are training in social skills and problem solving skills that help employees cope with social interaction, which might lead to stress.

"ASSERTIVENESS TRAINING" is another important component of social skills training. The training helps the individuals in responding in a straightforward manner with regard to what they believe, feel and wish. Another important subset of social skills to prevent the social stresses is "problem solving skills" These skills help the individual to respond with some action that will reduce the stressfulness of a situation.

Physiological Intervention Strategies

Stress management practitioners have suggested a set of intervention which help individuals in preventing the negative effects of stress by lowering physiological arousal, such as deep breathing, progressive muscle relaxation, physical exercises, biofeedback, yoga and meditation.

Biofeedback (Electromyographic)

Biofeedback as a technique of stress management developed out of the work in the field of psychology and physiology. Two types of biofeedback have been developed: Operant conditioning biofeedback and augmented feedback. Operant conditioning biofeedback involves using physiological information as a reinforcement to bring about the desirable physiological changes. Augmented biofeedback is more commonly used as a technique for stress management, which involves providing the individual with continuous feedback about physiological functioning (Brown, 1984).

Biofeedback has been found to be effective in helping individuals in restoring their bodies to non-stressed states. In their study, Matteson and Ivancevich (1987) found that biofeedback training reduced chronic tension, headache and significantly decreased the interference of stress related symptoms. However other studies have not found significant positive result of biofeedback training. It is a time consuming and costly method. Better results could be obtained spending the money and effort on other conventional stress management interventions (Shrivastava, 1999).

Yoga and Meditation

Yoga and transcendental meditation are the system of Indian philosophy and practice. These techniques have been in use in India since ancient times as the techniques of relief from stress and for improvement in physical and psychological health. In contemporary societies, importance and need of yoga has been realized by the people all over the world. Yoga has now become popular technique for stress management. The word "Yoga" means union of humans being and universal energy. It teaches the means by which one can learn to communicate with the Absolute or with universal energy (Patel 1993). Yoga attempts to bring within its perspective all three sides of humans' life, i.e., body, mind and soul. The physical dimension of human life also includes the natural elements such as air, water, food, and sunshine without which humans cannot sustain physical life, and a healthy body is necessary to house the inner soul. Yoga, by presenting us with various values, techniques and disciplines teaches us ways of establishing harmony among various sides of life. Different types of yoga have been developed by Indian Yogis, such as "Hatha Yoga"- the physical path for the development of the body; "Gyan Yoga" – the intellectual path; "Bhakti Yoga" – devotional path; "Karma Yoga" – the path of practical actions for unfolding of mind and realization of soul. The different path for developing mind are based on the fact that mind has three different aspects, i.e., knowing, feeling, and willing. In some people intellect predominates, in others emotion and still others action. For intellectuals, the Yoga of knowledge (Gyan) is prescribed, for emotional people the devotional (Bhakti) yoga of love and faith and for the people of action the yoga based on daily action (Karma) is prescribed. Shrivastava (1999); Stephen P. Robbins (10th edition, 2002).

Meditation

Meditation has been part of most of Eastern and Western cultures and religious. It is probably the oldest method of yoga. Recently medical people have realized that it can be used without any religious conotation in the promotion of health. Meditation involves taking a comfortable position either sitting, lying down or standing. But sitting is the most useful and common posture. The practical advantages of meditation are that we can function more efficiently, feel more complete in ourselves and realize more of our potentials. We feel closer to ourselves and are better able to relate to other. Our personality structure is strengthened and becomes more integrated. We are able to think and express ourselves with more clarity. We are more effective in our work and clear in our goals. Other physiological advantages include induction of oxygen consumption, respiratory rate, cardiac output (indicating metabolic rest), a marked decrease in blood lactate level (reduction in anxiety), increase in electrical resistance of the skin (indicating autonomic rest), increase in alpha brainwaves (indicating mental rest) (Wallace & Benson, 1972).

Meditation In Action

In this approach, at frequent intervals during the day if we observe our mind to see what it is doing it becomes clear that mind is busy with wishful thinking daydreaming and fantasies of the future. Such useless activity wastes time and energy and lowers the quality of our work. By learning to concentrate on everyday tasks that it was the most important thing at that moment and by understanding that each task is a part of the total harmony with the universe, we become closer to reality. When a person is completely engrossed in whatever he or she is doing he is meditating in the action.

Among the modern forms of meditation, "Transcendental meditation" (TM) is most widely known and studied. It may be more accurately described as 'TRANSITIONAL' because it retains certain cultic features such as "PUJA". Among the clinically oriented meditation techniques, "Clinically standardized meditation" (Carrington,

1978) and the "Respiratory one method" (Benson, 1975) have been the most widely used to date. These techniques were devised with clinical objectives in mind and are strictly non-cultic. The "clinically standardized meditation" is relatively permissive techniques and may be subjectively experienced as almost effortless. In this method, the trainee selects a sound from standard lists of sounds and then repeats this sound mentally without internally linking the sound to the breathing pattern or pacing it in any structured manner. In "respiratory one method" the trainee repeats the word "one" to himself mentally, and at the same time intentionally linking this word with each exhalation. Thus, it is a relatively disciplined form of meditation with two objects the chosen word and the breath. Buddhist "mindfulness" meditation is also a common non-concentrative method. But it is a less standardized method being used in clinical settings. It is more difficult method to learn. Success of the trainee depends more on the individual expertise and personality of the trainer.

Relaxation

The state associated with transcendental meditation (TM) is achieved when physical and mental relaxations are at a peak. A meditation technique developed by Benson (1975) is similar to TM. In this techniques the individual assumes a comfortable position and begins deep breathing. The individual focuses passive attention on a single word, although not a sacred word as is the 'mantra' in TM. Benson proposed that using this technique summons forth a state labeled the "relaxation response", said to be the opposite to the body' s response to stress . This technique can be taught by a TM instructor (Matteson & Ivancevich, 1987). Relaxation is a form of meditation, a state of concentration. By using the mind to focus upon an object, image, or thought, all distraction associated with everyday life counter -balances the stress response (Shrivastava, 1999).

Organizational Role Stress

The concept of role is the key concept in understanding the integration of the individual in a system. The first requirement in linking individual and organization is to locate the individual in the total set of ongoing relationship and behaviors comprised by the organization. Every organization is composed of a number of position and specific roles associated with these positions. Katz and Kahn (1966) have accordingly extended that an organization is a system of roles. Position or office is essentially a relational concept defining one position in terms of its relationship to other and to the system as a whole. Each position in the organization is associated with a set of activities which constitute the role being performed by the person occupying that position. In fact no role is totally independent and sufficient in itself. Performance of one's role is determined also by the patterns of interpersonal connectedness within which that role behavior takes place. It may be directly related to certain others, less directly to still others and only remotely concerned to remaining offices in the organization. These offices make up the role set for the particular role. Kahn, Wolfe, Quinn, Sonek and Rosenthal (1964) were the earliest to draw attention to organization stress in general and role stress in particular. These researchers after systematic exploration identified two basic sources of role stress, i.e., role conflict and role ambiguity.

Coping With Role Stress

It has been a general observation that job role causes maximum stress to the executive. But this stress can be effectively dealt with through various coping strategies. In pursuit, Pestonjee (1992) has suggested some specific skills and coping strategies. It has been a general observation that job role causes maximum stress to the executive. But this stress can be effectively dealt with, which could be quite effective in dealing with different types of role stress experienced by the executives Table below depicts the variety of role stress and coping skill and strategies to deal with them.

Role Stress and Coping Skills and Strategeies

1.	Role ambiguity (feedback)	Defining one's goal clearly in view of the organizational goal.
2.	Role ambiguity (task)	Be more proactive than reactive, ask for information from superiors, subordinates and colleagues.
3.	Person role conflict	Re-clarify and increase the ability to integrate one's values with others, discriminate between legitimate and illegitimate expectations held by others.

(Contd.)

(Contd.)

4.	Inter-role conflict	Setting up limits on demands of each roles; weighting one demand against the other.
5.	Role conflict (inter-sender)	Ability to look for possible consequences before taking a decision; ability to disintegrate view points, etc.
6.	Role overload	Ability to set priorities; increase one's assertiveness; better time management skill; self delegation.
7.	Personal inadequacy	Identifying and developing technical and managerial skills required.
8.	Resource inadequacy	Ability to manage with existing resources; accepting task conditionally; realizing one's limitations.
9.	Role shrinkage	Ask for new tasks; develop specialized skills to become a specialist.
10.	Role isolation	Involve others in decision making; develop participative managerial skills.
11.	Role stagnation	Ask for a change in role; delegate obsolete duties and tasks; start training one's subordinates.

Summary

Stress is a dynamic condition in which an individual is confronted with an opportunity, constraints or demands, related to what he or she desires and for which the outcome is perceived to be both uncertain and important. Occupational stress definéd as any characteristics of job environment which poses a threat to the individual. There are many organizational factors that cause stress such as task, role and interpersonal demands, organizational structure, organizational leadership and the organization's life stage. The stress researchers and practitioners have introduced systematic techniques for management of stress of life in general and of job life in particular. The individuals reduce stress by self-management, self-awareness, time management, biofeedback, yoga, meditation. Self-management suggests expanding social support network. Self-awareness also helps to reduce the stress. Biofeedbacks guide the individual to control biological response system and help the individual to restore their bodies to no stressed states.

There are different types of yoga which teaches us to establish harmony among various sides of life. Meditation is a relaxation techniques which has the objective to reach a state of deep relaxation. Organizational role is also one of the causes of stress. There are different types of organizational role stress and it has various coping strategies.

References and Further Reading

1. Kaila H.L. (2005). A Reading for HR Professionals. Delhi: Kalpaz Publications.
2. Shrivastava A. K. (1999). Management of Occupational Stress Theories and Practices. New Delhi; Gyan Publishing House. pp. 9, 10, 20, 24-28, 85-118,148-149.
3. Stephen P. Robins (10th Edition, 2002). Organizational Behavior. Delhi; Pearson Education (Singapore) Pte. Ltd. pp. 576-583.

9

Depression among Executives

Introduction

½ to 2/3rd of the dollar cost of depression takes the form of lower productivity, replacement and disability payments. If this is what the numbers have to say, then we better know what depression is.

While studying depression the following questions need to be answered:

Why is depression a well-kept secret among executives? What is the predictors and prevalence of depression among managers and organizational leaders? What are the health and performance risk of depression in managerial population? (Jennings 1967).

Well lets first try to answer the basic question of what depression is?

Definition

The definition of depression is "a mental state characterized by a pessimistic sense of inadequacy and a despondent lack of activity" (Feldman 1986).

The other definition of depression could be: "response of an individual to frustration" (Feldman 1986).

So we see that depression is basically a state of mind which brings some kind of pessimism and some sort of frustration in the mind of an individual. Undoubtedly it affects the mood and thinking capacity of an individual, thereby leading to reduced productivity and related problems.

What is a depressive disorder?

A depressive disorder is an illness that involves the body, mood, and thoughts. It affects the way a person eats and sleeps, the way one feels about oneself, and the way one thinks about things. A depressive disorder is not the same as a passing blue mood. It is not a sign of personal weakness or a condition that can be willed or wished away. People with a depressive illness cannot merely "pull themselves together" and get better. Without treatment, symptoms can last for weeks, months, or years. Appropriate treatment, however, can help most people who suffer from depression.

It has been seen that most people have suffered from acute depression occasionally. Individuals may be really depressed after getting poor performance evaluation, or getting job rejection letters, or breaking up a marriage. It is the number one problem for people in all kind of organizations. Many physicians acknowledge that depression is affecting their job performance, family life and health. Start with sluggish economy, pressure to maintain profitability and increased responsibilities. Add concerns about travel and workplace security and you have got a pressure cooker environment.

The toll of depression can be counted many ways. It robs spouses of partners, children of parents. It estranges sufferers from themselves, in addition to robbing all pleasure from their life.

Not only this, Depression also takes a huge toll in the workplace as well. It costs employers $44 billion a year in lost productive time, versus $13 billion lost from those without depression.

It's not that depressed workers are frequently absent. It's just that even when they're there, they're not. "A total of 81.1% of the lost productive time costs are explained by reduced performance while at work," a team of researchers recently reported.

The phenomenon has been called presenteeism -a kind of absent presence, being on the job but not working productively. As a result, depression is a leading cause of disability, but an invisible one. The costs are hidden in plain view—an excess of $31 billion among individuals actively engaging in work. That figure is over and above the direct medical cost of depression.

A disproportionate share of workers with depression, the study found, experience physical symptoms as part of their disorder. The most common group of physical symptoms includes pain, weakness and fatigue. Sensory or motor impairment was only slightly less common. A still significant number of workers reported such physical symptoms as ringing ears or head-fullness.

Physical symptoms are a common presence in depression, a product of dysfunction in nerve pathways that extend down into the body as well as up into the brain. But the physical symptoms may also be linked to depression as a way to manage it; they help people assume a "sick role" that legitimizes reduced performance.

Depression was most prevalent among workers with the lowest levels of education. It was also associated with lower annual salaries. Increasing scientific evidence supports a linkage between shiftwork and depression. A follow-up survey of 15 cases of depression revealed that depression among shiftworkers was higher than that of the general population. The survey investigated three categories: 1) depression directly related to shiftwork; 2) reactive depression, probably exacerbated by shift work; and 3) reactive depression linked to a major life event.

Those surveyed were asked: "All other things being equal, would you have preferred to give up working shifts and get a day time job?" Three out of seven whose depression was connected to a major life event responded, "definitely yes." One out of four whose depression was intensified by shift work answered similarly. Three of four whose depression was directly associated with shift worker also said, "definitely yes."

In summary, depression, among shift workers for the most part occurred during shift work. Eighty-six percent of category three cases happened after stopping shift work. Evidence of marital conflict related to the shift worker's schedule accompanied category one depression. Those in this category also reported a significant disruption in social and/or domestic life.

Statistical Data Showing Intensity of Depression

Percentage of families of depressed patients manifesting significant family dysfunction: 50-75%.

Proportion of families that continue to have significant dysfunction even after recovery of depressed member: 40-50%.

Direct workplace cost of depression in terms of time lost per year: Over 172 million days.

Assuming treatment, amount of time it takes for recovery of work function: 4 to 6 months.

Difference in long-term symptomatic effectiveness between drug therapy and cognitive psychotherapy: None.

- Two-year relapse rate of depressed patients treated by medication: 50%.
- Two-year relapse rate of depressed patients treated by cognitive therapy: 21%.

The above numbers do show us the intensity of depression in the organizations and its impact on the family life and the recovery time taken. From the above schedule it is quite clear that depression has a long term influence on the body and mind not only of the patient i.e. the executive at work but also the people who are in constant contact with him.

Depression adversely affects functioning in all domains, but only recently has the magnitude of the impact on work productivity become clear. Lost labor time among those with depression is huge. In a recent issue of the Journal of the American Medical Association, Walter F. Stewart and colleagues calculated the cost of labor loss. His extensive survey of U.S. workers puts the bill at $44 billion.

The calculations were as follows:-.

- 8.27 in billions of dollars, cost of lost productive time due to absenteeism in workers with depression.
- 35.73 in billions of dollars, cost of lost productive time due to presenteeism in workers with depression.
- 5.6 hours per week in lost productive time experienced by all workers with depression.
- 1.4 hours per week in lost productive time experienced by workers with major depression.
- 1.5 hours per week in lost productive time typical of workers without depression.
- 77.1 percentage of individuals with depression who report some lost productivity time.
- 82.1 percentage of lost productivity time among depressed individuals due to reduced performance while at work.

Types of Depression

Depression is not a one-size-fits-all condition. Mental health professionals have long recognized that patients tend to display reasonably distinct clusters of clinical symptoms, and they increasingly regard such clusters as subtypes of depression.

The boundaries between subtypes are often fuzzy, with some overlap of symptoms, and not every depression expert agrees on the classification system. But clinical research suggests that parting depression into subtypes is useful in guiding treatment and in gauging the long-term outcome for patients.

At a symposium presented at the recent meeting of the American Psychiatric Association, doctors discussed five depression subtypes that together encompass the majority of depressed persons. These include:

- Atypical depression, which studies show accounts for 23 per cent to 36 per cent of all cases and is under-recognized.
- Anxious depression, which afflicts 40 per cent of patients with major depressive disorder and poses many treatment challenges.
- Melancholic depression, a severe form of disorder that is most common among persons hospitalized for depression.
- Vascular depression, a newly recognized variety that reflects the existence of silent cardiovascular disease and is most common among persons over the age of 60.
- Psychotic depression, a severe form of disorder distinguished by mood-congruent delusions and accompanied by specific changes in brain tissue.

The distinctions first emerged several decades ago on the basis of variations in response to then available treatments. But clinicians and researchers suggest that dissecting depression into subtypes may be even more valuable today. The subtypes may represent distinct biological pathways of disorder and may ultimately provide clues to the multiple ways depression can arise as well as express itself.

Atypical depression can manifest in both bipolar and unipolar depression, psychiatrist Jonathan W. Stewart. M.D., of Columbia University reported. Patients with this variety of disorder—about 10 million Americans—have what physicians label mood reactivity: they can be cheered up at least 50 per cent in response to positive events in their life, albeit temporarily.

In contrast to patients with classical depression, those with atypical depression overeat regularly and binge often, gaining sometimes substantial amounts of weight. They also sleep a lot, and experience an overwhelming fatigue for much of the day, feeling as if they cannot even lift themselves out of a chair.

In addition to such physical manifestations, atypical depression is marked by a longstanding pattern of extreme sensitivity to perceived interpersonal rejection that affects functioning at work, in love, and with friends. With a trail of stormy relationships patients are either never married or divorced, and are unemployed or underemployed. Given their fear of rejection, many withdraw from relationships entirely and refuse to go on job interviews.

This variety of depression begins early—median age of onset is 17—and takes a chronic course. Depression afflicts many family members, and it tends to be of the same chronic type.

Perhaps the landmark feature of atypical depression is its responsiveness to one class of antidepressants, the MAO inhibitors. While they are no longer considered a first-line treatment because of their onerous side effects, they are regarded especially useful for people with atypical depression who fail to respond to other drugs. Cognitive therapy in conjunction with drug treatment is also effective and helps restore function.

Biology of atypical depression has not been delineated, as patients appear normal on most physiologic tests. But patterns of response to mixed-up images of faces suggest that parts of the brain that interpret emotion are not working normally.

Anxious depression covers the large gray area where symptoms of depression and anxiety co-exist or overlap. Patients typically have feelings of worthlessness and pessimism, excessive worrying and guilt, and are unable to enjoy things. The disorder is expressed physically in diminished appetite, poor sleep with frequent awakenings, and restlessness and psychomotor agitation.

In one study of 255 depressed outpatients that he conducted, psychiatrist Maurizio Fava, M.D., of Harvard reported at the symposium, 51per cent were found to have anxiety along with their depression. It's not clear whether the anxiety follows on the heels of feelings of worthlessness. But in 40 per cent of the anxiously depressed, the anxiety disorder started first.

Among those whose anxiety takes the form of social phobia and generalized anxiety disorder, the anxiety tends to precede major depressive disorder. But in the case of panic disorder it usually follows the onset of the depressive disorder.

Patients are young—average age 20.6 versus 28.4 among those with major depression alone—significantly functionally impaired, and take more time to recover. They are less likely to respond to treatment and more likely to relapse, and experience less change in their depressive symptoms with treatment.

The disorder may have its origins early in life among children of a distinct temperament type who are frightened by novelty. Both the anxiety and depression may be the outcome of abnormality high levels of hormones driving the body's stress response system.

Anxious depression typically poses a treatment dilemma for doctors. Many seek to use antidepressants that have sedating properties, although it's not clear that they need to, said Dr. Fava. Studies show that all of the antidepressants work equally well against this type of depression, although high doses may be needed. Still, in practice physicians tend to prescribe a combination of drugs for such patients, usually a tranquilizer along with an antidepressant.

Given their anxiety quotient, depressives of this type are unusually sensitive to bodily sensations. As a result, common drug side effects—such as gastrointestinal distress—are often causing for discontinuing treatment. Even when treatment continues, remission can be a long time coming. Cognitive therapy can be very helpful.

Melancholic depression is often a synonym for severe depression, and it is far more common among those hospitalized for depression than among those in the community. Affected persons lack pleasure in almost all activities and do not react to pleasurable stimulation. They may experience extreme slowness of movement or agitation. Their depression is regularly worse in the morning and is accompanied by lack of appetite and weight loss.

Melancholic depressives may also ruminate over the same thoughts and experiences, and feel excessive guilt. Their depression takes on a life of its own: the more episodes they have, the more autonomous such episodes seem, less likely to be set off by stressful events. Patients do not respond to psychotherapy, at least not before successful drug treatment, reported J. Craig Nelson, M.D., of Yale.

Psychotic depression was once another term for severe depression, but the more refined the tools scientists apply to dissect the disorder, the more distinctive this variety appears, especially biologically. Not only is this type of depression severe, life- impairing and marked by suicide attempts, it is accompanied by delusions that reflect the depressed mood and guilt patients feel.

Biological tests show the patients have a distinct abnormality in the system that controls production of stress hormones, said Linda L. Carpenter, M.D., of Brown University. Imaging studies reveal significant brain atrophy. The decrease in brain tissue likely reflects the toxic effects of excess stress hormones, namely cortisol.

Despite the proliferation of antidepressant drugs, the best treatment for psychotic depression is electroshock therapy. But drugs now in development may offer some advantage. Dr. Carpenter specifically cites agents that interfere with cortisol by blocking receptors for it.

For some folks with depression, the best prescription might not be Prozac but rather lessons in interpersonal problem solving. That's because depressed people aren't helpless bystanders to their condition, contends Joanne Davila, Ph. D. A depressed person's actions—especially the mistakes—can create stress, and stress is one of the biggest contributors to depression.

Because interpersonal conflicts can be particularly stressful, Davila studied how depressed and non-depressed young women handle such problems, both at work (asking your boss for Friday off) and at play (telling your friend you want to see other guys). In depressed women, poor problem solving indeed intensified stress, increasing their risk of further depression, Davila and colleagues report in the Journal of Abnormal Psychology (Vol. 104, No. 4).

"We're not saying people are doing something wrong and making themselves depressed," notes Davila. "Depression is more complicated than that. But people can make changes in their lives that might protect them from getting depressed."

Davila, a researcher at UCLA, says the findings mirror the observations of many therapists, who see best results when they do more than just help patients feel better. By advising depressed individuals how to resolve interpersonal conflict more successfully, therapists, family, and friends can contribute to a long-term solution.

Forms of Depression

Depressive disorders come in different forms, just as in the case with other illnesses such as heart disease. This paragraph briefly describes three of the most common types of depressive disorders. However, within these types there are variations in the number of symptoms, their severity, and persistence.

Major depression is manifested by a combination of symptoms that interfere with the ability to work, study, sleep, eat, and enjoy pleasurable activities. Such a disabling episode of depression may occur only once but more commonly occurs several times in a lifetime.

A less severe type of depression, dysthymia, involves long-term, chronic symptoms that do not disable, but keep one from functioning well or from feeling good. Many people with dysthymia also experience major depressive episodes at some time in their lives.

Another type of depression is bipolar disorder, also called manic-depressive illness. Not nearly as prevalent as other forms of depressive disorders, bipolar disorder is characterized by cycling mood changes: severe highs (mania) and lows (depression). Sometimes the mood switches are dramatic and rapid, but most often they are gradual. When in the depressed cycle, an individual can have any or all of the symptoms of a depressive disorder. When in the manic cycle, the individual may be overactive, over talkative, and have a great deal of energy. Mania often affects thinking, judgment, and social behavior in ways that cause serious problems and embarrassment. For example, the individual in a manic phase may feel elated, full of grand schemes that might range from unwise business decisions to romantic sprees. Mania, left untreated, may worsen to a psychotic state.

Symptoms of Depression

- Persistent sad, anxious, or "empty" mood.
- Feelings of hopelessness, pessimism.
- Feelings of guilt, worthlessness, helplessness.
- Loss of interest or pleasure in hobbies and activities that were once enjoyed, including sex.
- Decreased energy, fatigue, being "slowed down".
- Difficulty concentrating, remembering, or making decisions.

- Insomnia, early-morning awakening, or oversleeping.
- Appetite and/or weight loss or overeating and weight gain.
- Thoughts of death or suicide; suicide attempts.
- Restlessness, irritability.
- Persistent physical symptoms that do not respond to treatment, such as headaches, digestive disorders, and chronic pain.
- General feeling of lethargy (people do the minimum required and without of joy or enthusiasm).
- Little creativity or innovation combined with resistance to change.
- Marginally acceptable productivity.
- High rates of absenteeism, lateness, long lunch hours.
- Limited communication between and within departments.
- Low to average turnover (depressed people don't make moves).
- Delayed decision-making.
- No expressions of happiness over significant achievements.

Corporate Triangle

Life in the corporate triangle is a convenient way to express the activity of the mind caught up with the pressures of a career crisis. The mental life of this executive pivots on a triad of pressures. An executive in a career crisis tends to focus on problems of authority and goal achievement activities of the corporation. These factors are in turn evaluated in terms of the kind of a person the executive believes

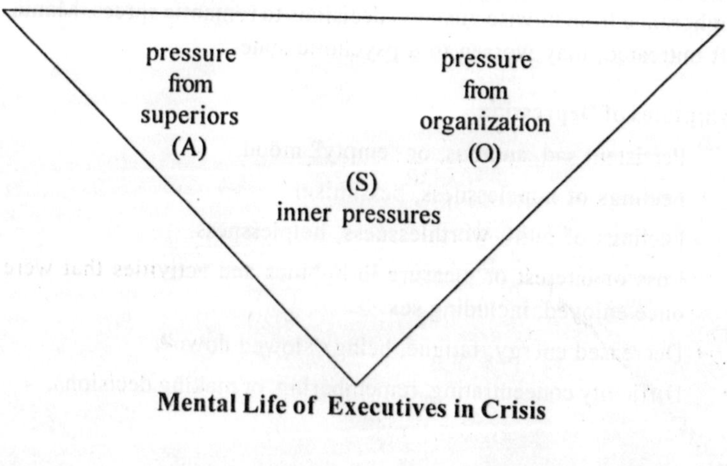

Mental Life of Executives in Crisis

he is and would like to become. The corporate triangle becomes activated abnormally during career crisis. It exists in all executives to some degree regardless of their difficulties. It grows out of a need to make sense of their highly complex environments which ultimately results into too much of burdening of the executives and finally leading to depression. (Jennings 1967).

Causes of Organizational Depression

Some types of depression run in families, suggesting that a biological vulnerability can be inherited. This seems to be the case with bipolar disorder. Studies of families in which members of each generation develop bipolar disorder found that those with the illness have a somewhat different genetic makeup than those who do not get ill. However, the reverse is not true: Not everybody with the genetic makeup that causes vulnerability to bipolar disorder will have the illness. Apparently additional factors, possibly stresses at home, work, or school, are involved in its onset. (Norfolk 1997).

In some families, major depression also seems to occur generation after generation. However, it can also occur in people who have no family history of depression. Whether inherited or not, major depressive disorder is often associated with changes in brain structures or brain function.

People who have low self-esteem, who consistently view themselves and the world with pessimism or who are readily overwhelmed by stress, are prone to depression. Whether this represents a psychological predisposition or an early form of the illness is not clear.

In recent years, researchers have shown that physical changes in the body can be accompanied by mental changes as well. Medical illnesses such as stroke, a heart attack, cancer, Parkinson's disease, and hormonal disorders can cause depressive illness, making the sick person apathetic and unwilling to care for his or her physical needs, thus prolonging the recovery period. Also, a serious loss, difficult relationship, financial problem, or any stressful (unwelcome or even desired) change in life patterns can trigger a depressive episode. Very often, a combination of genetic, psychological, and environmental factors is involved in the onset of a depressive disorder.

Causes of Depression Among Women Employees

Women experience depression about twice as often as men. Many factors may contribute to depression in women—particularly such factors as menstruation, pregnancy, miscarriage, postpartum period, and menopause. Many women also face additional stresses such as responsibilities both at work and home, single parenthood, and caring for children and for aging parents.

A recent NIMH study showed that in the case of premenstrual syndrome (PMS), women with a preexisting vulnerability to PMS experienced relief from mood and physical symptoms when their sex hormones were suppressed. Shortly after the hormones were re-introduced, they again developed symptoms of PMS. Women without a history of PMS reported no effects of the hormonal manipulation.

Many women are also particularly vulnerable after the birth of a baby. The hormonal and physical changes, as well as the added responsibility of a new life, can be factors that lead to postpartum depression in some women. Treatment by a sympathetic physician and the family's emotional support for the new mother are prime considerations in aiding her to recover her physical and mental well-being and her ability to care for and enjoy the infant.

Well these could be the hereditary or familial reasons for depression both in men and women. However the common causes for depression in an organization are:-

- Clinically depressed managers and executives.
- Prevalent substance abuse (drugs or alcohol) among managers and executives.
- Lack of regard for diversity.
- Tolerance of and reward for mediocrity.
- Dysfunctional behaviors of managers and executives.
- Highly controlling managers and executives.
- Organizational secrets.

Diagnostic Evaluation and Treatment

The first step to getting appropriate treatment for depression is a complete physical examination by a family physician. Certain medications as well as some medical conditions such as a viral infection can cause the same symptoms as depression, and the physician should rule out these possibilities through examination, interview, and lab tests. If a physical cause for the depression is ruled out, a psychiatrist or psychologist should do a psychological evaluation, usually.

A good diagnostic evaluation will include a complete history of symptoms, i.e., when they started, how long they have lasted, how severe they are, whether the patient had them before and, if so, whether the symptoms were treated and what treatment was given. The doctor should ask about alcohol and drug use, and if the patient has thoughts about death or suicide. Further, a history should include questions about whether other family members have had a depressive illness and, if treated, what treatments they may have received and which were effective.

Last, a diagnostic evaluation should include a mental status examination to determine if speech or thought patterns or memory have been affected, as sometimes happens in the case of a depressive or manic-depressive illness.

Treatment choice will depend on the outcome of the evaluation. There are a variety of antidepressant medications and psychotherapies that can be used to treat depressive disorders. Some people with milder forms may do well with psychotherapy alone. People with moderate to severe depression often benefit from antidepressants. Most do best with combined treatment: medication to gain relatively quick symptom relief and psychotherapy to learn more effective ways to deal with life's problems, including depression. Depending on the patient's diagnosis and severity of symptoms, the therapist may prescribe medication and/ or one of the several forms of psychotherapy that have proven effective for depression.

Medications

There are several types of antidepressant medications used to treat depressive disorders. These include newer medications—chiefly the selective serotonin reuptake inhibitors (SSRIs)—the tricyclics, and the monoamine oxidase inhibitors (MAOIs). The SSRIs—and other newer medications that affect neurotransmitters such as dopamine or nor epinephrine—generally have fewer side effects than tricyclics. Sometimes your doctor will try a variety of antidepressants before finding the medication or combination of medications most effective for you. Sometimes the dosage must be increased to be effective. Antidepressant medications must be taken regularly for as many as 8 weeks before the full therapeutic effect occurs.

Patients often are tempted to stop medication too soon. They may feel better and think they no longer need the medication. Or they may think the medication isn't helping at all. It is important to keep taking medication until it has a chance to work, though side effects may appear before antidepressant activity does. Once the individual is feeling better, it is important to continue the medication for 4 to 9 months to prevent a recurrence of the depression. Some medications must be stopped gradually to give the body time to adjust. For individuals with bipolar disorder or chronic major depression, medication may have to be maintained indefinitely.

Antidepressant drugs are not habit-forming. However, as is the case with any type of medication prescribed for more than a few days, antidepressants have to be carefully monitored to see if the correct dosage is being given.

For the small number of people for whom MAO inhibitors are the best treatment, it is necessary to avoid certain foods that contain high levels of tyramine, such as many cheeses, wines, and pickles, as well as medications such as decongestants. The interaction of tyramine with MAOIs can bring on a hypertensive crisis, a sharp increase in blood pressure that can lead to a stroke. The doctor should furnish a complete list of prohibited foods that the patient should carry at all times. Other forms of antidepressants require no food restrictions.

Medications of any kind—prescribed, over-the counter, or borrowed--should never be mixed without consulting the doctor. Other health professionals who may prescribe a drug—such as a dentist or other medical specialist—should be told that the patient is taking antidepressants. Some drugs, although safe when taken alone can, if taken with others, cause severe and dangerous side effects. Some drugs, like alcohol or street drugs, mays reduce the effectiveness of antidepressants and should be avoided. This includes wine, beer, and hard liquor. Some people who have not had a problem with alcohol use may be permitted by their doctor to use a modest amount of alcohol while taking one of the newer antidepressants.

Side–Effects

The literature reveals that the antidepressants may cause mild and, usually, temporary side effects (sometimes referred to as adverse effects) in some people. Typically these are annoying, but not serious. However, any unusual reactions or side effects or those that interfere with functioning should be reported to the doctor immediately. The most common side effects of tricyclic antidepressants, and ways to deal with them, are:

- **Dry Mouth:** it is helpful to drink lots of water; chew sugarless gum; clean teeth daily.
- **Constipation:** bran cereals, prunes, fruit, and vegetables should be in the diet.
- **Bladder Problems:** emptying the bladder may be troublesome, and the urine stream may not be as strong as usual; the doctor should be notified if there is any pain.
- **Sexual Problems:** sexual functioning may change; if worrisome, it should be discussed with the doctor.
- **Blurred Vision:** this will pass soon and will not necessitate new glasses.
- **Dizziness:** rising from the bed or chair slowly is helpful.
- **Drowsiness as a Daytime Problem:** this usually passes soon. A person feeling drowsy or sedated should not drive or operate heavy equipment. The more sedating antidepressants are generally taken at bedtime to help sleep and minimize daytime drowsiness.

The newer antidepressants have different types of side effects:

- **Headache:** this will usually go away.
- **Nausea:** even when it occurs, it is transient after each dose.
- **Nervousness and Insomnia (Trouble Falling Asleep or Waking often During the Night)**: these may occur during the first few weeks; dosage reductions or time will usually resolve them.
- **Agitation (feeling jittery):** if this happens for the first time after the drug is taken and is more than transient, the doctor should be notified.
- **Sexual Problems:** the doctor should be consulted if the problem is persistent or worrisome.

Herbal Therapy

In the past few years, much interest has risen in the use of herbs in the treatment of both depression and anxiety. St. John's wort (Hypericum perforatum), an herb used extensively in the treatment of mild to moderate depression in Europe, has recently aroused interest in the United States. St. John's wort, an attractive bushy, low-growing plant covered with yellow flowers in summer, has been used for centuries in many folk and herbal remedies. Today in Germany, *Hypericum* is used in the treatment of depression more than any other antidepressant. However, the scientific studies that have been conducted on its use have been short-term and have used several different doses.

Because of the widespread interest in St. John's work, the National Institutes of Health (NIH) is conducting a 3-year study, sponsored by three NIH components—the National Institute of Mental Health, the National Institute for Complementary and Alternative Medicine, and the Office of Dietary Supplements. The study is designed to include 336 patients with major depression, randomly assigned to an 8-week trial with one-third of patients receiving a uniform dose of St. John's wort, another third receiving a selective serotonin reuptake inhibitor (SSRI) commonly prescribed for depression, and the final third receiving a placebo (a pill that looks exactly like the SSRI and the St. John's wort, but has no active ingredients).

Psycho Therapies

Many forms of psychotherapy, including some short-term (10-20 weeks) therapies, can help depressed individuals. "Talking" therapies help patients gain insight into and resolve their problems through verbal "give-and-take" with the therapist. "Behavioral" therapies help patients learn how to obtain more satisfaction and rewards through their own actions and how to unlearn the behavioral patterns that contribute to or result from their depression.

Two of the short-term psychotherapies that research has shown helpful for some forms of depression are interpersonal and cognitive/ behavioral therapies. Interpersonal therapists focus on the patient's disturbed personal relationships that both cause and exacerbate (or increase) the depression. Cognitive-behavioral therapists help patients change the negative styles of thinking and behaving often associated with depression.

Psychodynamic therapies, which are sometimes used to treat depressed persons, focus on resolving the patient's internal conflicts. These therapies are often reserved until the depressive symptoms are significantly improved. In general, severe depressive illnesses, particularly those that are recurrent, will require medication (or ECT under special conditions) along with, or preceding, psychotherapy for the best outcome.

How to Help Yourself if You are Depressed

Depressive disorders make one feel exhausted, worthless, helpless, and hopeless. Such negative thoughts and feelings make some people feel like giving up. It is important to realize that these negative views are part of the depression and typically do not accurately reflect the situation. Negative thinking fades as treatment begins to take effect. In the meantime (Jennings 1967):

- Set realistic goals and assume a reasonable amount of responsibility.
- Break large tasks into small ones, set some priorities, and do what you can as you can.
- Try to be with other people and to confide in someone; it is usually better than being alone and secretive.
- Participate in activities that may make you feel better.
- Mild exercise, going to a movie, a ballgame, or participating in religious, social, or other activities may help.
- Expect your mood to improve gradually, not immediately. Feeling better takes time.
- It is advisable to postpone important decisions until the depression has lifted. Before deciding to make a significant transition—change jobs, get married or divorced—discuss it with others who know you well and have a more objective view of your situation.
- People rarely "snap out of" a depression. But they can feel a little better day by day.
- *Remember*, positive thinking will replace the negative thinking that is part of the depression and will disappear as your depression responds to treatment.
- Let your family and friends help you.

How Family and Friends Can Help The Depressed Person

The most important thing anyone can do for the depressed person is to help him or her get an appropriate diagnosis and treatment. This may involve encouraging the individual to stay with treatment until symptoms begin to abate (several weeks), or to seek different treatment if no improvement occurs. On occasion, it may require making an appointment and accompanying the depressed person to the doctor. It may also mean monitoring whether the depressed person is taking medication. The depressed person should be encouraged to obey the doctor's orders about the use of alcoholic products while on medication. The second most important thing is to offer emotional support. This involves understanding, patience, affection, and encouragement. Engage the depressed person in conversation and listen carefully. Do not disparage feelings expressed, but point out realities and offer hope. Do not ignore remarks about suicide. Report them to the depressed person's therapist. Invite the depressed person for walks, outings, to the movies, and other activities. Be gently insistent if your invitation is refused. Encourage participation in some activities that once gave pleasure, such as hobbies, sports, religious or cultural activities, but do not push the depressed person to undertake too much too soon. The depressed person needs diversion and company, but too many demands can increase feelings of failure.

Do not accuse the depressed person of faking illness or of laziness, or expect him or her "to snap out of it." Eventually, with treatment, most depressed people do get better. Keep that in mind, and keep reassuring the depressed person that, with time and help, he or she will feel better.

Where to Get Help

If unsure where to go for help, check the *Yellow Pages* under "counselling", "mental health," "health," "social services," "suicide prevention," "crisis intervention services," "hotlines," "hospitals," or "physicians" for phone numbers and addresses. In times of crisis, the emergency doctor at a hospital may be able to provide temporary help for an emotional problem, and will be able to tell you where and how to get further help.

Listed below are the types of people and places that will make a referral to, or provide, diagnostic and treatment services.

- Family doctors
- Mental health specialists, such as psychiatrists, psychologists, social workers, or mental health counselors
- Health maintenance organizations
- Community mental health centers
- Hospital psychiatry departments and outpatient clinics
- University- or medical school-affiliated programs
- State hospital outpatient clinics
- Family service/social agencies
- Private clinics and facilities
- Employee assistance programs
- Local medical and/or psychiatric societies

Coaching Tips to Add Vitality to Your Work Place

1. Recognize organizational depression and commit yourself to taking positive action to resolve the problem.
2. Conduct a climate survey. The caveat is that once you ask, you are obliged to act on the findings. Otherwise, you'll make the situation worse.
3. Include all levels of staff in solving the problem of organizational depression. Although they may at first be reluctant or distrustful, involving them is the ideal way to ensure outcomes.
4. Identify specific goals and objectives for a healthy workplace. This may include public statements about diversity, rewards for healthy behavior, or communications related to creating a healthy culture. Although these may at first be viewed as simply "slogans," eventually they will become institutionalized.
5. Provide coaching to senior executives who may require it. At the risk of sounding self-serving, coaching is the ideal way to prepare executives who may be unwittingly contributing to the problem of turning around a depressed organization.
6. Hold managers accountable for the emotional climate of the organization. Remember the maxim, what you measure is what you get. Not only should they be responsible for contributing to the solution, but for their personal behaviors as well.

7. Increase communication at all levels. Whether it's through a newsletter, meetings, or regular communications from the CEO, information is key to overcoming organizational depression.
8. Create a process, where small groups come together and are empowered to solve problems on the spot, is just one great idea for how you can do this. Avoid suggestion boxes – physical or on-line. They only increase the likelihood of complaining rather than focus on problem resolution.
9. Implement an incentive program. The system need not be complex or expensive, merely one that recognizes and rewards behaviors consistent with goals. Pick up a copy of Bob Nelson's book, 1001 Ways to Reward Employees. It will stimulate your thinking in this direction.
10. Expect and work through resistance. Change isn't easy and almost always takes twice as long as you'd like it to. Just keep in mind, you're in a marathon, not running a sprint.

Summary

The time to worry is when you stop worrying. Depression prods us into action. If this action is blocked by some external agency, we become frustrated and this makes us re-double our efforts to secure our goals. The Chinese use two pictures to depict the concept of "crisis" They link the symbol for danger with the symbol for opportunity, thus expressing their belief that every crisis provides an opportunity. Those who learn to cope with depression have the confidence and ability to seize the opportunities of life without suffering its hurts. (Jennings 1967).

References and Further Reading

1. Feldman, D.C. (1986). Organizational Behaviour, New York: McGraw Hill publication, 470.
2. Griffin, R.G.(1998). Management, Texas: Houghton Mifflin Company, 460-463.
3. http://www.mayoclinic.org/news.2003-jax/1827.html
4. http://www.blackwellpublishers.co.uk/pdf/jms-special.pdf
5. http://cms.psychologytoday.com/articles/pto-1996036-000021.html
6. http://www.mhamilw.org/Workplace/0102.html
7. http://www.mentalhealthroundtable.ca/aug round pdfs/Roundtable%20 report Jul 20.pdf

8. http://scotlandonsunday.scotsman.com/index.cfm? id=321712002
9. http://www.cmshealthcare.com/articles/DMNewsDDM8250Reprint.pdf
10. http://www.shiftworker.com/articles-and-/reseach reports.html
11. http: www.m-rm.com/editspa i.html
12. http://www.dreamjobs.tv/tips194.html
13. Jennings, E. E. (1967). Executive Success, Michigan: Appleton – century – crofts publications, 79,80,81.
14. Khanna, K.K. (1984). Executive Psychosis. New Delhi: National publishing house, 105 – 111.
15. Norfolk. D (1997). Executive stress, London: Associated business programmes, ltd. 15, 16, 17.

10

Personnel Records, Reports and Audit

Introduction

Managers require information on the general health of the organization under their care from time to time. They require feedback that accurately reflects how well the parts of an organization are moving. Personnel records and reports enable them in obtaining the requisite information concerning the use of human resources in various departments and divisions. Personnel audit helps in finding out the usefulness of personnel programmes and practices followed by the organization. The inadequacies and deficiencies in personnel programmes could thus be easily traced and rectified promptly.

Personnel Research

There are two important areas in connection with personnel research which are the functions of the personnel specialist or the operating line manager concerned with controlling manpower.

1. The maintenance of personnel records or statistics; and
2. Evaluation or audit of the personnel programme.

Personnel Records and Reports

A record is a piece of writing or chart which provides ready information and which preserves evidence for future reference or use. Personnel records provide information relating to the use of human resources in an organization - eg; personnel history cards, training records, performance records, absence data, turnover records, wage and salary records, etc.

A report is a statement describing an event, a situation or a happening in a clear manner. It describes clearly as to what has happened or is happening. It provides both qualitative and quantitative information.

Purposes of Records

Records management is the planned control of records. It includes decision making regarding the retention, transfer, microfilming and destruction of records. More essentially, records management concerns itself with the creation, distribution, maintenance, retention, preservation, retrieval and disposal of records. As Little field et al commented, "records management includes forms, reports, reproduction of written material, filing records, retention and microfilming services".

The purposes of record management are:

1. To keep an orderly account of progress - The historical function of records.
2. To facilitate the preparation of the statement of the true conditions.
3. To enable making of comparisons between one period and another, to improve the productivity of business operations.
4. To facilitate the detection of errors and frauds.
5. Legal requirements.
6. Miscellaneous functions such as the settlement of disputes, memory of business to serve as a tool to make policy decisions, etc.

Fundamental Principles of Record Keeping

For effective records management, the following points about record keeping must be followed:

1. Justification - The purpose of keeping and maintaining records must be justified.
2. Records must be subject to verification.
3. Records must be properly classified so that they are useful to senior management.
4. The records should make availàble all the required information accurately and quickly.
5. Records must be produced and maintained at a reasonable cost.

Significance of personnel records

1. To supply information required to management and unions to review the effectiveness of personnel policies and practices and develop them.
2. Supply the information required by various agencies on the accidents, employment position, strikes, absenteeism etc.
3. To provide information about manpower inventory for manpower and succession planning.
4. Conduct research in personnel and industrial relations areas.
5. Identify training and development needs.
6. Revise pay scales and benefits from time to time.

Essentials of Good Records

1. Simple and yet meet the needs of the organization.
2. Accurate.
3. Economical to maintain.
4. Useful to facilitate decision making.

Essentials of Good Reports

1. Conformity to organizational objectives.
2. Unbiased.
3. Data based.
4. Clarity and simplicity.
5. Timely.

Types of Personnel Records

1. Job application and test score.
2. Job description and job specifications.
3. Interview results.
4. Employment history.
5. Medical reports.
6. Attendance records.
7. Payroll.
8. Employee ratings.

9. Training records.
10. Accident and sickness records.
11. Grievances and disputes records.
12. Contracts of employment.
13. Records to be kept under various statutes.

In connection with job description, eg: records which might be kept as a result of job analysis include detailed job descriptions, man specifications and time schedules for jobs.

In connection with recruitment and selection, it may be necessary to keep records such as manning & replacement tables; completed employee applications when they applied for a job giving their historical background; qualification's record; the interviewer checklist or report.

In connection with wage and salary administration, details are required for preparing the payroll. Records must include the type of salary changes and decisions on salary reviews, besides the time record or clock cards.

In connection with personnel evaluation & training, records are required of employee ratings, performance appraisals, employee training records and training time- tables.

Records have to be maintained regarding leaves, transfers and promotions. Record must be kept of requests for leave as well as the actual leave granted. Other records in this connection include seniority record; employee review record and performance evaluation.

In connection with health and safety, accidents reports, sickness reports, medical reports, medical history and time losses through accidents would supply relevant information.

Again, records have to be kept for discipline and terminations. In connection with terminations, exit interviews can considerably help the personnel management. There is always a reason why a person leaves or resigns from an organisation. A study of such interviews might indicate a fixed pattern and suggest possible improvements in compensation, supervision, training and promotion policies. An analysis of industrial disputes as well as the number and the nature of grievances can similarly help improve the personnel management function.

Ten Essentials of Effective Records

1. Be clear about the objectives and possible use of the records.
2. Keep the records at a minimum consistent with the requirement of the organisation.
3. Be sure that the benefits outweigh the cost of the records decided upon.
4. Be sure that the information is available immediately it is needed.
5. Be sure that the records are kept up-to-date.
6. Design the forms in such a way that they are easy to complete and provide data which can be used easily.
7. Give specific instructions on how the form is to be completed.
8. Identify each form by a number and avoid entering of data which are not likely to be used.
9. Centralise the responsibility for both control and design of the forms.
10. Avoid duplication of entries in different forms.

Personnel Audit

Personnel records and reports provide information regarding the utilization of human resources in an objective way. However, in most cases, this is not sufficient. A critical evaluation of manpower programmes might be required to find out the areas where improvements are needed. In place of informal impressions gathered and summarized through records and reports, a systematic and analytical search is made to find out the effectiveness of personnel management.

Audit (Vérification): the systematic, independent review and appraisal of all departmental (personnel) operations, to determine the efficiency, effectiveness and economy of the departmental (personnel) management practices and controls.

Audits of personnel management as a function would normally be conducted once ever three to five years by the departmental internal audit group and by the central agencies. The audits by the internal audit group would focus on the adequacy of all personnel management controls (including the monitoring activities), the extent of compliance with legislation central agency and departmental personnel management policies and directives, and on the efficiency, effectiveness and economy of personnel management. Treasury Board Secretariat and Public Service Commission audits would determine the extent of compliance with legislation and service-wide personnel management policies and practices and, in classification and staffing, how well formally delegated authority is being managed.

The scope of these audits by departments and the central agencies would include Human Resources Planning, Staffing, Classification, Pay and Benefits, Staff Relations, Training and Development and all other personnel-related activities.

Personnel management at the Responsibility Centre level would be audited each year by the internal audit group as part of individual audit of departmental operations.

According to Seybold, personnel audit refers to an examination and evaluation of policies, procedures and practices to determine the effectiveness of personnel management, covering three things:

1. Measurement and evaluation of personnel programmes, policies and practices.
2. Identification of gap between objectives and results.
3. Determination of what should or what should not be done in future.

Objectives of Personnel Audit

The basic objective of personnel audit is to know how the various units are functioning and how they have been able to meet the policies and guidelines which were agreed upon, and to assist the rest of the organization by identifying the gaps between objectives and results, for the end product of an evaluation should be to formulate plans for corrections of adjustments.

The objectives of personnel audit are:

1. To review the organizational system, human resources sub-system in order to find out the efficiency of the organization in attracting and retaining human resources.
2. To find out about the effectiveness of various personnel policies and practices.
3. To know how various units are functioning and how they have been able to implement the personnel policies.

4. To review the personnel system in comparison with organizations and modify them to meet the challenges of personnel management.

Need for Personnel Audit

Though there is no legal obligation to audit personnel policies and practices, some of the modern organizations have accepted it due to compelling reasons:

1. Increasing size of the organization and personnel.
2. Changing philosophy of management towards human resources.
3. Increasing strength and influence of trade unions.
4. Changing personnel practices throughout the world.
5. Increasing dependence of the organization on the human resources system and its effective functioning.

Benefits

1. Identifies the contributions of HR.
2. Improves the professional image of HR.
3. Encourages greater responsibility and professionalism among members of HR.
4. Classifies HRs duties and responsibilities.
5. Stimulates uniformity of personnel policies and practices.
6. Finds critical personnel problems.
7. Ensures timely compliance with legal requirements.
8. Reduces Human Resource costs.

Major Areas of Personnel Audit

1. Planning - Forecasting and scheduling to meet organization and personnel needs.
2. Staffing and development.
3. Organizing and maintaining structures for co-ordinating, collaborating.
4. Administration - Style of leadership.
5. Research and innovation.

Personnel Audit Process

The personnel audit should probe much deeper, evaluating personnel policies, programmes, philosophy, practices and concepts comparing with standards and with those of the personnel records of the said organization and other organizations.

The process involves:

1. Identifying indices, indicators, statistical ratios and gross numbers in some cases.
2. Examining the variations in time frame in comparison with a similar previous period.
3. Comparing the variations of different departments during different periods.
4. Examining the variations of different periods and comparing them with similar units and industries in the same region.
5. Drawing trend lines, frequency distributions and calculating statistical correlations.
6. Preparing and submitting a detailed report to the top management and to the managers for information and necessary action.

Personnel practices and procedures can be evaluated by asking the questions of the following type:

1. What are they (ie policies, procedures)
2. How are they established?
3. How are they communicated?
4. How are they understood by employees and managers?
5. Are they consistent with management's organizational philosophy and HR management philosophy?
6. Are they consistent with the existing trend towards HR management and research?
7. What are the controls that exist?
8. What measures exist to modify them to meet organizational requirements?

Frequency of Audit

Rather than as a post mortem after conflict, management should conduct a regular audit to find out significant trends. These trends could lead to remedial steps to counter serious incidents against the organization. Along with an annual audit, certain parameters such as absenteeism should be reviewed every month or quarter.

The Audit Climate

Finally for a personnel audit to be successful, there must be a right climate created for accepting it as something useful. Sometime management feels that such an audit is an indication of want of faith by top management. This is an emotional viewpoint. The objective of such an audit is not merely to ascertain weaknesses but also the strengths of the manpower management programme. In fact, the existence of such an audit indicates the desire of persons in charge of the personnel management function to do better and improve their performance. Some argue that such an audit is not necessary. For example, they say that whether there is good employee relationships or not is observable and needs no audit. As against this, the use of objective yardsticks, such as the rate of absenteeism and employee turnover when compared with such figures in other similar organisations, can throw more light than what is merely observable. Thus both quantitative and qualitative yardsticks can be used in this evaluation. Quantitative can thus include the number of accidents, the employee turnover, the extent of use of facilities such as canteen and recreational opportunities.

Social Values and attitudes are changing. Personnel management policies must be geared to such changing scene. For eg: in a climate where age and seniority are given extreme reverence, insisting on merit as the only criterion for promotion might prove ineffective.

In the final analysis, the personnel management function is increasing in importance and securing a more sophisticated and scientific outlook. Human resources being the most valuable asset of an organisation, productivity and ultimate profitability of the entire organisation depend considerably on the effectiveness with which the personnel management function is executed.

Personnel Research

Personnel research is the task of searching for and analyzing facts related to the end that personnel problems may be solved or principles governing their solution derived.

Objectives of Personnel Research

1. Measure current conditions in HRM.
2. Evaluate effects and results of current policies and practices.
3. Discover ways and means of strengthening the abilities and attitudes of employees at a high level on a continuing basis.
4. Provide an objective basis for revising current programmes and activities.

Techniques

1. Historical studies.
2. Case studies.
3. Survey method to measure structure, responsibility, reward, risk, team spirit and standards.
4. Statistical studies.
5. Mathematical models.
6. Simulation methods.
7. Action research method.

Evaluation: the periodic, independent review and assessment of personnel management policies to determine whether the intended results are being achieved and are making the expected contribution to the achievement of the public service personnel management objectives.

Examples of policies which are evaluated are Training and Development, Performance Pay, Occupational Health and Safety, Human Resources Planning, Staffing Delegation, Probation and Transfers. Evaluations of particular policies usually occur every three or four years but could be undertaken more often, if necessary.

What Should I Keep in Personnel Files?

You should keep a personnel file for each of your employees, containing every important job-related document, including job applications, offer letters, employment contracts, benefits and salary information, government forms, performance evaluations and disciplinaþ+1Xry actions.

Auditing Human Resources Using the Scaled Comparison

The Scaled Comparison asks a person filling out a questionnaire to Compare two HR activities.

Importance of HR Activities

The first question asks about the importance of the HR activities to the accomplishment of business objectives. As much as HR professionals love all of the work they do, there is no other standard against which their work will be evaluated.

Question: Which Human Resource work adds more value to achieving the company's business objectives?

	Agree	Disagree	Don't know	disagree	agree	
Effectively manage benefit costs	○	○	○	○	○	Ensure pay reflects individual performance
Create benefits that attract/keep people	○	○	○	○	○	Coach line mgmt to resolve employee issues
Assess/address employee and org issues	○	○	○	○	○	Ensure HR systems work equitably for all
Ensure competitive pay bia benchmarking	○	○	○	○	○	Deliver accurate benefits on time
Manage Performance Rating System	○	○	○	○	○	Develop/implement high perf work systems
Develop/implement high perf work systems	○	○	○	○	○	Ensure pay reflects individual performance
Effectively manage benefit costs	○	○	○	○	○	Coach line mgmt to resolve employee issues
Create benefits that attract/keep people	○	○	○	○	○	Ensure HR systems work equitably for all

Performance of HR Activities

The second question asks the person completing the questionnaire to indicate which of the various activities HR is performing better than the other. This will prioritize all activities with the one being delivered the best at the top of the list.

Although some of the issues in the second example are different that the issues in the first, both questions display the same list and each activity appears multiple times on each page.

Question: Which work is Human Resources currently doing better?

	Agree	Disagree	Don't know	disagree	agree	
Effectively manage benefit costs	○	○	○	○	○	Develop/implement high perf work systems
Coach line mgmt to resolve employee issues	○	○	○	○	○	Deliver accurate benefits on time
Create benefits that attract/keep people	○	○	○	○	○	Ensure competitive pay bia benchmarking
Assess/address employee and org issues	○	○	○	○	○	Assess/address employee and org issues
Manage Performance Rating System	○	○	○	○	○	Ensure HR systems work equitably for all
Ensure HR systems work equitably for all	○	○	○	○	○	Develop/implement high perf work systems
Effectively manage benefit costs	○	○	○	○	○	Deliver accurate benefits on time
Coach line mgmt to resolve employee issues	○	○	○	○	○	Ensure competitive pay bia benchmarking

The Reports

Ideally, the work that is most important to the accomplishment of business objectives should also be the task being performed the best. The profile allows you to clearly analyze the "gap" between the importance of the activity and how well the HR area is delivering it.

The next illustration shows the same data in slightly different format. Although there are strong statistical data supporting these reports, experience has shown that survey results are most useful when they require little numerical or statistical understanding in order to interpret them.

As is common with many such surveys, important differences exist in different parts of the organization, among workers and managers with very different perspectives. The analysis of subgroups shows these differences, so decision-makers can know how HR work is perceived in various parts of the company.

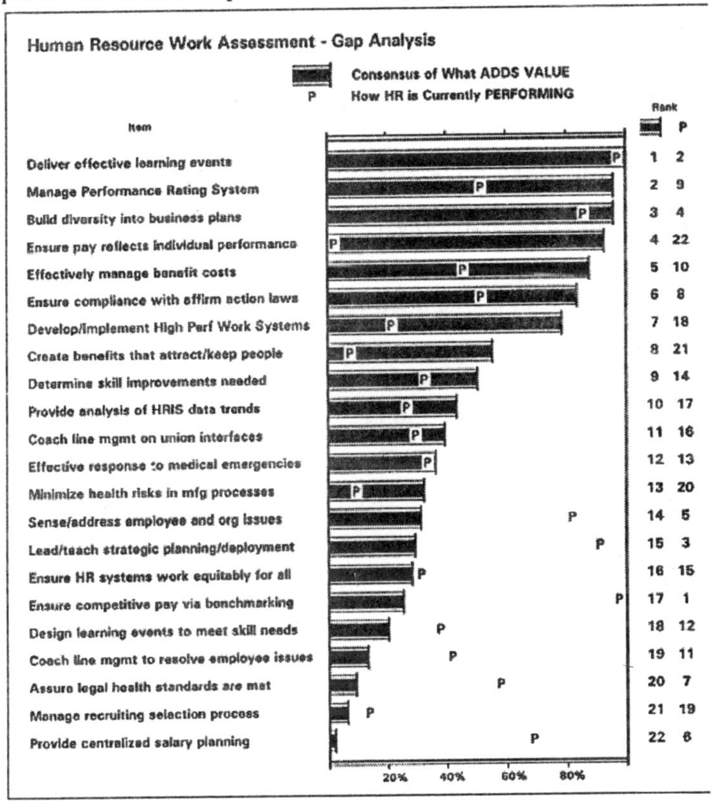

Underlying all of the reports shown above is the actual scaled comparison score, a true interval index, and supported by actual reliability assessment with each report. You never have to rely on assurances of reliability or studies conducted in some other time and place. You will know the reliability of your results.

The examples shown here pertain to the evaluation of HR work performance. Any staff group, whose output is absent, concrete measures of performance, could be audited in the same way. All staff functions provide a service to the larger organization, which receives the "service" as its "customers". This evaluation tool uses that perspective to perform a sensitive and accurate assessment of the quality of service from staff areas.

Few of us enjoy dealing with paperwork, but taking the time to properly create and maintain your employees' personnel files will pay off in the long run. You will have all the important documents relating to each employee in one place, easily available when it's time to make decisions on promotions or layoffs, to file tax returns, or to comply with government audits. And if you have to fire a problem employee, careful documentation will protect you from legal danger.

What Goes in a Personnel File?

You should begin a personnel file for each of your employees on the date of hire. All important job-related documents should go in the file, including:

- job description for the position.
- job application and/or resume.
- offer of employment.
- receipt or signed acknowledgment of employee handbook.
- performance evaluations.
- forms relating to employee benefits.
- forms providing next of kin and emergency contacts.
- complaints from customers and/or co-workers.
- awards or citations for excellent performance.
- records of attendance or completion of training programs.
- warnings and/or other disciplinary actions.
- notes on attendance or tardiness.
- any contract, written agreement, receipt or acknowledgment between the employee and the employer (such as an employment contract or an agreement relating to a company-provided car).

Although an employee's personnel file should contain every important job-related document, don't go overboard. Remember that, employees have the right to view their personnel files. And in the worst case scenario, that file may turn into evidence in a lawsuit brought by a disgruntled former employee. Indiscrete entries that do not directly relate to an employee's job performance and qualifications — like references to an employee's private life or political beliefs, unsubstantiated criticisms or comments about an employee's race, sex or religion - will come back to haunt you. A good rule of thumb: don't put anything in a personnel file that you would not want a jury to see.

How to Maintain a Personnel File?

You should establish a time to periodically review each employee's personnel file, perhaps when you conduct the employee's evaluation. During this review, consider whether the documents in the file are accurate, up to date and complete. Some questions to consider:

- Does the file reflect all of the employee's raises, promotions and commendations?
- Does the file contain every written evaluation of the employee?
- Does the file show every warning or other disciplinary action taken against the employee?
- If your policies provide that written warnings or other records of discipline will be removed from an employee's file after a certain period, have they been removed?
- If the employee was on a performance improvement plan, a probationary or training period, or other temporary status, has it ended? Has the file been updated to reflect the employee's current status?
- If the employee handbook has been updated since the employee started working for you, does the file contain a receipt or acknowledgment for the most recent version?
- Does the file contain current versions of every contract or other agreement between you and the employee?

Auditing Human Resources

- It is the systematic assessment of your organization's HR service excellence. A good HR Audit should help you:
- Identify the HR programs that are most important to achieving your organization's objectives.

- Find out how well your HR department is delivering those programs.
- Benchmark your HR work to ensure continuous improvement.
- Promote change and creativity.
- Focus the HR staff on important issues.
- Bring HR closer to the line functions of the organization.
- Now you can assess HR work performance with the scaled comparison

In this section, we are not discussing whether HR programs are in compliance with existing laws and statutes. Any good textbook on Human Resource Management can give you a checklist of programs, benchmarks, reporting requirements and positions that will comply with legal requirements for HRM. This kind of audit is worthwhile, and needs to be done periodically, but it is not particularly challenging nor mysterious.

What is important, however, is to determine whether the HR function is adding value to the larger organization with its work and performance. It's no secret that evaluating Human Resource performance (or any staff functions, for that matter) is a real challenge.

The best organizations meet the challenge by changing the paradigm by which they view the HR / Personnel area. First, they stop seeing HR as a department with a budget, personnel, and tasks. Instead, they define it as an organization with resources, customers, and services to deliver. Then it becomes a matter of finding out what the "customers" think of the "services" they are receiving.

The Scaled Comparison is one of the premier tools for evaluating the quality of external customer service for entire organizations, and serves equally well as an internal customer service survey.

The evaluation is performed by both internal HR employees as well as individuals in other organizational units who have contact with HR. This allows comparison of perceptions of value and quality between HR and other units.

This tool is available online or in paper and pencil format.

Using the Scaled Comparison, instead of traditional surveys, you have the advantages of:

A consensus, not an average - A consensus is what you would expect to emerge from face-to-face interactions between disagreeing people trying to reach a workable solution that is acceptable to everyone. You don't reach a consensus with a simple numerical average of checkmarks.

Ideal state defined by business objectives - The organization can compare its HR performance with an "ideal" determined by its own business objectives, rather than by a consultant or some other external viewpoint.

Small subgroups - Most surveying techniques require that groups or subgroups have at least 20 to 30 subjects in them. With the Scaled Comparison, subgroups as small as 5 or 10 people may be studied. This permits the delineation of viewpoints in and between small, but important decision-making groups.

Large number of HR tasks and programs - Conventional methods become cumbersome if they attempt to study more than a handful of HR programs, especially from more than a single perspective. With no significant increase in respondent time or effort, 40 to 50 or more different tasks or programs can be studied using the Scaled Comparison.

A "custom" study at an "off-the-shelf" price -You get a study that uses exactly the questions and HR tasks and programs you want, worded exactly the way you want them, at or below the cost of a generic questionnaire.

Complete control of manipulation - The Scaled Comparison protects the organization against errors in the results due to

intentional manipulation.

inconsistent judgments.

misunderstood instructions or concepts.

Human Resource Audit

An HR "Early Warning System" that works! Your tool to asses the present. Your blueprint for the future. Your commitment to excellence. Policies..Programs...Practices...People If you are guiding your HR function through compliance and employee relations issues, you know how challenging your work can be. So how do you know if you are on a solid foundation? With the Human Resource Audit, you can determine where you are, prioritize what you have to do, and know for certain you have looked at the right issues. The Result? Your comfort level and professional contribution will be enhanced, and you will be confident about moving forward.

Evaluate and Improve Your HR Practices In:

- Staffing.
- Compensation and Benefits.
- Performance Management.
- Employee Development.
- Employee Relations.
- Safety.
- Reporting and Recordkeeping.

How Does the Audit Process Work?

- Interview key staff.
- Review relevant documentation.
- Help you complete a comprehensive questionnaire.
- Compile data a prepare and customized written report.
- Make specific recommendations to improve the efficiency and performance of your HR function.

Following the comprehensive assessment of these systems, identify areas for improvement and provide practical solutions.

Immediate Audit Benefits

- Streamline HR work processes.
- Monitor compliance with established regulations and procedures.
- Develop user-friendly HR systems.

Moving from Recommendations to Results. As you evaluate the findings from your organizational audit, one needs to prioritize and implement what one choose to do. The goal is to provide specific, cost-effective options by pairing it with the services and individuals who can be most helpful.

Conclusion

Monitoring is defined as the ongoing and recurring review by the manager of activities and operations against plans, procedures or performance standards to determine whether they are being performed or are functioning as intended and are producing the desired results.

The intent is to determine at regular intervals (for example weekly, monthly, quarterly) the level and quality of performance and results and, when required, to take corrective action.

Monitoring of personnel management activities and operations will take many forms. In staffing and classification, for example, it would include the review of a sample of staffing or classification decisions and records to determine the quality (correctness) of decisions made in accordance with staffing or classification standards, directives and guidelines. It would also include a review of departmental staffing or classification policies and procedures and a check of their implementation. Finally, it would gather and analyze data to identify results, turnaround time and workload.

References and Further Reading

1. Davar RS; (1988) Personnel Management, (Tenth Edition) Vikas Publishing House Pvt Ltd.
2. http://www.msec.org/msecservices/human_resource_audit.asp
3. http://www.decpoint.com/auditinghr.html
4. Rao VSP; (2000) Human Resource Management, (First Edition) Excel Books.

11

Balancing Work and Life Issues

Background

People have family and personal responsibilities and needs outside of work, whether it is the caring of children and/or elderly parents, or the pursuit of personal interests, activities or hobbies. Finding ways to accommodate these responsibilities and needs can make a real difference to employees and to an organization. Work-Life balance is about creating supportive, healthy work environments for employees who are striving to better integrate their work and personal responsibilities. By implementing proactive programs and initiatives that support employees, organizations can strengthen employee commitment and loyalty, resulting in higher productivity, improved customer satisfaction and healthier bottom lines.

Introduction

Discussion about the meaning of work-life balance often draws on the soft components of work-life balance such as free gym memberships and coffee machines at work.

However, for unions the "fundamentals" of decent work such as secure employment, decent pay, leave and working conditions supported by affordable care arrangements for family members, significantly enhance workers' ability to balance work with the rest of their lives. This chapter has adopted a definition of work-life balance focusing on what measures are needed to create an environment where all workers, without discrimination, are able to choose employment arrangements that maximize their full potential in paid employment and family, social and cultural life.

How do we balance career and family life? At last, compulsions and common sense are turning corporate attention. Helping them is the new tribe of work/life professionals. Implemented solutions reduce stress, absenteeism, and conflict at work and at home. Productivity and profits increase.

In a research published, the 55-year old Society for Human Resource Management (SHRM) found the seriousness of the problem. 90 per cent of working adults were concerned that they do not spend enough time with the family. For many it's too late. Marriages crack and children left with a single stressed parent.

Work/life balance experts help a world where responsibilities increase while time to fulfill them does not. They work "in business, academia, or at the public sector to promote a healthier balance between work and personal life," as their trade association 'Alliance for Work-Life Progress' says. The term 'work/life balance' first appeared in 1986. It's defined as a "state of equilibrium in which the demands of both a person's job and personal life are equal."

Harmonising work and life becomes even more necessary in this century. Approach to life must keep pace with rapidly changing demands from career and home. Which is why the '9 to 5' routine is giving way for 'work/life balance' alternatives. More companies need to offer work life balance options like flexible working hours, compressed workweeks, family leave and telecommuting.

Flexible working time makes pragmatic sense in India's bursting metros. In Mumbai, an average home-office-return commute ranges from two hours to six hours or even more. The commuter lands in a disheveled, tired heap at office and home. Multiply this accumulated stress by a week, month, a year and we have a ticking social bomb. Companies could benefit from allowing those who can and need to work from home to do so. Better Internet and telecommunications facilities makes that easier to happen.

Work/life balance looks at corporate welfare beyond maternity leave, medical insurance and provident funds. It recognizes problems of single parents, those caring for the elderly, disabled or sick family members at home. Efficiency could suffer with distractions work through problems at home.

The reverse problem is the mind unable to shut off work after the office shuts. It comes with the territory of increasing workload and tensions in turbulent economic times. According to the American Institute of Stress, one million workers skipped work annually due to stress-related complaints. American companies lost more than five million workdays due to sick leave, with cause of more than half of them being stress-related. It's a universal problem.

A solution is 'Total Life Planning' that visionary companies have begun implementing. The SHRM research calls the concept a paradigm shift in society. It's a package of programs and services encouraging employees to look at life holistically. It helps assess relationships, emotional and physical health, career, spirituality and personal financial situation. Work finds its harmonious place in the larger scheme of things.

When companies started to consider work-life issues in the 1980s and 1990s, there was an intuitive sense that it was an important thing for employers to do, although there was no strong data to back up this feeling. Unsupported claims of "reduced absenteeism", "improved productivity" and "greater potential for recruitment and retention" were made to counter perceptions among senior management that work-life balance was a "fluffy" human resources issue.

Over the past decade, however, an abundance of data and the results of research studies supported these claims and point to work-life policies as being good for business. Several reliable data collection instruments and survey tools and an increasing body of research now exist to help us make the economic and social arguments for work-life balance. The results of the research and of these surveys support contentions that work-life balance is linked to reduced absenteeism and enhanced productivity. They indicate that the challenges of recruiting and retaining top talent in an increasingly competitive labour market are driving workplace change and workforce demands for work-life balance. These factors are now motivating employers to integrate work-life balance measures in their business strategies. As stated by Courtney Pratt, CEO, Toronto Hydro, "This (facilitating work-life balance) is not corporate social work. It's a business imperative."

Absenteeism

The Conference Board of Canada's Survey of Canadian Workers on Work-Life Balance (1999), found that twice as many Canadians reported moderate to high levels of stress as a result of trying to balance their work and home lives, a sharp increase compared to 1989 (46.2 percent in 1999; 26.7 percent in 1989). These stress levels are reflected in health problems and absences. Respondents who report a high degree of stress in balancing work and family life also report missing an average of 7.2 days of work while those who report very little stress in balancing work and family have missed, on average, only 3.6 days.

Statistics Canada: *Work Absence Rates, 1987-1998, (Analytic Report No. 10* states that Canadian workers lost an average of 5.7 days in 1998; women averaged 6.7 days lost, while men were absent for 4.9 days. The presence of children, especially pre-school children, was a primary indicator of time lost: employees with pre-schoolers lost an average of 6.4 days, compared to 5.6 days for employees without children. The ageing workforce also contributed to increasing absenteeism. Workers between 55 and 64 are absent for an average of 6.9 days per year, while all age groups combined report an average of 5.7 days.

According to the Watson Wyatt: Staying @ Work Study (September 2000), a survey of large employers in the US, short-term absences have doubled in the last three years. It concludes that the best way to address absenteeism and reducing absence rates for all groups is to provide work-life balance measures/programs.

Recruitment and Retention

In the Executive View Study conducted by Canadian Facts and sponsored by The Globe and Mail, 1850 CEOs and business leaders were asked "What issues about your business are most likely to keep you awake at night?" Interestingly, the most common response was not profitability or competition but the demands of attracting, training and retaining staff. Seventy-one per cent of leaders anticipate problems in retaining skilled workers.

As a result of the competition for talent, the ageing workforce and the shrinking of the labour pool, companies have seen their recruitment costs rise dramatically. Estimates from human resource professionals and consultants indicate that to recruit a new staff member it costs them between two and four times the annual salary for the position.

When employees are dissatisfied with their work experience they leave. Organizations see experience and knowledge walk out the door and down the road to their competitors. Consequently, more than ever, employers are recognizing the need to offer more than just "a job".

Prospective employees are looking for a company that recognises their commitments both inside and outside the workplace. As a result, work-life programs and policies are considered as tools for companies seeking to recruit and retain skilled employees.

In the PriceWaterhouseCoopers 1999, International Student Survey, 57% of students stated that work-life balance is their primary goal, and don't believe this competes with long-term career development and personal growth goals.

In AONs Canada @ Work 2000, a growing number of respondents (29%) rank work-life balance as the first or second most important factor in taking a job. The good news is that over 69% indicate that their organization had demonstrated increased efforts over the last year to support work-life employee needs.

Productivity

In a 1999 study by Health Canada, it reported 40 percent of working Canadians say they experienced high levels of work-family conflict. This conflict is particularly acute for women; however, it is becoming more of a concern for men with 49 percent reporting some kind of work-family stress.

In a workplace that focuses on hours worked, bodies in seats and "face time" (being able to see employees when they work), productivity is often confused with working long hours. This creates a barrier for employees looking for flexibility in how they work, since long working hours are not compatible with employee health, personal and workplace well being, or work-life balance.

When building a business case for work-life balance, the main factors to consider are costs and stakeholder impact. Absenteeism, recruitment and retention issues and low productivity all impact organizations' bottom-line. Customer/client commitment is based on a positive experience with representatives of the organization they are dealing with. Employees who report that they have achieved work-life balance are more satisfied and more willing to 'go the extra miles' for their employers.

What is Work Life Balance All About?

Work-life balance is about adjusting working patterns. Regardless of age, race or gender, everyone can find a rhythm to help them combine work with their other responsibilities or aspirations.

Increasingly, employers are developing a wide range of work-life balance options, covering flexible working arrangements and flexible benefit packages. Here are just a few:

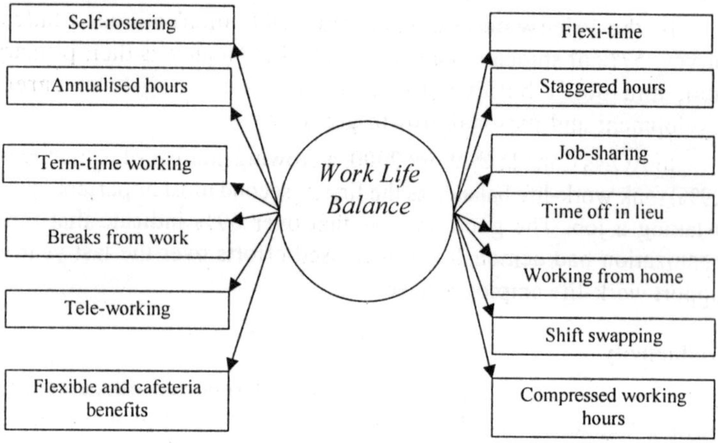

Flexi-time lets people choose when they work, usually outside the agreed core times. This means staff can vary their start, finish and break times each day.

Staggered hours means employees can all have different start, finish and break times. This allows employers to cover longer opening hours. It also offers employees more flexibility, as long as they're consulted first.

Time off in lieu is when employees take time off, in agreement with managers, to make up for extra hours worked. It's often used to compensate employees who attend meetings in the evenings.

Compressed working hours lets people work their total number of hours over fewer days. For example, you can work full-time hours over four days a week instead of five, or work nine days a fortnight instead of ten. With shift-working, employers can extend the use of their plant or facilities by letting staff work one after another through a 24-hour period. Some businesses are realising that longer opening hours and more flexible shifts mean everyone has more choice.

Shift swapping lets staff negotiate their working times and shifts amongst themselves, whilst keeping the needs of the business or service in mind.

Self-rostering involves working out the number of staff and type of skills needed each day, then letting employees put forward the times they would like to work. Shift patterns are then compiled, matching staff preferences to the agreed staffing levels as closely as possible. Self-rostering is used in some hospitals and care services.

Annualised hours means that total working hours are calculated over a year rather than a week. This means people can work according to the peaks and troughs of activity over the year.

Job-sharing involves two part-time employees sharing the duties of a post normally done by one. Job-sharers divide pay, holiday and other benefits.

Term-time working makes it possible for permanent employees to take unpaid leave during school holidays.

Working from home has been made easier due to new technology. It is possible for all kinds of work. Examples are: assembly work, sewing, or providing a personal service to paid consultants working with new technology. Some employees, such as service engineers, are mobile, others work in their home.

Tele-working involves working at home, and using a telephone and computer to keep in touch with work.

Breaks from work are often due to maternity or parental and paternity leave. But some employers also offer unpaid career breaks and sabbaticals.

Flexible and cafeteria benefits include childcare information or vouchers, funding and time off for learning, pension or insurance contributions, laundry services, use of staff facilities, and in-house medical and dental care. 'Cafeteria benefits' means a person can pick and choose those benefits that best suit their needs.

Costs and Benefits of Work Life Balance to An Organization

In a representative survey of US employers only a minority (18%) perceive the costs of flexible work arrangement policies as outweighing the benefits, while nearly half (46%) perceive the benefits from such policies as outweighing costs. Employers and employees agreed that while organizational goals have priority, employers have a responsibility to help people balance work and other aspects of their lives.

When developing a work-life business case for an organization, it is important to consider the tangible and intangible benefits. Start by linking your work-life strategy to your organizations goals and objectives. Then consider all the possible benefits that could arise from implementing your strategy such as:

- The potential for increased service coverage if some employees arrive earlier and others stay later.
- The possibility that telecommuting employees (especially those in sales and service functions) may be closer to their customers' offices, thereby reducing necessary traveling time.
- Greater flexibility in employee schedules may help meet customer demand.
- Improved employee health and well being.
- Reduced stress, reduced absenteeism and reduced numbers of short-term disability claims.
- Increased employee commitment, satisfaction and resiliency.
- More effective workload management, reduced interruptions and distractions in the workday.
- Increased capacity to meet work targets and make customer needs their top priority.

Organizations may also want to link their strategy to other employer obligations such as:

- Accommodation under employment equity and/or human rights legislation.
- Occupational safety and health.
- Workplace health and well-being.

Employer Benefits

Employers benefit from having a more motivated, productive and less stressed workforce, as well as:

- Reduced staff turnover rates
- Less loss of knowledge workers to competitors
- Lower recruitment and training costs, associated with reduced turnover
- Broader recruitment pool

- Improved quality of applicants
- Increased return on investment in training as employees stay longer
- Reduced absenteeism
- Reduced use of sick leave
- Reductions in worker's stress levels
- Reduced liability for stress under the Health and Safety in Employment Act
- Increased return rate from parental leave
- Reduction in worker stress from conflicts between work and family roles
- Improved morale or satisfaction
- Greater staff loyalty and commitment
- Greater flexibility in deploying staff such as an ability to offer extended hours of business to customers
- Improved corporate image, which can lead to greater sales or improved stock price of ethical investment choice

All of the above contribute to more effective staff and as such, combine to enhance the productivity of the business.

Employee Benefits

Employees benefit from being happier at work and at home, as well as:

- Greater responsibility and a sense of ownership
- Better relations with the management
- Improved self-esteem, health, concentration and confidence
- Loyalty and commitment
- Not bringing problems at home to work, and vice versa
- The time to focus more on life outside work
- Greater control of their working lives

Costs of Implementing Work Life Balance In An Organization

The costs associated with implementing work life balance in an organization are:

- Direct costs of policies which involve payments, such as childcare subsidies or paid parental leave.
- Costs of extra spaces associated with increased facilities such as breastfeeding rooms or childcare facilities
- Costs of equipment to facilitate working at home
- Costs of investigating work-life balance policies.
- Costs of implementing new work-life balance policy systems. This may include costs associated with changing processes or culture.
- Fixed costs associated with the number of staff
- Maintenance or transaction costs for managers in implementing work-life balance practices.
- Disruption costs for temporarily filling absent colleagues posts
- Temporary reduction in productivity from disruption
- Reduced morale of those employees not benefiting

So how do businesses make decisions about whether or not to introduce work-life balance policies? Ideally, firms would identify all the costs and benefits involved in implementing work-life balance policies, undertake some form of cost-benefit comparison and implement the policies if the net impact is positive. Obtaining an accurate measure of the savings gained from work-life balance policies is problematic and many companies do not or cannot make explicit calculations of the costs and benefits. While the costs of introducing work-life balance policies are relatively direct and easy to measure, the benefits are often more difficult to identify and measure. As not all the benefits may have been identified or measured the net impact of these policies is often regarded as negative. Given the difficulties in comparing the costs and benefits of work-life policies, and assessing their net impact, employers often make decisions based on their values, attitudes or beliefs. Some employers implement work-life balance policies because they intuitively make sense. Some employers undertake an evaluation of their work-life balance policies after they have been implemented, in order to justify the decision.

How Do Work-life Balance Policies Affect Business Performance?

There are different routes by which work-life balance policies affect business performance. The pathways are often inter-connected;

business performance may be influenced by any, some or all of these routes.

The ways that work-life balance policies affect business performance are:

1. By being necessary in a competitive labour market,
2. Reducing costs and thus increasing profitability,
3. Improving labour productivity levels and thus increasing profitability,
4. Reducing the risks of workplace accidents and stress, hence reducing liability for health and safety issues.

Competitive Labour Market

In a competitive labour market, there is evidence that firms enhance their ability to attract the best recruits if they offer flexible policies, alongside competitive remuneration packages. In a strategic model, if a critical mass of firms in an industry offer work-life balance policies, it would be difficult for the other firms to hold out and not offer work-life balance programmes.

Cost Reduction

There are many cost savings available to firms and other enterprises through implementing work-life balance policies. They rest upon the assumption that work-life balance policies will improve staff retention.

Reducing staff turnover leads to lower costs, as recruiting new staff is a costly process. Staff loss leads to direct costs associated with recruiting, such as advertising and interviewing as well as indirect costs such as the loss of institutional knowledge and contacts. Greater staff retention also reduces training costs. Having staff staying longer in a firm, increases the returns on investments made in their training. There are also cost savings if work-life balance policies reduce absenteeism.

Productivity Improvements

The arguments that work-life balance policies will increase productivity are more complex and take different routes. The literature search has not found any sources that develop a coherent theory of how work-life balance influences productivity. Instead, each study seems to have a variation on general theories.

Productivity is difficult to measure and these studies generally do not measure the underlying mechanisms through which productivity gains are made. The studies do not necessarily support any one of these productivity theories over another. There appear to be at least three basic ways of thinking about the relationship between work-life balance and productivity:

1. Examine how work-life balance policies affect another variable such as job satisfaction or organizational commitment, and then correlate these variables to productivity.
2. Consider how work-life balance fits into an exchange theory model, inducing workers to increase their discretionary effort and raise productivity.
3. In the absence of work-life balance policies, there will be productivity losses.

There are variations on these three themes, which are discussed below.

Job Satisfaction

When work extends into family time, it can create stresses which then extend into the workforce. One meta-analysis suggests that there is a consistent negative relationship between work-family conflict and job satisfaction. As far as work-life balance policies can reduce the conflict between work and family, they can increase job satisfaction. There is no strong empirical evidence of a positive association between high employee satisfaction and high productivity, but job satisfaction does have a clear negative relationship to absence and turnover.

A satisfied workforce may be valuable because employees are then less likely to be absent and consequently affect the bottom line. Other commentators suggest that work-life balance policies can increase organizational commitment. Higher levels of organizational commitment are then correlated with lower turnover and better job performance.

Exchange Theory

Work-life balance programs are posited as a means to encourage workers to expend extra effort, beyond the minimum required to maintain their jobs. An exchange framework is used to explain this general mechanism. In situations with some mutual trust and commitment, more general investments by the employer may be rewarded by greater employee effort. Akerlof's gift exchange model offers a possible explanation for why this may be the case. His model assumes that workers develop sentiments for the firm. Gift giving is governed by norms of reciprocity. Workers can give firms the gift of extra effort in response to the gift of work-life balance policies from the firm.

More recently, frameworks focus on general exchanges between employer and employees. Where firm investments go beyond specific monetary incentives, to include investments in general well-being and career development, firms may see greater discretionary efforts from employees. There are some empirical studies to support these claims.

High Performance Management

Another variant, using the exchange framework, examines "high-commitment" or "high-performance" management styles which involve greater mutual commitment between employers and employees. Employees only provide the necessary degree of commitment if they are treated with sufficient consideration in return. Work-life balance policies are perceived as an indication of concern for employee's welfare and as such could assist in engaging employee commitment.

Reducing Negative Spill-over

A further way of arguing for the productivity gains of work-life balance policies, is to argue that in their absence, work-life conflict leads to stress and negative spill-overs from the home and a consequence of this is a decrease in productivity at work. There is a body of research that links work-life conflict to productivity loss. There are fewer studies of the firm level productivity gains from implementing work-life balance policies. This theory of the connection between work-life balance policies has strong empirical support.

Countering the Effects of Long Hours

A number of firms have made aggregate productivity gains from increasing the hours of work of their employees. However the evidence suggests that we have already reached, or passed the point of diminishing returns in many industries, particularly those working more than 50 hours per week. The relationship between extended hours of work and productivity is complex.

Historically, most work was relatively less skilled and more routine. This would suggest that increased hours of work may not have had as much of a negative impact on productivity. As workplaces have become increasingly complex from a cognitive perspective, they now require much higher levels of problem solving and teamwork. The impact of extended hours on fatigue and subsequent performance and productivity is well documented.

Studies show that employee productivity per hour for 10-12 hour shifts is significantly lower than for an 8 hour shift. Fatigue, which is often caused by extended working hours, negatively affects:

- The ability to comprehend complex situations without distraction
- The ability to monitor events and improve strategies
- Risk Assessment and Accurate Predictions of Consequences
- Thinking laterally and being innovative
- Controlling mood and behaviour
- Monitoring personal performance
- Recollecting the timing of events
- Effective communication

In other words, there are clear benefits to businesses from staff not working excessive hours, having breaks, enough time at home every day for rest and recuperation and holidays. Work-life balance policies are a way of reducing excessive hours and allowing employees to recover from the negative effects of short periods of working extended hours.

What is the Strength of the Evidence?

Much of the evidence for the claims of the costs and benefits of work-life balance policies comes from case studies. There is clearly extensive information that could be used to prepare a business case for work-life balance policies in these case studies.

However, the evidence must be seen in the context of the particular case study. Case studies are not necessarily representative and so the results cannot be generalized to all situations.

There are specific situations in which the business case is strong but it is more difficult to make robust generalisations about the business benefits of work-life balance policies. This finding confirms the diversity of firms. Just as there is no "one-size fits all" model of work-life balance for individuals, we cannot expect there to be one generic business case for firms.

Formal and Informal Policies

Other studies have attempted to make a more general case through the use of larger sample sizes and econometric techniques to assess the benefits of work-life balance policies. These studies face a number of challenges in quantifying both the benefits and the policies. Almost all the studies rely on reports of the formal work-life balance policies available to employees. Informal work-life balance policies often exist, but they generally aren't measured.

The culture of a workplace has a large effect on the use of work-life balance policies. Work-life balance policies are not very effective in an unsupportive workplace because they either will not be used or they would harm an employee's prospects. Employees may not necessarily feel free to use these policies for various reasons. For example, they may feel that doing so would lead to negative impacts on their career progression, as they would be perceived as lacking commitment to the company.

Productivity

Individual productivity is hard to measure. Measures such as profits, are the result of the contribution of a number of people. Researchers either use firm productivity measures such as profits, or rely on self-reported productivity measures.

Konrad and Mangel's US study used firm profitability (as revealed by public disclosure laws) as a measure of productivity. This meant that their study of the relationship between work-life balance and productivity had a bias towards larger firms. 7% of the variation in productivity of the firms in their random sample, was explained by the presence of work-life balance policies. They did not however directly measure the underlying mechanisms through which work-life programs increased productivity. The authors of these econometric studies generally caution that the associations between work-life balance policies and productivity are correlations and not proof of causation. It may be that more profitable firms are better able to afford work-life balance policies. The association between providing work-life balance policies and employee productivity may go either way. The policies may encourage a greater output by workers or the policies may attract more productive workers. However, it is almost impossible to set up a large, randomized econometric study to prove a causal relationship between work-life balance policies and productivity. Productivity has multiple causes and work-life balance policies can only be part of the equation. The econometric studies discussed above offer strong evidence to support the business case.

Business Opinion on Cost-effectiveness

Another way of assessing the strength of the business case is to assess how many businesses offer work-life balance policies and ask businesses if they believe they are cost-effective. Bearing in mind that the direct costs of implementing work-life balance policies are more easily measured than the benefits, employers may consistently underestimate the cost-effectiveness of work-life balance policies. This means that business opinions on the cost-effectiveness of work-life balance policies may not be a very robust measure of their actual cost-effectiveness.

Galinsky and Bond found that around 90% of US companies offer at least one policy which would fall under the work-life balance policy umbrella. Similarly, in the UK, nine out of ten employers in 1996 provided at least one family-friendly arrangement. In a study of a representative sample of US businesses employing more than 100 people, Galinsky and Bond found that only 17% of companies think that the costs of leave programs that exceed the statutory minimum outweigh the benefits. 42% thought the programs were cost-neutral and another 42% believed there was a positive return on these investments. Of the companies offering flexible work arrangements, 18% viewed the costs as outweighing the benefits, 36% saw them as cost-neutral and 46% claimed a positive return on investment.

Components of Work Life Balance

Component #1 - Emergency child-care

Definition:

Employees may sometimes need emergency childcare because their child-care centre or usual caregiver cannot look after their child or because they have to work overtime. A company generally makes arrangements with a community organization or private company that specializes in this type of service.

Considerations:

- This measure may help lessen the stress experienced by employees since they know they have access to emergency child-care services.
- It may help lower the rate of unexpected employee absenteeism.
- However, this measure must not be used to force an employee to use the service or authorize a manager to change the employee's schedule without notice because the manager knows that the employee can use the service.
- The costs associated with such a measure may be high.
- The managers must promote and be able to refer their employees to such services

Component #2 - Emergency eldercare

Definition:

Employees may need emergency care for an elderly person whom they care for because they cannot do it themselves (for example, they have to work overtime unexpectedly). Such services may entail outside-the-home or in-home care. A company may make arrangements with a community organization or private company that provides such services.

Considerations:

- This measure may help lessen the stress experienced by employees.
- However, this measure must not be used to force an employee to use the service or authorize a manager to change the employee's schedule without notice because the manager knows that the employee can use the service.
- This measure may help lower the rate of unexpected employee absenteeism.
- The costs associated with such a measure may be high.

- The managers must promote and be able to refer their employees to such services.

Component #3 - Financial assistance for child-care expenses

Definition:

Some employers offer financial assistance to their employees rather than set up a child-care service. This assistance may be paid directly to the employees or may subsidize a space in an existing childcare centre.

Considerations:

- This measure may help lessen the stress experienced by employees since they can manage their personal life more effectively.
- It allows employees to choose the child-care service that best meets their needs. Some employees may prefer to have their children looked after close to home or by a member of their family.
- This measure may be easier to administer than a child-care service and may also not be as costly.
- The managers must promote and be able to refer their employees to such services.

Component #4 - Information and referral service

Definition:

Employees who have dependants may need an information and referral service so that they can obtain information, advice and recommendations about available services. More and more businesses and community organizations are specializing in this type of service.

Considerations:

- This measure may help lessen the stress experienced by employees since they can manage their personal life more effectively. It also helps lower the rate of absenteeism by reducing the number of calls and visits employees need to make before choosing a service.
- This measure is inexpensive and easy to implement. It fits in well with a program designed to help employees balance their work and personal life.
- Confidentiality is very important.

- The information in the service's data banks must be comprehensive and updated regularly.
- The managers must promote and be able to refer their employees to such services.

Component #5 - Workplace child-care

Definition:

Employees may have their children looked after at or near the workplace. The child-care centre may be owned by the company or be managed by a board of directors that includes representatives of the company and parents whose children go to the centre. It is sometimes also open to children in the community. It must comply with provincial and municipal regulations. Work-related childcare centres accept preschoolers and infants.

Considerations:

- This measure may help lessen the stress experienced by employees. Parents may have easier access to a child care service.
- A work-related childcare centre may accommodate the company employees' schedules more readily.
- It may be perceived as an important employee benefit and be conducive to the recruitment of new employees.
- If the centre is open to children in the community, this measure may help improve the company's image.
- For a company, the costs of such a measure may be high. Employers generally contribute by paying an amount that covers the rent, start-up costs, etc.
- It is important to assess employees' needs carefully by conducting a proper survey.
- Managers must promote and be able to refer their employees to such services.

Component #6 - Gradual retirement

Definition:

Phased or gradual retirement allow older employees, usually with long service records, to progressively reduce their working time and workload over a period of time instead of abruptly shifting from full-time employment to retirement.

Considerations:

- From the employer's point of view, phased retirement programs can be useful in retaining skilled older employees who would otherwise retire (especially in sectors where there is a shortage of entry-level job applicants), in reducing labour costs, or in arranging the training of replacement employees.
- Gradual retirement also allows employers to plan attrition and to a certain extent maintain employee morale when a company restructures its operations.
- This practice can also be beneficial for older workers, not only in easing the transition to retirement, but also in balancing their work and family responsibilities, particularly if they must care for an ageing spouse or elderly relative(s).

Component #7 - Job sharing

Definition:

Two employees share a full-time job. This practice involves not only sharing job duties and responsibilities, but also pay and holidays as well.

Considerations:

- Employees sharing a job must be able to work as a team and communicate effectively.
- This practice may increase productivity particularly if employees who are sharing a job have complementary skills.
- It can also be attractive if a job must be filled full-time or if there are few part-time jobs in the company. It can prove an incentive to the retention of experienced employees who want to reduce significantly reduce their hours of work for personal reasons (e.g. employees who are considering gradual retirement).

Component #8 - Voluntary part-time work

Definition:

Employees choose to work fewer hours than the standard 37.5 or 40 hours per week. This practice may be temporary (that is, established for a specific period) or permanent.

Considerations:

- Employees with health problems or with disabilities can maintain some link with the labour force.

- Employees may have more time to care for their dependents and may be less stressed.
- Employee benefits are often established on a prorata basis for part-time employees. Part-time work may limit or reduce access to some employee benefits or governmental programs (e.g. employment insurance, pension plans). This practice may also have a negative impact on promotion and training opportunities.
- This practice may help increase operational flexibility of companies during times of heavy workload.
- It may facilitate re-entry in the labour force for employees who had interrupted their labour market participation.
- It may increase productivity by helping to reduce tardiness and absenteeism, by increasing employee morale and it may also serve as an incentive to recruitment and retention.

Component #9 – EAP

Definition:

The Employee Assistance Professionals Association defines an employee assistance program (EAP) as:

A worksite-based program designed to assist in the identification and resolution of productivity problems associated with employees impaired by personal concerns, including, but not limited to, health, marital, family, financial, alcohol, drug, legal, emotional, stress, or other personal concerns which may adversely affect employee job performance.

Considerations:

- EAP services are usually provided by an external company specializing in this type of support, information and counseling service. EAP services are confidential and can be offered to either individuals or groups of employees. Most plans offer access to employees and their family members via a 24-hour, toll-free line. Counselors will meet or discuss the problem with the employee and if longer-term or specialized treatment is required, EAP counselors will link callers with appropriate community resources.
- The cost of an Employee Assistance Program is often based on utilization.
- The benefits of EAPs to an organization can include:

- Decreased costs related to turnover, absenteeism, accidents and stress related disability;
- Increased employee productivity;
- Prevention of problems, which could negatively impact the employee's work and/or home life; and enhanced morale and commitment to the organization

Component #10 - Wellness/health promotion

Definition:

Health and wellness are much more than the absence of illness. Health is an essential life ingredient that is influenced daily by personal circumstances, attitudes, beliefs and actions; and by the cultural, social, economic, and physical environments in which an individual exists.

A healthy workplace provides mutual benefits for employers and employees within a common belief that good health practices by both will lead to individual and organizational self-fulfilment and productivity. Health promotion is the process of enabling employees to increase control over and to improve their physical, emotional and social health.

Considerations:

- Programs should be designed for all employees, whether it is to improve the health of those with serious health problems or to assist those employees who are generally well to maintain their good health.
- People's habits affect their health. Some important habits involve eating, smoking, alcohol and drug use, physical activity and sleep. Individuals may develop counter-productive or unhealthy habits in relation to any of the above that can impair their personal and work lives and will likely require a sustained effort and commitment on the part of the individual to achieve success in breaking the habit. Thus, results of health promotion programs and activities might not be evidenced in the immediate or short-term, as they often require a long-term approach.
- At home and work, physical and social environments have major influences on a person's health. The physical environment can affect people directly in many ways, and includes noise levels,

toxic substances, air quality and workplace design. The social environment has an impact on employee wellness through such factors as work schedules, coordinating home and work responsibilities, deadlines, work organization, available training and support. The social environment also has an effect through interpersonal relationships, including supervisor communications, feedback from co-workers and family relationships. People are also affected indirectly by worry, nervousness and stress.

Therefore, the types of wellness/health promotion activities that can be implemented within an organization are numerous and target different aspects of an individual's physical, emotional, and social environment. Some examples of health promotion and/or wellness activities include:

- Creation, promotion and maintenance of organizational occupational Health and Safety Committees;
- Providing advice to employees and managers on dealing with issues concerning the use or wearing of scented products in the workplace;
- Workshops/seminars on HIV/IDS in the Workplace, dealing with stress in the workplace, time management, team building, safe winter driving, smoking cessation, first aid, cardio pulmonary resuscitation (CPR), elder care, or retirement planning;
- Promotion of an organizational Employee Assistance Program;
- Flu immunization and blood donor clinics;
- Promotion of Workplace Injury Prevention Initiatives such as ergonomic or workplace assessments for employees by health professionals;
- Promotion of a healthier lifestyle by encouraging employees to walk, run, or jog; and
- Enforcement of a smoke-free work environment.

Component #11 - Annualized hours

Definition:

Flexible working time arrangements can also be provided in the form of "annualized" hours. These essentially allow employees to choose, within certain boundaries, their days and hours of work, with the proviso that they work a specified number of hours

in a year. This can also be calculated over a shorter averaging period, be it on a monthly, biweekly, or other basis. Such arrangements combine elements of flexitime and compressed workweeks and can have the added advantage of reducing recourse to overtime.

Considerations:

- Employers may also benefit from such arrangements if they can be used to meet seasonal variations and peak hours.
- Moreover, output and product quality can be improved if employees work during their most productive periods of the day.

One potential disadvantage of annualized hours for supervisors is the difficulty in monitoring and co-coordinating the work of employees.

Component #12 - Compressed workweeks

Definition:

A compressed workweek is an arrangement whereby employees work longer shifts in exchange for a reduction in the number of working days in their work cycle (i.e. on a weekly or biweekly basis).

Considerations:

- This can be beneficial for employees in terms of additional days off work (e.g. longer weekends allowing "mini-vacations") and reduced commuting time, whereas employers can extend their daily operating hours, with less need to resort to overtime.
- Compressed work week arrangements may be particularly useful for employees who wish to reduce the number of days per week spent at work, but who can not financially afford to decrease their working hours.
- Compressed workweek provisions are not necessarily designed as a means of balancing work and family responsibilities. In some cases, they may be initiated by an employer solely in order to improve operational efficiency and to maximize production.

Component #13 - Flexitime

Definition:

Flexitime is an arrangement whereby employees can vary the scheduling of their working hours within specified guidelines.

Essentially, it allows employees, on an individual or collective basis, to determine (or be involved in determining) the start and end times of their working day. It is the result of an agreement between the employee and the manager and usually takes the form of a pre-arranged alternative schedule.

Considerations:

- Employees have some discretion that allows them to plan their workday around their personal lives. They can manage their work hours more efficiently by introducing, in agreement with the manager, a work schedule that is in the best interest of both the employee and the organization.
- This practice has been credited with reductions in tardiness and absenteeism, increases in employee morale and deemed an incentive for recruitment and retention.
- An employer may introduce flextime in order to maintain or increase work efficiency and improve services offered to the public.
- This practice may be inappropriate in some industries or workplaces where the nature of the work requires that employees be present at given times for instance in the case of assembly line work.

Component #14 - Telework

Definition:

Telework, also referred to as telecommuting, is an arrangement whereby an employee, at least on a periodic basis, fulfils his or her regularly scheduled job responsibilities at a remote location which is not operated by the employer (a teleworkplace)—usually an employee's own residence.

Working from home has been practised for decades in certain sectors, such as the garment industry. However, the rapid development of computer and information technologies in recent years has made teleworking feasible in an increasing number of job categories.

Considerations:

- Telework can be advantageous for employees by allowing them: to organize their work day around their personal and family needs;

to decrease work-related expenses; to reduce commuting time; and to work in a less stressful and disruptive environment.

- It may also help to accommodate employees who, because of particular disabilities, are unable to leave home. Although telework cannot normally be combined with child or eldercare-related tasks, it may nevertheless let employees work in closer proximity to their children and relatives, offering some peace of mind and giving the family a chance to spend more time together at lunch time as well as before and after school.
- Apart from improved productivity, efficiency and employee morale, employers can also benefit from lower overhead costs and from reduced disruptions in case of bad weather and other emergencies. The fact that employees who telework can use this added flexibility to capitalize on their personal peak productivity periods can also favourably influence a company's bottom line.
- Not all occupations are amenable to such an arrangement. Moreover, employers may be concerned by the initial implementation costs, potential legal liabilities, and difficulties in supervising and appraising the performance of teleworkers. Unions may disapprove of work-at-home clauses if they perceive them as leading to greater isolation of employees, reduced job security and promotion opportunities, and diminished health and safety protection.
- Employees may work at home full-time or part-time. This measure can be permanent or temporary but it is not appropriate for all types of employment.

Component #15 - Flexible benefits

Definition:

Flexible benefit plans are an alternative way for companies to deliver benefits by using "flexible" options that are not always available with traditional "one-size fits all" plans. Employees are able to select the type and level of coverage from among a menu of available benefits commonly including such options as: health, dental, life insurance, accidental death and dismemberment, and long-term disability.

These programs are generally implemented to permit employees to build an individualized benefit program that most closely meets their coverage needs and budget requirements and to change their benefit elections over time as their life circumstances change.

Flexible benefit plans are generally paid for using credits (sometimes termed flex credits) that are assigned to each employee by crediting them to a form of health spending account. The employee then allocates his/her flex credits to various benefits according to what they need. Unused credits are commonly deposited back into the health care spending account, cashed out, or carried forward.

Another form of flexible benefit plan is structured in such a way that the employer provides a base level of standard coverage for all employees, but allowing individual employees to select a level of coverage for each benefit, ranging from no coverage to a premium level of coverage with a dollar value being assigned to each level of coverage above or below that standard.

Considerations:

- Flexible benefit plans offer employees the opportunity to select those benefits they need, while helping the employer manage benefit plan costs and meet the diverse needs of its workforce.
- Employers can define the level of funding for the plan each year, rather than having it dictated by increases in the premium costs of insurance benefits. This is usually a defined contribution based on a flat dollar amount per employee or a percentage of each employee's salary.
- Employers can help control plan costs by choosing benefits with cost control features and by designing or pricing these benefits attractively.

Generally, employees are offered the choice to examine their benefits choices on an annual basis.

Component #16 - Leave for personal reasons

Definition:

Leave for personal reasons can provide employees with periods of time off, with or without pay, to deal with family obligations or other personal commitments.

In general, this type of leave does not exist in labour standards legislation. However, labour standards legislation may include a variety of other leaves intended to help employees meet their personal obligations.

Among these other leaves available are:

- Annual vacation leave,
- Bereavement leave
- Leave for family responsibility
- Court/jury leave
- Marriage leave

Considerations:

- The total number of days of personal leave available in one year is limited, as is the number of days employees may take consecutively.
- Access to personal leave allows employees to avoid the necessity of having to use vacation time for personal needs.
- This measure improves employee morale and helps recruit and retain staff. It may also help reduce conflict between employees who have access to leave for family responsibilities and those who do not because they have no dependants.
- This leave can be combined with leave for family responsibilities.

Component #17 - *Maternity leave*

Definition:

The purpose of this type of leave is to allow mothers to take time off work following the birth of a child.

An employee who gives birth is, under certain conditions, entitled to maternity unpaid leave. Employees must give their employer notice in writing a few weeks prior to the start of such leave. When she comes back to work, the employee usually returns to her former position or is assigned equivalent duties, with the same salary and benefits.

- Generally, the employee must have worked for the same employer for a certain period.
- In certain organizations, a pregnant woman or nursing mother may ask her employer to temporarily modify her duties or to assign her to another position, if continuation of her present duties puts her health or that of her unborn child or nursing infant at risk. This request must, however, be accompanied by a certificate from a qualified physician. If it is impossible to reassign the employee or to modify her duties, she may take leave immediately.

- Labour standards legislation stipulates that benefits may continue throughout the leave period, provided the employee makes all the contributions she would normally have made, within a reasonable period of time. In some jurisdictions she may also be required to pay the employer's share of these benefits.
- An employer may not dismiss, lay off or demote an employee because of her pregnancy or intention to take maternity leave. The employer also may not use an employee's pregnancy as grounds for denial of promotion or training.

Considerations:

- During maternity leave, eligible employees may receive Employment Insurance maternity benefits for 15 weeks, after serving a 2-week waiting period.
- Some employers provide a supplemental unemployment benefit plan that partially or wholly makes up the difference between Employment Insurance maternity benefits and the worker's salary.

Component #18 - Parental leave

Definition:

Parental leave is designed to provide either or both parents with time to spend with their newborns. For the mother, parental leave provisions commonly stipulate that the leave be taken immediately after maternity leave, thereby extending the total leave period. For the father, parental leave provisions allow time off to help with the care of the newborn; sometimes collective agreement language that is gender-specific to the father is referred to as paternity leave.

- Employees who meet eligibility requirements are entitled to unpaid parental leave usually ranging from 12 to 52 weeks.
- Employees must give notice in writing to the employer a few weeks prior to the start of such leave. When they come back to work, employees must normally return to their former position or be assigned equivalent duties with the same salary and benefits.
- Some organizations allow employees to continue their participation to benefit plans during the leave, provided they make all contributions they would normally have made, within a reasonable period of time. In some organizations the employee may be required to pay the employer's share of these benefits.

Considerations:

- During their parental leave, eligible employees may receive 35 weeks of Employment Insurance parental benefits.
- A limited number of employers have a supplemental unemployment benefit plan that partially makes up the difference between Employment Insurance parental benefits and the worker's salary.

Component #19 - Paternity leave

Definition:

Paternity leave enables a father to take a few days or weeks off work after a child is born.

- Paternity leave was replaced by parental leave in the 1990s in many organizations.
- Generally, parental leave is considered to be similar to long term paternity leave for fathers who wish to take time off work to care for their child.

Considerations:

- This leave enables a father to take time to look after his child and the child's mother.

Component #20 - Sick leave

Definition:

Sick leave enables employees to take time off work when ill. It is not really leave for family obligations although it may sometimes be used as such.

Considerations:

- Some companies offer employees, as part of their benefit plans, the opportunity to be off work for a set period of time for illness without loss of wages.
- Generally, some of these days may be taken each year without a medical certificate.
- If the employee needs to take a longer sick leave because of health reasons, he may be entitled to take longer unpaid sick leave. He may then be eligible for Employment Insurance sickness benefits or benefits from other compensation plans for work-related illness or injury.

- Some employees may allow their employees to use part of their banked sick leave for certain family obligations.
- Sick leave may also be combined with maternity leave if there are complications related to the birth of a child.

Component #21 - Vacation

Definition:

Vacations are one of the most common labour policies and practices. Companies may help their employees by allowing them sufficient flexibility to:

- Break their leave up into shorter periods;
- Take vacation at the same time as their spouse;
- Take annual leave during the summer when children are at home.

Considerations:

Breaking vacation time into shorter periods means that managers do not have to replace certain essential employees. This measure enables employees to divide up vacation time in a way that best suits them. Allowing employees to take vacation during the summer makes it easier for managers to plan for hiring seasonal workers.

How Does An Organization Get Started On Work Life Balance?

Factors to Consider

- The impact on customers of new ways of working
- Flexibility - must everyone start and finish at the same time?
- The management and training time needed to co-ordinate a more flexible workforce
- Back-up arrangements for sickness or leave
- Planning and scheduling to cover busy periods

Process

The recommended process for employers and human resources practitioners to follow when looking at introducing work-life practices into an organization is described below. The model is most applicable to medium and large-sized employers who do not currently have a work-life balance program in place or for employers who want to formalize the steps involved in introducing new work-life balance practices. Small employers can also use the model however, the process might be less formalized than what is presented below and would not require going through all of the steps.

- Step 1: Planning
- Step 2: Assessment
- Step 3: Consultation with Stakeholders and communication
- Step 4: Development
- Step 5: Launch and Implementation
- Step 6: Review and Evaluation

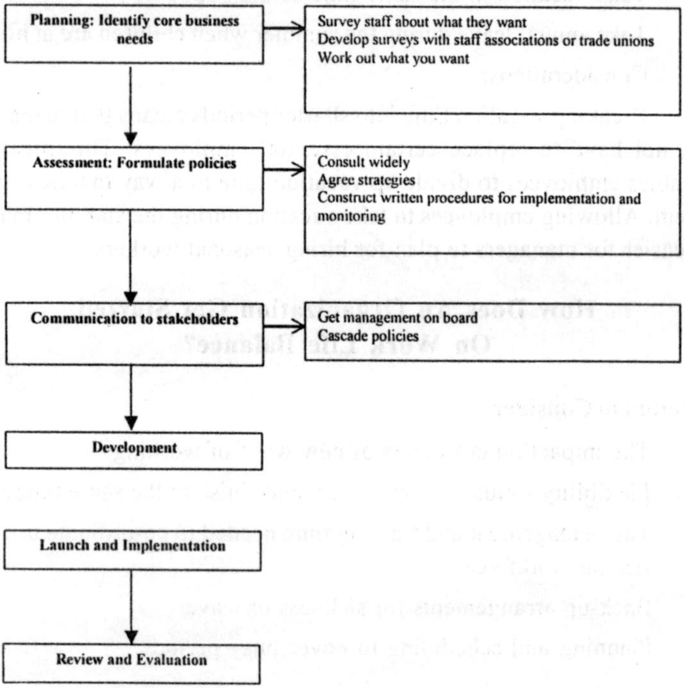

Step 1: Planning

Review the business and develop a business case for work-life balance - Identify the specific problems and issues that are affecting the efficiency of the business to determine if there is a solid business case for introducing work-life balance into the organization. Examine issues such as absenteeism, accountability, recruitment and retention, productivity and what the benefits might be of introducing work-life balance into your own organization.

Identifying the Benefits in Your Organization

When developing your work-life business case, it is important to consider the tangible and intangible benefits. Start by linking your work-life strategy to your organizations goals and objectives. Then consider all the possible benefits that could arise from implementing your strategy such as:

- The potential for increased service coverage if some employees arrive earlier and others stay later.
- The possibility that telecommuting employees (especially those in sales and service functions) may be closer to their customers' offices, thereby reducing necessary traveling time.
- Greater flexibility in employee schedules may help meet customer demand.
- Improved employee health and well being.
- Reduced stress, reduced absenteeism and reduced numbers of short term disability claims.
- Increased employee commitment, satisfaction and resiliency.
- More effective workload management, reduced interruptions and distractions in the workday.
- Increased capacity to meet work targets and make customer needs their top priority.

You may also want to link your strategy to other employer obligations you may face such as:

- Accommodation under employment equity and/or human rights legislation.
- Occupational safety and health.
- Workplace health and well-being.

Questions and Factors to Consider in Step 1

Not all managers, employers, and human resources practitioners will necessarily need to prepare a business case depending on the individual situation. Ask the following questions:

- What is the purpose of your project? Is it to understand the needs of your workforce, develop a work-life balance program or practice, refine or review current work-life balance programs or practices, or a combination of the above? The approach chosen will be dependent on what needs to be done.
- Is a business case needed to convince senior management of the importance of work-life balance practices or is there already senior management support? For smaller employers (who are the decision-makers), it might not be necessary to develop a business case, but rather to examine the benefits and costs of implementing work-life balance practices.
- Are there any other types of deliverables or processes that can be used at the planning stage to feed into the development of a business case or support justification for the need for work-life balance practices or programs? For example, work-life balance planning and research activities can also be included or linked to other organizational processes such as:

  Human Resources Planning;

  - Employment Systems Review (Employment Equity);
  - Occupational Health and Safety Committees; and/or
  - Workplace Health

While the focus of these processes is not solely on work-life balance issues, all of them include a work-life balance component.

Develop a team and organize your resources - Include members who are involved in different organizational processes on your planning team and seek participation from senior management to get their buy-in from the outset. For example, HR planners, communications advisors, finance and accounting personnel, information technology professionals as well as a senior manager can be included to champion the project. Determine if hiring an outside consultant or specialist in work-life balance programs might be beneficial.

Administrative and Management Responsibilities

Step 2: Assessment

Assess where your organization is at in terms of culture and openness to work-life balance practices and programs - Assess current culture and determine where the organization would like to be.

Determine which specific areas of the organization will benefit from the introduction of work-life balance policies - Consider how culture, resistance to change, and internal processes might be affected by introducing new work-life balance practices into the organization.

Employee Needs and Demand for Work-life Balance Initiatives

Selection and Suitability of Candidates

Step 3: Consultation with Stakeholders

Determine employees' and other stakeholders' opinions - Find out if current work-life balance practices are working and what sort of work-life balance practices employees want. Consult and communicate with employees and relevant unions, as well as community and government organizations. Your methodology might include one or more of the following:

- Surveys;
- Focus groups;
- Interviews;
- Formal committees; and/or
- Informal discussions.

As a result of the consultations, determine which work-life balance options are most suitable for your workplace - as some might not suit your workplace or industry and others might not be realistically affordable

Management Practices and Support

Logistical Arrangements and Responsibilities

Step 4: Development

Establish and develop formal/informal policies - After consulting with employees and deciding on the most appropriate work-life balance practices, develop written policies and tools to support the chosen practices. It is also very important to ensure that the work-life balance practices comply with all relevant legislation, for example industrial relations, occupational health and safety, employment equity and anti-discrimination statues.

Develop tools to assist with Culture Change in order to move beyond policies and programs - Make sure that when developing the written policies, also develop vehicles and methods to help in implementing the written policies and in facilitating change to the desired culture. For example, training programs for managers, communications products such as briefing memos or information sessions for managers and employees, and feedback mechanisms will all take time to develop. Don't put a policy in place without first considering what else can be done beforehand to increase the potential for success and for assisting in affecting the culture change needed.

Examine and propose changes and solutions to other organizational processes that might affect culture - For the new policies or programs to be successful and to affect the desired culture, other organizational and human resources processes or procedures might need to be adjusted in order to be consistent with the new work-life balance programs or practices. For example, performance appraisals or evaluations might need to be adapted to place more of a focus on quality of work as opposed to using criteria such as "face time" or "hours worked" in the office.

Step 5: Launch and Implementation

Put option/s into practice - Put practices into operation in the workplace. It is crucial to inform employees of the available benefits and fully explain which options have been implemented including the intended outcomes. Ensure senior and middle managers are targeted as part of your communications strategy.

Program Communications

Program Evaluation

Step 6: Review and Evaluation

Review your new work-life balance practices - Consult with employees to determine whether the practices you have implemented are effective and if any adjustments need to be made. Follow-up with employees and managers to determine their level of satisfaction with the new practices or programs and monitor usage regularly to gauge the success of the program. Review your position if you have made progress.

Accountability

According to Nora Spinks, of Work-Life Harmony Enterprises, "unless there are "teeth" to work-life strategies, they are only a piece of paper". In building your business case and developing your work-life balance strategy, it is therefore important to remember to clearly articulate roles and responsibilities and identify accountability measures. The more clarity, the more convincing your business case will be. Some accountability measures that have been used successfully include:

- Defining what accountability means to your organization. This could mean holding managers/supervisors accountable for "Walking the Talk".
- Incorporating measurements in performance appraisals. For example, these could be based on employee satisfaction survey results, absenteeism rates, productivity rates, and/or work unit turnover rates. The results could then be tied to incentives, bonus calculations, and flexible compensation.
- 360° Feedback or Balance Scorecard methods of assessment.
- Policy usage reporting and program utilization satisfaction reporting.
- The implementation of a process to annually review organizational processes and procedures including meeting schedules, workload distribution, application of technology etc. Review how each process helps or hinder work-life balance.
- Put work-life issues regularly on business agendas at all levels in a company. Discuss it, evaluate it, and treat it as seriously as you would any other important organizational issue.

In smaller organizations, informal approaches can also be very successful if the work environment fosters openness and dialogue with regard to both personal and business needs. These could then be accommodated by flexible or modified work arrangements or other means of support available to you:

Case Studies

Case Study #1 – IBM India

IBM India Fosters Work/ Life Balance for Employees–IBM is sponsoring many "fun 'n' learn" activities for its employees and their children to encourage a work/ life balance, under the aegis of IBM Global Work/ Life Fund. The company emphasises on Work/ Life balance as a key component to enhance the quality of life and productivity of every IBM employee across the globe. This year these activities will be organised through GenieKids, a forerunner in innovative and effective child-development.

Commenting on IBM's support of work/ life programme, Abraham Thomas, managing director, IBM India said, "IBM is committed in providing our employees with an attractive and comfortable working environment to maintain a healthy and productive lifestyle. This initiative will help our employees deal with the demands of home and family better in these times of hectic schedules and work pressure. Work/Life balance is a strategic initiative that helps IBM attract, motivate and retain the very best talent in the technology industry."

The Resource Centre houses a library, activity based games, pottery classes, computer classes, etc. IBM employees can also attend parenting workshops.

The IBM Global Work/ Life Fund is a US$50 million fund launched in the year 2000 by Ted Childs, vice president, IBM Global Workforce Diversity. This fund aims to facilitate the development of innovative programmes around the world for IBM employees.

Case Study #2 – Nokia

The well being of employees is important and also fundamental to the Nokia Way. As an employer, Nokia recognizes the importance of the balance between work content and personal interests and needs, as well as the impact of that balance on employee well being.

Nokia is offering services, programs and guidelines to support employees' possibilities to maintain work-life balance according to their changing needs and life situations. These work-life balance solutions may alter by country according to local needs, legislation, employment market situation and common practices. Typically they include:

- Teleworking
- Mobile working
- Flexible working hours
- Sabbaticals,
- Study leaves

- Health care services as well as recreational activities and other activity clubs.

Nokia also offer fitness facilities and programs as well as other sporting, social and cultural activities, which promote workplace relationships as well as personal development and comfort. The Nokia Helping Hands volunteer program gives employees a chance to contribute time, effort and expertise in a global network of community partnership schemes. These well-being services may also include laundry service, cafeteria, take-away food, day care and on-site concierge services, amongst others.

Case Study #3: Otis

Otis believes in providing employees with an environment where their individuality is respected and their full contribution and participation is encouraged. They should leave work each day with pride in the efforts of their team and its contribution to our bottom line. Otis strives to balance their challenging and rewarding work life with other interests and commitments—to communities, loved ones, and employees. For Otis Elevator Company, helping employees find that balance is an essential corporate commitment.

Otis understands the necessity for a balance between work and home. Through their work-life initiative, Otis has developed programs for flexible work arrangements, telecommuting, childcare, elder care consultation, financial planning, dependent family care days, wellness and fitness. These programs help to maximize both personal growth and the employee's contribution to the company.

Some of the Otis Work Life Balance programs are:

Life Choices

Life Choices provides confidential information and referrals to UTC employees and their immediate families, free of charge, during business hours and is available for emergencies 24 hours a day, seven days a week. It provides counseling and information on a wide array of personal and family issues and concerns.

Some services include adoption assistance, concierge services, adult services, childcare / parenting education, college financial aid service, elder care, financial planning assistance and the Homework Hotline.

The Employee Assistance Program (EAP)

EAP is a voluntary, confidential counseling service for employees and their families who are experiencing difficulties, including alcoholism, drug dependency, financial problems, personal or medical issues, stress-related issues and other concerns.

Flexible Work Arrangements

Otis realizes that the workplace of the future will require more flexibility. In order to attract and retain the best and brightest people, they offer work arrangements that meet their varied needs. Some options are:

- Flextime Work Hours and Telecommuting
- Job Sharing

Case Study #4: Glaxo Smithkline

"Staff morale is high as employees take more ownership and responsibility for the way they deliver their work."

Martin Swain, Human Resources Manager

By introducing work-life balance policies at its Slough factory, GlaxoSmithKline has boosted staff morale, reduced unauthorized absenteeism and increased individual initiative and proactivity amongst its workforce.

GlaxoSmithKline asked employees to come up with their own thoughts on improving their work-life balance. All ideas were considered as long as there were no negative impacts on safety, quality, production or cost.

Shift workers can now 'swap' shifts to allow more flexibility within existing shift patterns and office staff.benefit from the introduction of consolidated time, with a set number of flexible hours. As the workforce gradually take more ownership and responsibility for the way they deliver their work, the new 'give and take' culture is proving a notable success

Case Study #5 - HSBC

"Providing a childcare programme has contributed considerably to reducing the number of women who leave after maternity from 70%

to 15% in 13 years at HSBC. This represents a massive budget saving – the average service of a maternity leaver is 11 years and the cost to the bank of replacing each one is estimated at around a year's salary."

Jan Jones, Diversity Manager

Family-friendly initiatives at HSBC, in particular the childcare programme, have proved highly successful by supporting the business through retention of skilled staff.

The programme has been operating since 1998, and provides some 850 nursery places, 300 of them on the bank's premises. Most of the nursery facilities are joint ventures with either the public or private sectors, with the bank buying a guaranteed number of places. Dedicated childcare managers allocate these places to achieve maximum business benefit.

The bank supports the childcare programme with other work-life balance initiatives such as part-time and flexible working, job sharing, paternity and family leave. It also offers all UK-based employees access to Open Line, an in-house confidential advice, research and referral helpline which assists employees in effectively managing the challenging dual demands of home and work responsibilities

Case Study #6 - Unilever UK

"The arrangement works perfectly, the role is covered for the full five-day week and the organization has saved approximately £30,000 in the recruitment and training of external applicants."

Linda Emery, Diversity Manager

Nine out of ten women return to employment at Unilever UK following maternity leave since the company introduced an enhanced maternity package and career break scheme in 1990. This is a dramatic increase in numbers from 1988 when only 6% of female managers had childcare responsibilities.

Since then a wide range of other flexible working practices has been established, largely in response to employee requests. These include part-time working and reduced hours, term-time working, additional unpaid leave, job-sharing, flexitime and home working.

Employee assistance programmes are also available - an occupational health service operates at each site, and some have crèche and childcare support. Staff help lines providing services such as counseling are also provided.

"The feedback is generally very positive," says Linda Emery, Diversity Manager. "You need senior management commitment and need to be aware of any barriers to delivery, such as a long hours culture".

One major example of success was when two very highly qualified and skilled senior personnel submitted a proposal to jobshare. Traditionally, Unilever had not considered part-time roles appropriate to senior posts. However, management supported this solution as neither woman would have returned to work without the jobshare option.

Case Study #7 - Marks and Spencer

"Our work life balance policies have given significant commercial benefit to the organization. This has been measured in the number of staff that we are able to retain after maternity leave or a dependency break, and we save on the costs of recruitment and retraining."

Alison Houston, Head of HR Corporate Governance

As a household name, Marks and Spencer ensures it is seen as a popular employer across the country by offering a wide range of choices in working patterns to help its staff to find a healthy work-life balance.

The retailer has developed an extensive range of work-life balance initiatives that make a major contribution to the morale and loyalty of its 75,000 staff across 294 stores. These include benefits such as flexible working, home and part-time working, jobshare, educational sponsorship, secondments, career leave and flexible retirement options. A confidential employee helpline is also in place to advise and support staff on work-life balance issues.

Parents are able to take time off to attend appointments during pregnancy and IVF treatment, and are eligible for additional maternity leave, paternity leave, company maternity pay and adoption leave. Time off is also available for foster carers.

Nearly 80% of the workforce is female, and mothers going back to work following maternity leave have a range of options, including gradual return and term-time working. A "child break" scheme is in place for those who do not wish to start work again immediately. Similar support is provided for those with other caring responsibilities.

Marks and Spencer aims to create an environment at work where people can find time to enjoy what they do; flexibility enables the company to make individual arrangements with each member of staff to help achieve this.

Case Study #8 - Lloyds

"Traditionally, work-life balance and, in particular, flexible working policies can be seen to be to do with women and parents so we are quite pleased it's being taken up by men and managers."

Sally Evans, Senior Manager, Equality & Diversity

Lloyds TSB has been running its Work Options scheme since 1999. Some 34% of the workforce work flexibly. Of those on a Work Option, 16% are men, and 18% are managers.

A range of factors has influenced the work-life balance agenda, including customer expectations, requiring increasingly innovative and flexible delivery channels and intensive competition in recruiting and retaining quality staff. Productivity and motivation can be increased and absenteeism and stress can be reduced, through effective work-life balance strategies

Options introduced by Lloyds TSB include reduced hours, job sharing, variable hours, compressed working and teleworking. Any employee can put forward the business case for flexible working to their line manager, and a solution will be found that works for botn the bank and the employee. The reason for requesting flexible working is not relevant to the decision making process – applications will be accepted unless there is a clear business detriment. Since the organization estimates that it costs between £48,000 and £50,000 to replace a senior employee, it's clearly a business strategy that works.

Individuals and applicants are encouraged to think creatively about how they wish to work and team-based applications to work flexibly have been particularly successful. A prime example is the 12-strong manpower and information team who work a compressed nine-day fortnight. The benefits have been tangible: The level of service we are giving HR business partners is better than it's ever been, which means they work better in their business units, which ultimately has a good impact on the organization as a whole.

Case Study #9 - Sainsburys

"Finding, recruiting and training an employee is expensive. Losing that investment, together with accumulated experiences, is a costly and often unnecessary waste".

Glyn House, Employment Brand Manager

The Sainsbury's business operates 24 hours a day, 365 days a year. Flexible working is therefore essential to business success, with some 70% of colleagues working part time and numerous examples of flexible working at all levels of the Organization.

In order to beat the competition, Sainsbury's must be a leader in attracting and then retaining talented people. Flexible working is therefore vital as today's workers demand that they are able to balance both their home and work commitments. Sainsbury's continually encourages its stores, depots and the business centre to develop working solutions that enable colleagues to plan their daily lives, alongside solutions that ensure that sufficient people are available to meet the demands of customers.

Sainsbury's offers a range of work-life benefits including career breaks, job sharing, dual store contracts, leave for fertility treatment and time off for emergencies.

Sainsbury's believes it is important for staff to take the lead in shaping their work-life balance. Anyone is able to suggest to their line manager a working pattern that would suit them, and as long as there is a strong business case and it fits in with colleagues, it will seriously be considered.

Case Study #10 – Legal And General

"Legal & General believe that the flexibility of our employees has been key to our success as it gives benefits to both individuals and the company, enabling fast reaction to events."

Geoff Tucker, Head of Remuneration

Legal & General is actively committed to equal opportunities, with three women board members and a significant number of women in senior management. It recognizes the need to persuade women with young children to keep their career going forwards, and offers flexible and part-time work to encourage them to stay in the workforce.

A tenth of the workforce works part-time, including many maternity returners, building their hours around the needs of the individual and the business. Staff are now counted as full-time equivalents rather than on the individual headcount to foster management acceptance of part-time working.

Although formal flexitime was introduced at the company in 1970, by the mid-90s it was found to be too restrictive. The company then introduced proper flexible working which enhances the work-life balance of its employees. The scheme is based on the individual, their team and the manager agreeing the hours needed to get the work done. This can be regular hours at one extreme, or leaving when the work is completed at the other.

In practice, it means that the needs of individuals can be met, as long as the team can do the work. A staff opinion survey showed 51% were satisfied with the company's family-friendly approaches. 61% were satisfied with the flexible working approach.

Case Study #11–Barclays Bank

"The goal of becoming an employer of choice needed to extend to all people policies, and particularly those that impact on the life and families of employees."

Anne Woolcott, HR Policy Manager

"People policies" at Barclays Bank are based on a simple premise – that staff who are happy and feel valued are more likely to stay.

The bank recognizes that its ability to compete as a global financial services organization depends upon its willingness to attract, retain and develop the very best employees. This means that policies have to be in place to support employees in balancing work and home commitments.

Two-thirds of the 57,000 workforce across the UK are women, but the bank recognizes that caring is not just a woman's issue. All employees can apply for paid carer leave for up to five days a year, responsibility breaks for a maximum of six months and career breaks for up to five years. All employees can also request flexible working arrangements not just those with young children. New fathers are eligible for 2 weeks paid paternity leave, the first week at full pay and the provisions for maternity and adoption pay are well in excess of the statutory minimum. In addition, couples who both work for Barclays can swap maternity leave between them – for example, the mother may return to work early and her partner take any remaining leave. All parents with children under fourteen are also eligible for parental leave.

Barclays buddying scheme offers everyone who is going on maternity or adoption leave a 'buddy' who will have experienced maternity leave themselves and will be able to offer practical support and guidance during the period of leave and at the time the individual returns to work. These policies mean that Barclays retains key staff, with 80% of the women taking maternity breaks returning to full or part-time work

Case Study #12 - APS

"Recruitment is becoming easier and costing us less. We now have the employment agencies calling us because they have people asking if we have vacancies."

Paul Hayden, Marketing and Commercial Manager

Offering a package of work-life benefits has helped Automated Packaging Systems to attract and retain staff in an area of high employment. It has also reduced absenteeism.

Among the benefits for employees are 'banked hours', where staff members can store up hours which can then be taken off to meet domestic or other commitments, or simply to take a holiday. Other policies include flexible working hours, provision of childcare information, help with childcare transport and time off for care of dependants.

One beneficiary is a single parent who was able to take five months off to care for her son who was receiving treatment for cancer. "I was able give my son the full-time care that he needed without feeling any pressure to come into work or even having to consider leaving," she says.

The whole philosophy at APS – from top management to the factory floor – is to organize around high performing teams. Everyone knows what they have to deliver – it is up to the teams to decide when and how they deliver it. With an absenteeism rate of 1.5% in 2001 (down from 1.9% in 2000), high rates of staff retention and year on year growth in the company's turnover, it is clearly a philosophy that works.

A Research Study on Work life balance

The questionnaire used for this study was given to a sample size of 30. It was distributed randomly across departments and across levels in Tata Chemicals Ltd, Mumbai.

The questionnaire used for this study contained questions regarding the participant's existing caring responsibilities, their workload, their major concerns regarding their personal life & work life, the level of stress experienced, the level of support the organization provides toward the major concerns of their life and the services they would like the organization to provide towards a balance between their personal and work life.

Demographics

The age group varied from 23 to 56 years old and had 18 males and 12 females in this study. All the questionnaires were anonymous and so components like name and work level was not used. Though age was included most of the participants did not fill it in.

Results of the Research

Caring Responsibility

15 respondents had caring responsibility towards their children and 20 of them had caring responsibilities towards other dependents.

Recommendation #1: The organization should provide for childcare and elder care services so that the tension of providing for care for the dependents outside work is alleviated.

Recommendation #2: The organization should provide for financial assistance for child care and elder care.

A recent study showed that employers in UK who provide childcare referral services for their employees save an estimated £2 for every £1 they spend on the service and reduce costs - possibly by £50 million in the course of a year - as a result of reduced sickness absences.

Taking Work Home

16 respondents, forming 53% of the respondents, took work home out of which 8 respondents worked under ten hours, 6 respondents

worked between ten to fifteen hours, 1 respondent worked between twenty to twenty five hours and 1 respondent worked between twenty five to thirty hours. (Please refer to Chart 1 Below)

Chart 1 - Amount of work done at home per week

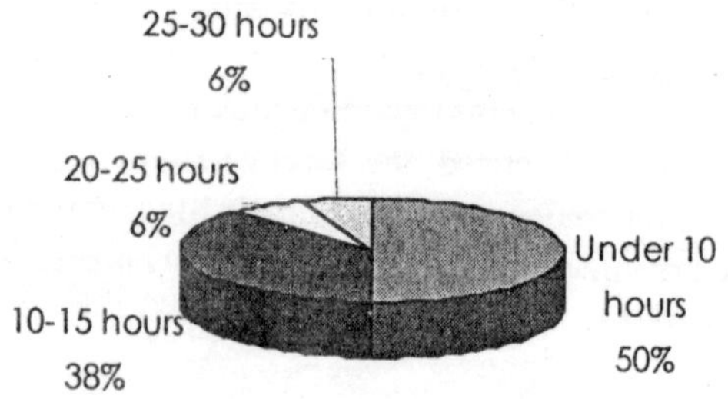

Lunch Breaks

22 respondents made sure that they took their lunch everyday, 4 took it four times (4/5), 1 respondent took it thrice a week and 3 respondents took their lunch twice a week. (Please refer to Chart 2 below)

Chart 2 - Number of lunch breaks per week

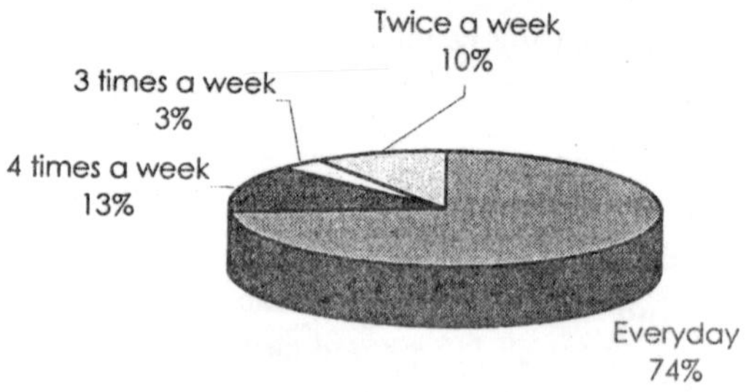

Reasons Behind Additional Work

- No support staff.
- Incomplete assignments and job responsibility.
- Sudden workload and month end.
- More workload and more pressure at work.
- No clarity.
- Last minute requirements.

- Lack of clarity on the deliverables for the person and his boss.
- Over-commitment of his time.
- Job requirements.
- Too many assignments and too little time.
- Passion to work.
- Peer pressure.
- Delay in decision making.
- Deadlines.
- Unexpected assignments.
- Urgency of work.
- Excess unplanned work.
- Need to give certain details.
- Lack of resources.
- Lack of planning.
- Commitment to the job.
- Very late working hours when boss is around.
- Small time limit for jobs.
- Bottleneck for approval from decision makers.
- Excess work.

Recommendation #3: The organization should look at implementing job sharing and flexi-time so that the work is evenly distributed, especially during the month end and the peak period. The organization should also look at hiring temporary resources to alleviate the workload during the peak period. The potential for increased service coverage if some employees arrive earlier and others stay later. Increased employee commitment, satisfaction and resiliency by providing training/support in managing their workload, clear communication on objectives and targets and making sure that it is successful.

Recommendation #4: The organization should look at creating a process for projects, deadlines and decisions to shorten the unnecessary work and the delays in decision-making. Additional resources to help employees increase productivity by completing the assigned work on time, thus contributing to the overall performance of the organisation. To increase capacity to meet work targets and make customer needs their top priority.

Recommendation #5 : The possibility that telecommuting employees (especially those in sales and service functions) may be closer to their customers' offices, thereby reducing necessary travelling time. In addition, the organization should look at compressed week, temporary reduced hours under certain circumstances, part time work and annualized hours.

Available and Successful Policies in the Organization

In the list of what was available in the organization and which has been successful, the following is observed:

Chart 3 - Available and successful policies

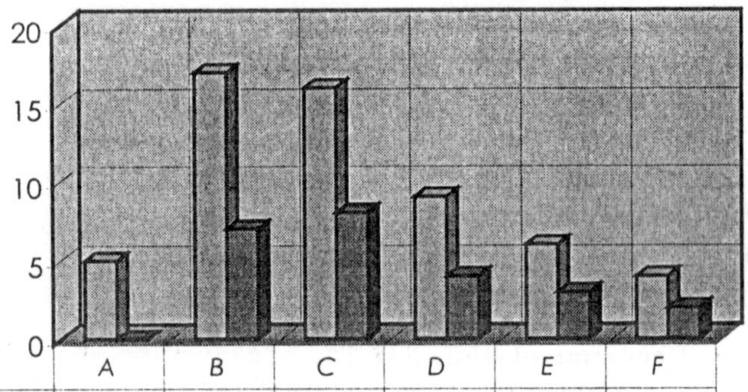

	A	B	C	D	E	F
Available	5	17	16	9	6	4
Successful	0	7	8	4	3	2

A. Discussion of workload planning and allocation: 5 persons responded that it was available but not successful.

B. Clear communication on objectives and targets:. 17 responded that it was available out of which 7 found it successful.

C. Clear and attainable deadlines: 16 responded that it was available out of which 8 respondents found it successful.

D. Training/support in managing your workload: 9 responded that it was available out of which 4 respondents found it successful.

E. Extra staff: 6 responded that it was available out of which 3 respondents found it successful.

F. Level of workload that can be completed within contacted hours: 4 responded that it was available out of which 2 respondents found it successful.

In this list of services available in the office- it is seen that most of the listed are not available. Even if available, it is not seen as a successful activity by the participants.

Recommendation #6 : It is recommended that the organization concentrate on the six areas highlighted and come up with processes to make these areas successful. Subsequently, the organization should look at the other areas and try to implement these policies in the workplace.

Balancing Family Life with work life

19 respondents (63%) found it difficult to balance their family/ private life with work, while 11 (37%) responded that they didn't face any difficulty. Individuals who didn't face any difficulty were those who belonged to the older age group, who believed that their spouses should understand and accept this kind of life.

24 (80%) responded that their employer is sympathetic when they need to reschedule work and 6 (20%) responded that their employer is not sympathetic.

8 (27%) responded that they felt they were unable to cope, out of which 1 respondent identified the source as "at home" and 7 identified the source as "at work". 22 (73%) responded that they did not experience any such feeling.

11 (37%) respondents suffered ill health that they felt was related to the way they worked.

Details of the ailments are:

- 11 indicated that they suffered from headaches,
- 10 indicated that they had 'lack of concentration',
- 7 displayed irritability with colleagues/family/friends,
- 6 responded that they experienced fatigue and persistent cold,
- 4 experienced depression and 4 had sleeplessness,

- 2 respondents had short term sickness and 2 had suicidal thoughts,
- Also found a respondent each in asthma, blackout, heart problem, increased smoking/drinking/eating, long-term sickness absence and loss of weight category.

Only 3 respondents in the above category had sought help out of which 2 sought help from the doctor and one from his parents.

Recommendation #7 : It is recommended that the organization provide a comprehensive medical insurance scheme, as well as an in-house counselor to counsel the employees on stress related illnesses.

Errors at Work

5 responded that they have been so tired or pressured at work that they have made a serious error. Some of the brief descriptions are:

- Mistake in Financial modeling in Excel.
- Wrong data was entered.
- Sent an executive to the airport to catch a flight to Egypt without making sure he had a visa.

The consequence of their act was that they had to give explanations to their immediate superiors regarding what they had done. Since the errors were corrected in time, it did not cost the organization.

Statements respondents Identified with

Out of 30, 21 respondents identified with the statements – "Family and friends have commented on the hours I work", "Work is an important part of life" and "I enjoy challenges of my job"

- 20 respondents identified with the statements – "I am so busy that I come in to work even when I am ill" and " I feel more fulfilled when I am busy"
- 18 respondents identified with the statement – "I have missed family and social occasions through work"
- 15 respondents identified with the statements – "I am in control of the role work plays in my life"
- 14 respondents identified with the statements – "I do not always manage to take all of my annual leave or TOIL entitlement", "I

make choices about how I divide my time" and "I make sure work does not dominate my whole life".

- 13 respondents identified with the statements – "I have cancelled holiday or cut them short through work".
- 12 respondents identified with the statements – "My workload is generally well planned and under control".
- 11 respondents identified with the statements – "I would like to control the hours I work but do not know how" and "sometimes I resent the hours I spend at work away from family and friends"
- 10 respondents identified with the statements – "I do not see my children as much as I would like", "I find my job very rewarding" and "When I return to work after a holiday, I don't feel rested".
- 9 respondents identified with the statements – "When I take time off I miss my work".
- 8 respondents identified with the statements – "If conditions remain as they are I will consider changing jobs".
- 7 respondents identified with the statements – "I feel my job here is insecure", "When I am not working I do not know what to do with my time" and "When I go on a holiday, it takes me several days to wind down".
- 6 respondents identified with the statements – "My partner/ spouse has to take an unfair share of childcare" and "Overwork often leaves me too tired for sex".
- 5 respondents identified with the statements – "I have pretended to be ill in order to take a day's break" and "My partner/spouse has to take an unfair share of domestic work".
- 4 respondents identified with the statements – "I would change to a less demanding career if only I could afford the pay cut" and "Work has affected my relationship with my partner/spouse".
- 3 respondents identified with the statements – "I have had medical advice to cut down my working hours".
- 2 respondents identified with the statements – "My working life has played a part in breaking up any relationship/marriage", "My working relationship with my manager or colleagues is poor" and "Working so hard has affected my relationship with my children".

Biggest Improvement to Work

As to what would be the biggest improvement to work, the following are the results:

- 22 participants felt it is "Better planning of workload"
- 18 participants felt it is "Being given clearer objectives", "Better communication with management/staff" and "Open discussion of workload allocation".
- 17 participants opted for "Flexible working options"
- 15 participants opted for "Being able to control my workload" and "Having more time to spend with family"
- 14 participants opted for "Being given clearer deadlines" and "Better training in technology".

Recommendation #8 – In addition to a redesign on the work processes within the organization, it is seen that there is a need for flexible work options in the organization which will allow the employees to have a healthier work life balance. 50% of the participants asking for more time with their family is a clear indication that work needs to be done on work-life balance.

- 13 participants opted for "More positive attitude towards managing workloads and solving problems".
- 12 participants opted for "Confidential independent counseling services" and "Option to work from home".
- 11 participants opted for "Additional resources/staff", "Bigger salary", "Less cost cutting" and "More sympathetic responses to complaints".
- 9 participants opted for "Better Management behavior" and "More holidays"

The other suggestions by the participants are

- Good appraisal system
- Provision of a laptop (resources)
- More delegation of power

Workload

Compared to a year ago, the workload has increased for 18 participants, decreased for 2 participants and for the rest (10 participants), it has remained the same.

Work vs Personal Life

Compared to life outside work, 17 participants found work more fulfilling, 4 found work little more fulfilling, 8 found it less fulfilling and one participant found it equally fulfilling. (Please see Chart 4 below)

Chart 4. Working Personal Life

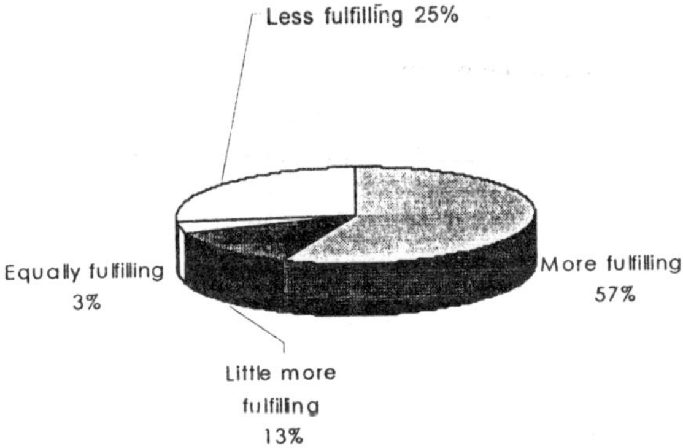

Policies to be implemented

Chart-5 Policies

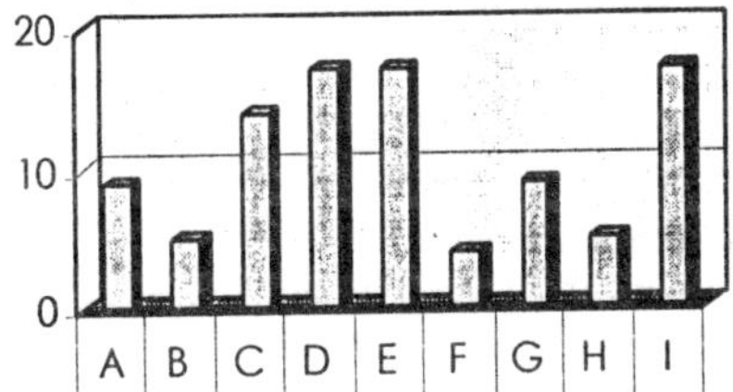

	A	B	C	D	E	F	G	H	I
Policies	9	5	14	17	17	4	9	5	17

- 17 participants opted for "Coaching and training in controlling workload" (D), "Employers should take effective action to eliminate stress" (E) and "The right to flexible working arrangements" (I).
- 14 participants opted for "All working beyond contracted hours should be paid for, and at a higher rate" (C).
- 9 participants opted for "A public campaign to end the 'macho' culture of long hours" and "Less focus on the bottom line" (A)
- 5 participants opted for "A shorter week" and 'More and better childcare facilities" (H).

- 4 participants opted for "It should be easier to sue employers for stress due to overwork" (F).

Other Comments

- Management and employees should create an environment of fun - relieve stress.
- Informal communication and get together.

As seen from the results, a majority of employees (19 out of the 30 respondents forming 63% of the respondents) have clearly responded that they experience difficulty in balancing their work life and personal life.

16 out of 30 (53%) take work home and some among the rest said they stay back till late to complete their work, thus making a conscious effort not to take back work. However it again leaves with them with less time for personal activities.

21 participants have said that family and friends have commented on the hours they work, making it very evident that they spent more than a good deal of time at work, missing social functions and leaving an unfair share of work to their partners. This has led to break up of relationships and there was also a comment made that he did not have a relationship because he couldn't find the time to!!

Conclusion

Although the availability of part-time and casual work has enabled many workers to work fewer hours and spend more time caring for dependants, to study or pursue other interests – developing solutions relating to work-life balance is a much larger issue. The issues affecting workers relating to work-life balance is not a problem exclusive to one area, but touches on all corners of the workforce and affects workers in many ways. In our view, developing solutions to address work-life balance issues requires a genuine commitment from the government, unions and employers addressing a wide range of areas. The key concerns identified by unions are, pay, modes of employment, hours of work, income levels, workplace culture and wider family, life and community responsibilities. Nevertheless, this by no means exhaustive and simply reflects the priority areas identified by unions. While a range of practical measures can be adopted by unions, employers and the Government, it is also important to note aspects of this discussion which are more difficult to resolve relating to entrenched values and cultures within workplaces.

Changing the way work-life balance issues are viewed, and respecting rights in the workplace requires greater employer and worker education and will take time. But as the benefits outweigh the costs, one hopes that the recommendations will be implemented by organizations to reap the benefits of work life balance.

References and Further Reading

1. A. Roger Merrill, Rebecca Merrill (2003) *Life Matters : Creating a Dynamic Balance of Work, Family, Time & Money.*
2. Anderson, Sandy (1998) *The Work-At-Home Balancing Act.*
3. Bevan Stephen, Dench Sally, Tamkin Penny and Cummings John (1999) *Family Friendly Employment: The Business Case.*
4. Bredin, Alice (1998) - *The Home Office Solution: How to Balance Your Professional and Personal Lives While Working at Home.*
5. Carnoy, M. (2000) *Sustaining the Economy: Work, Family and Community in the information age,* New York: Russell Sage Foundation.
6. Department of Trade and Industry United Kingdom, Work Life Balance Campaign resource site.
7. Dex and Scheibl (1999) *Managing Work/Life Balance.*
8. Employers for Work Life Balance UK - www.employersforwork-lifebalance.org.uk.
9. Galinsky E. and J.T. Bond, (1998) *The 1998 Business Work-Life Study: A Sourcebook,* Families and Work Institute.
10. Government of Canada website on Work Life Balance in Canadian workplaces - http://labour.hrdc-drhc.gc.ca/worklife/
11. Government of New Zealand Work Life Balance Project - http://www.dol.govt.nz/worklife/index.asp
12. Hardill, Irene (2003) *A tale of two nations? Juggling work and home in the new economy.*
13. *Harvard Business Review on Work and Life Balance* (2000).
14. Kala H.L. (2005). women, Work and Family. New Delhi: Rawat Publications.
15. Ken Blanchard, Marjorie Blanchard (1999) *The One Minute Manager Balances Work and Life.*
16. Organization websites (www.ibm.com, www.nokia.com).
17. Shirley Dex and Fiona Scheibl (1999), *Business performance and family-friendly policies,* Journal of General Management vol. 24 No. 4.
18. T.Hogarth, C,Hasluck and G.Pierre with M.Winterbotham and D.Vivien, (2001), *Work-Life Balance 2000: Results from the Baseline Study.*

12
Organization Development

- Definition of Organization Development
- History of Organization Development.
- Assumptions Underlying Organizational Development
- Relevant System and Concepts
- Approaches to Organizational Development
- Organizational Development Interventions
- Impact of Current Technology on OD

Definition

Change not only occurs in technology, marketing but also in human values, attitudes, relationships, social system, organizational climate and culture. Hence all are aware of and are concerned with that changes in values have tremendous impact on organization as changes in technology and marketing, as such the management has to meet the challenges of changes. Management can effectively meet these challenges through systematic and planned change effort. Organization development has emerged to help the planned change for organizational effectiveness, thus it is said that the organization development is the modern approach to management of change and human resource development. Organization development concentrates on people dimensions like norms, values, attitudes, relationships, organizational climate etc.

History of Organization Development

Douglas McGregor served as resource person to help Union Carbide Corporation to create an organizational development capability where OD department was set up in 1962. French and Bell who have done most of the work in OD feel that laboratory training and survey feedback are the main stems of OD. Sensitivity training programmes were conducted for managers under the OD movement.

Survey feedback method emphasises the collection, organization, and analysis of data. Such an approach pertains to assessment of attitudes held by members, identification of discrepancies among the members, perception and solving the differences. Survey feedback approach to OD collects data from employees in an organization, analyzes, give feedback on their attitudes and perception and attempts to solve differences in them.

The basic steps involved in this process are:

- A questionnaire is prepared, based on the views of organizational members and an appraisal of an situation covering the members attitudes and perception.
- The questionnaire is then completed by all members of organization or the unit.
- The data from this questionnaire is tabulated with reference. to an individual's specific family and to the entire organization and distributed to the employees.
- The data then becomes the basis for group discussions in organizational family groups and in some cases expert counseling of individual managers to identify problems and clarifying the issues that may be creating the difficulties in people.
- Finally the group discussions approach is expected to result in members identifying the possible implication to the questionnaire findings and agreeing upon commitments to various actions that will remedy the problems identified.

The survey feedback technique has been reported to have gained momentum in recent years. In a company in 1977 more than 1 lac employees from production workers to senior management participated. Robbins reports a survey in general electric company of 20000 employees in which more than 50 percent were found to be unhappy with their promotion opportunities. As a result, unit manager at GE conducted regular monthly meetings and actively worked to improve communication. A year later, the number who were unhappy dropped to 20 percent even though no one person was promoted or changed the jobs. While the survey feedback approach has been found to change attitudes, long term change in behavior have not resulted from mere group discussion of the results. As Friedlander and Brown note little evidence that survey feedback alone leads to changes in individual behavior or organizational performance.

Assumptions Underlying Organizational Development [OD]

Practitioners believe that OD assumptions are implicit and need to be examined, it is important for managers to identify these assumptions so that they will be aware of their impact. OD assumptions need to be shared with managers and employees so that those groups will clearly understand the basis for the OD program

The wide range of assumptions can be made, but certain ones are relatively common at the individual, group, and organization level. A sample of them is described here and is summarized below. OD assumptions typically hold a highly positive viewpoint regarding the capabilities, unused potential and interests of all individuals. This stems from the humanistic values that are implicit in OD theory. Groups and teams are seen as vital building blocks of an organization, but since they are powerful and complex they are not always easy to change. Traditional organizations are viewed as rigid bureaucracies that have sometimes stifled employee development and growth, but possibilities are seen for positive growth and development.

Individuals level

- People want to grow and mature.
- Employees have much to offer [e.g. energy and creativity]that is not now used at work.
- Most employees desire the opportunity to contribute [they desire, seek and appreciate empowerment].

Groups level

- Groups and teams are critical to organizational success.
- Groups have powerful influences on individual behavior.
- The complex roles to be played in groups require skill development.

Organization level

- Excessive controls, policies are detrimental.

- Conflict can be functional if properly channeled.
- Individual and organizational goals can be compatible.

Values of OD Movement

- Organizational movement is especially composed of various professionals like behavioral researchers, consultants, and business executives. There are a number of values of this profession. The important among them are:-
- People are basically good: OD movement believes the assumption of theory y of McGregor. It emphasizes supportive and relative opportunities, for growth and opportunity are to be provided to the employees in an organization rather than using control and punishment.
- Need for confirmation and support: every new employees need confirmation and support of others. He is conditioned to believe that no news is good news as he may be afraid of the negative aspects of support and security. Hence as the new employee is being appointed, he is to be taken into confidence, invited to work place and into association for discussion on his personal and work related decisions.
- Accepting differences among people: people have different backgrounds, experiences, opinions, ideas, viewpoints and personality. Organization is benefited by the differences in background, personality and viewpoints of employees.
- Expressing feeling and emotions :allowing people to be rational to express their feelings, sentiments, emotions, anger. Full range of expression of feeling results in high motivation, commitment and creative ability. The people may be allowed to exhibit the anger, emotion and exhalation.
- Authenticity, Openness and Directness: most of the people exhibit duplicity, tell half-truths and mask their true motives. Such behavior inhibits the growth of individual and productivity as the resources are misused in this process. Honesty and directness enable people to put their energies into real problems and improve effectiveness.
- Fostering Cooperation: Some executives adopt the rule of divide and manage. Thus they believe in win-lose competition for

various employee benefits. This style results in wastage of human and other resources. Hence, executives should create and develop cooperation among employees for effectiveness.

- Giving Attention: Giving attention to process activities not only at the time of assigning and bringing among employees but also at the later stages.
- Confronting Conflict: Some executives suppress the conflict. But it has its long-run effect on employee morale. Hence, identifying the root causes of the problem and working out a satisfactory solution rather than suppressing the conflict are needed.

In some organizational cultures, these values are highly prized and taken seriously by management, examples include the open door policy at IBM, shared ownership and practice of supporting innovative concepts by encouraging entrepreneurial behaviour, companies that appreciate human values demonstrate this through positive change.

In other organizations however such values are espoused but not practiced, this is typical of the older "sunset" corporation, now need a face to revitalize themselves and of long established government agencies and public institutions. When such organizations fall on hard times, they sometimes conclude that they must improve their people management and seek OD assistance.

The organization that has already discovered the importance of human values and their impact on performance, already knows how to use OD assistance, even many troubled corporations using buy-outs, downsizing and the like are coming to recognize their needs for OD. The subject for human values and performance is beginning to discuss much more freely.

The process for organizational change, however is complicated, even such successful giants as Procter and gamble, IBM and GE with all their highly trained managers, have not discovered the secret to how values are linked to actual performance. It simply is not obvious on the surface, thus although corporate commitments to values and people may be highly desirable, this does not guarantee success. That is why corporate wide training program seldom affects the behaviour of first line and mid line managers. Learning what corporation believes about people management is one thing and another to use this when one is back on the job and one is faced with deadline, pressures, limited resources, daily conflicts among individuals and departments and the frustration of having to settle for less than one has planned for.

The issue of concern for OD and thus for managers is determining not merely the correct values to teach managers, but the linkage between human values and human behavior. Douglas McGregor demonstrated years ago the set of values that has a positive impact on the work behavior of most of the persons. Moreover they may actually have theory y type managers, the performance of managers is the true test of the manager's real values.

Not enough attention was paid to the linkage of values and behaviour. Just because a person freely chose values from among alternatives. And then displayed these by publicly espousing them, did not mean that the individual has actually integrated values into her or his behavior.

That is why OD practioner must approach the subject of values from the perspective of the impact of values on the workplace. This is also why the subjects of motivation, ownership, decision-making, leadership, team work and the like are so important to the field.

Relevant System and Concepts

Planned Change : in dealing with plan for organizational development purposes, the three issues become crucial in practical terms are: how to change, how to manage the total changes and how to consolidate and stabilize outcome of changes to plan and execute and consolidate effectively the required change interaction.

- Organizational changes such as new structures, process of reward system, attitudes etc occur only through individual changes in the key members as the organizational change is always worked out through individual changes
- The adult changes involve attitudes, values and self image, and unlearning of already formed responses in these areas is inherently uncomfortably, painful, stressful and disturbing.
- Change is multistage cycle and all stages must be negotiated before a stable change can take place.

Integration of The Process, The Role, and The Organization

Individual process of change is a cognitive process and also motivational or emotional or affective predisposition of such a change.

Moreover a change itself is of no organizational consequences unless it is expressed through sustained action, which involves the conative process of the individual. In other words the multistage cycle involves in sequence the affective, cognitive and conative mental process of an individual ultimately the integration of them in the total personality.

Approaches to Organizational Development

Survey Feedback

One tool for assessing attitudes held by organizational members, identifying discrepancies among member's perceptions, and solving these differences is the survey feedback approach.

Everyone in an organization can participate in survey feedback, but of key importance is the organizational family – the manager of any given unit and those employees who report directly to him or her. All members in the organization or unit usually complete a questionnaire. The questionnaire typically asks the member for their perceptions and attitudes on a broad range of topics, including decision-making practices, communication effectiveness, coordination between units, and job satisfaction.

The data from this questionnaire are tabulated with data pertaining to an individual's specific "family" and to the entire organization and distributed to employees. These data then become the springboard for identifying problems and clarifying issues that may be creating difficulties for people.

Finally, group discussion in the survey feedback approach should result in members identifying possible implications of the questionnaire's findings.

Process Consultation

No organization operates perfectly. The purpose for process consultation is for an outside consultant to assist a client, usually a manager, "to perceive, understand, and act upon process events" with which he or she must deal.

Process consultation (PC) is similar to sensitivity training, its assumption that organizational effectiveness can be improved by dealing with interpersonal problems and in its emphasis on involvement. But process consultation is more task directed than sensitivity training.

Consultants in process consultation are there to "give the client insight into what is going on around him, within him and between him and other people".

Importantly, the process consultant need not be an expert in solving the particular problem that is identified. The consultant's expertise lies in diagnosis and developing a helping relationship.

Team Building

Team building utilizes high interaction group activities to increase trust and openness among team members. Team building can be applied within groups or at intergroup level where activities are interdependent.

Team building can also address itself to clarifying each member's role on the team. Each role can be clarified and identified. Teams may be formal work groups, committees, task forces and any other permanent or transient aggregation of personnel. Team building begins when members of a group admit that they have a problem and gather data to provide insight to it. Work teams have been used effectively to combat a variety of important organizational problems. For these efforts to be successful, however, all group members must participate in the gathering and evaluating of information as well as the planning and implementing the action plans.

Sensitivity Training

It is also called T-Group training. T-Group training consists of ten to twelve members and a professional trainer called facilitator. The facilitator is generally professional behavioral scientist. The group usually meets over a period of two weeks but not regularly. The purpose of the sensitivity training is to sensitize people to perceptions and the behavior related aspects of themselves and others. The sessions are generally unstructured, without any agenda. As the members interact with each other, the facilitator moderates the discussion and provides an opportunity for each participant to express his or her opinions, beliefs and ideas. He also takes a note of expressions and reactions of the participant during interactions and at the end of the session provides feedback on their behavior. The feedback helps members of the group to know more about themselves as well as of others and learn about group dynamics. This kind of training helps them to improve their listening skills, learn to talk openly and accept individual differences. T-Group training is basically used in organization to reduce interpersonal conflicts, enhance group cohesiveness and improve organizational productivity and efficiency.

There is a need for sensitivity training both in organization and outside as interpersonal differences and frictions are common part of life. Beyond a certain limit each frictions result in strained or negative social relation which can interfere with organizational effectiveness. In extreme cases, such frictions and antagonisms among employees can bring the organization to a standstill. Such bad blood which generally make life more difficult and stressful than necessary can reduce the level of productivity in all cases.

The objectives of sensitivity training are:

(a) Better insight into one's own behavior and the way one appears to others.

(b) Better understanding of group processes.

(c) Development of skill in diagnosing and intervening in group processes.

Transactional Analysis Approach

It is a theory of personality and systematic psychotherapy for personal growth and personal change. Three-part model of personality is used in organization as an effective tool to understand why people behave in a certain manner. This also provides an effective tool for analyzing and improving communication and style of management. It encourages people to take responsibility for their own life. This approach helps to actualize the potential of people in organizations, encourages them to take responsibility for goal setting and achievement of goal, both personal and organizational. Transactional analysis is also a decisional model for individual and organizational development. This means that individual destiny and organizational destiny is governed by decisions made at different stages of development. Sometimes this decision becomes strong influence so that as time changes, this limits the flexibility in problem solving. This approach finds wide range of applications in organizations like superior-subordinate relationship, customer relations, team building, employee involvement, audit etc.

Organizational Development Interventions

Role Analysis Technique

This technique is adopted to clarify the duties and responsibilities of team members and improve team performance. Sometimes individuals play multiple roles such as superior, subordinate, colleague, expert, administrator etc. Each role demands a certain type of behavior. When a person assumes a new role, he does not know about the behavior expected of him by others. This results in role ambiguity. Ishwar Dayal and John Thomas designed this technique to help new teams define the role of their members, and establish teams to resolve problems of role ambiguity and confusion. This technique assumes that defining and clarifying their roles can enhance cooperation and coordination among the team members. The role being defined is known as focal role. Role analysis technique consists of 3 steps:

Step 1: The incumbent of focal role attempts to analyze his roles. He describes his formal duties and responsibilities in his role, the significance of the role to the organization and its place in achieving goals of the organization. The other members of the team give their suggestions to the duties and behaviors described by the focal role incumbent. The discussion continues among team members till they arrive at a consensus on the role definition.

Step 2: The focal incumbent describes the behavior that he expects from other members of the team so that he can perform well. The other members may seek clarifications or make some suggestions to modify the behavior expectations by focal role incumbent.

Step 3: All the team members express the behavior they expect from the focal role incumbent. The focal role incumbent may make some suggestions and subsequently, the entire team discusses and finalizes the expectations of focal role.

The focal role incumbent prepares a written description of his role, including the results of the above steps. It is known as role profile. According to Dayal and Thomas the role profile consists of discretionary activities of the role, obligatory duties towards other roles and expectations of focal role from other roles in the team or organization.

Role Negotiation Technique

This technique is designed by Roger Harrison, which is used to deal with situations. The technique is based on the assumption that people prefer to resolve conflict even if it means making some compromises from their side, rather than leaving the conflict unresolved. By using role negotiation technique, the consultant negotiates between conflicting parties and reaches a settlement where each party agrees to make specific changes in its behavior in return for changes in the behavior of the other party.

Role negotiations techniques consist of the following:

Contract Setting: in this step, the consultant lays down some ground rules for negotiations between members of the teams in conflict. Some of the rules may be:

During negotiations, one should not comment on personal beliefs and feelings of other members but should focus only on work behaviors; one should keep one's priorities straight, and be sure whether one wants the person to be more supportive, less interfering or remain unchanged; each expectation should be submitted in written form, one should not expect change from others without making similar concession from ones own side etc.

Issue diagnosis: in this step, the parties are given issue diagnosis forms. In the form, each party writes what type of change in work behaviors he expects from others and in what way the change affects his own performance. The content of all the issues diagnosis forms is shared among all the members. The content may also be displayed to bring to the notice of all members.

Influence trade or negotiation period: in this stage the conflicting parties discuss the most important changes they require from each other. They highlight the changes they are willing to bring in their behavior and the changes they expect from the other person on return. The number of behavioral changes expected from each other may decline during the process of negotiation. Once all the parties are satisfied with the contents of the agreement, the process of negotiation comes to an end. All the agreements are written and the agreement copies are distributed among the members.

Thus role negotiation technique is highly effective in situations where power and influence related issues jeopardize interpersonal relationships and behavior of employees in the organization.

Force Field Analysis

Is one of the oldest and most widely used interventions for understanding problematic situations and planning corrective actions. This technique is based on the assumptions that there are two forces namely; driving forces and restraining forces that play a role in attaining a desired state of equilibrium in the organization. This technique was developed by Kurt Lewin. According to him, social forces and events have a major effect on organizational phenomenon such as productivity, morale of a team, and the degree of prejudice in a community. These organizational phenomena stabilize at the point of equilibrium. Bringing out certain changes in the driving and restraining forces that govern equilibrium can bring the point of equilibrium.

Third Party Peace Making

These activities involve the use of a third party consultant to help resolve a conflict between two others. The consultant uses a variety of mediator and conflict resolution skills and strategies.

Life and Career Planning

These activities help individuals to articulate their personal goals and then analyze how they can go about achieving these in the organization. Specific programs here involve life/ career inventories, assessment of capabilities and skills, and determination of training needs.

Organization Mirror

This approach is useful when a particular unit is having difficulties with a number of organizational units. The focal unit invites the other units to a meeting. This technique is very useful when a particular work unit seems to experience difficulties with other work related groups. Information feedback is quick, and agreed upon plans to resolve problems usually lead to real actions and better understanding.

Impact of Current Technology on OD

The use of microcomputers to support OD is a relatively recent phenomenon. Application of microcomputers that serve as management development tools are developed at a rapid pace. These tools tend to be designed for individual use, and are expert systems based on psychological theories of how individual behaves in a work environment. These software packages use the concept of interactive programmed learning, and are capable of branching. They instruct the user to answer the series of question and use the responses to provide a diagnosis and opportunities to experiment with new approaches to various situations through new stimulation.

Microcomputers are now being used to support people understanding of the group processes by allowing complex computations to be performed quickly and flexibly.

Technology in the form of microcomputers is now exploding into our lives at an unprecedented rate. As recently as a decade ago, computers were large machines enclosed in air conditioned rooms that require swarms of persons to maintain them to do new tasks. In most cases, the management information system [MIS] specialist was the person who told the organization's management what they should ask for computer and how long it would take to provide the information. When the computer completed its task, management often did not use the information generated because it did not really perceive the need for it.

References and Further Reading

1. Ghosh PK [1991] Industrial And Organizational Psychology. New Delhi: Himalaya Publication.
2. Jerald Greenberg, Robert Baron, Behavior in organization, 6th edition, prentice hall, New York.
3. John B. Miner, industrial organizational psychology, 1992, McGraw Hill, Inc. New York.
4. John W. Newstorm / Keith Davis, Organizational Behavior, 9th edition, 1996, Tata Mc Graw Hill publishing Co. ltd, New Delhi.
5. Keith Davis [1999]. Organization Behavior, United States Of America.
6. Kurt Pawliks, Mark R. Rosenweig, The International Handbook of Psychology, 2000, Sage publications ltd London.
7. Stephen .P. Robbins, Organizational Behavior, 7th edition; 1996, Prentice Hall of India, pvt ltd, New Delhi.

8. Subba Rao [2000] Human Resource Management, New Delhi; Himalaya Publication.
9. Tansik Chase & Aquilano, Management, A life cycle approach, 1980, Richard D Irwin Inc., Ontario.
10. Walter Sikes [1989]. Organizational Development, United States of America.

13

Change Management

Introduction

Change Management is about how to get users to accept a new business process—and the technology that enables it. The guiding principal of change management is that human beings make companies work, not technology. Technology is just a tool, and users have to be excited about it, believe in it, [be] trained in it, and supported in it. Change management is about making sure all of those things are included from the beginning as part of the project.

To design a successful strategy of change, managers must become skillful at diagnosing the forces pressing for change and the resistances to change. The change problem might be large or small in scope and scale. It might focus on individuals or groups, one or more division or departments, the entire organization, or one or more aspects of the organization's environment. For example, is the company facing an immediate threat to its survival? It is important that managers effectively diagnose the external and internal forces that threaten the company's survival. Secondly, managers must assess and implement strategies for combating these forces.

Change management experts focus attention, specifically, on resistances to change—both organizationally and those of individuals within the organization. The change management model operates under the premise that people and organizations are innately adverse to change. The general argument is that when confronted by rapid change, people [and organizations] get frustrated, freeze up, get rigid and rebel against the changes.

Managers must be adept at addressing the inevitable resistance of staff to a change. Change management argues that the most effective way to make needed changes is to identify existing resistances to change and to focus efforts on removing or reducing as many as possible. Consultants working in this arena assist organizations to effectively address and overcome the forces that are commonly associated with organizational and individual resistance to change:

Individual resistances to change include:

- Selective attention and retention
- Habit
- Dependence
- Fear of the unknown

Organizational resistances to change include:

- Threat to power and influence
- The organizational structure itself
- Resource limitations
- Fixed investments not easily altered
- Interorganizational agreements

Theories of Change Management

1. Force Field Analysis

A technique developed by Kurt Lewin, assumes that in any situation there are both driving and restraining forces that influence any change that may occur. Driving forces are those forces affecting a situation that are pushing in a particular direction; they tend to initiate a change and keep it going. In terms of improving productivity in a work group, encouragement from a supervisor, incentive earnings, and competition may be examples of driving forces. Restraining forces are forces acting to restrain or decrease the driving forces. Apathy, hostility, and poor maintenance of equipment may be examples of restraining forces against increased production. Equilibrium is reached when the sum of the driving forces equals the sum of the restraining forces.

This equilibrium, or present level of productivity, can be raised or lowered by changes in the relationship between the driving and the restraining forces.

Once you have determined that there is a discrepancy between what is actually happening and what you would like to be happening in a situation – and have done some analysis on why that discrepancy exists – then force field analysis becomes a helpful tool. Before embarking on any change strategy, it seems appropriate to determine what you have going for you in this change effort (driving forces) and what you have going against you (restraining forces). We have found that if managers start implementing a change strategy without doing that kind of analysis, they can get blown out of the water and not know why.

Here are a few guidelines for using force field analysis to develop a change strategy.

1. If the driving forces outweigh the restraining forces in power and frequency in a change situation, managers interested in driving for change can often push on and overpower the restraining forces.
2. If the restraining forces are much stronger than the driving forces, managers interested in driving for change have two choices. First, they can give up the change effort, realizing that it will be too difficult to implement. Second, they can pursue the change effort, but concentrate on maintaining the driving forces in the situation while attempting, one by one, to change each of the restraining forces into driving forces or somehow to immobilize each of the restraining forces so that they are no longer factors in the situation. The second choice is possible, but very time-consuming.
3. If the driving forces and restraining forces are fairly equal in a change situation, managers probably will have to begin pushing the driving forces, while at the same time attempting to convert or immobilize some or all of the restraining forces.

2. Logical Incrementalism

Another theory that has received wide acceptance in designing change implementation strategies in James Brian Quinn's logical incrementalism. This theory recognizes that the process of implementing change in a large organization is complex and time-consuming. Internal and external forces can exert significant pressure to resist a significant pressure and to resist a senior management team's plan for strategic reorganization of the company. Logical incrementalism describes the process and focuses on the evolution of the change as broad goals are more narrowly refined and adapted. The stages of logical incrementalism are:

1. General concern-a vaguely felt awareness of an issue of opportunity.
2. Broadcasting of a general idea without details – the idea is floated for reactions pro and con and for refinements.
3. Formal development of a change plan.
4. Use of a crisis or opportunity to stimulate implementation of the change plan – retirement of a senior manager or a sudden loss of market share can facilitate rapid acceptance and implementation of the change.
5. Adaptation of the implementation progress.

Change Process

Unfreezing

The aim of unfreezing is to motivate and make the individual or the group ready to change. It is a thawing – out process in which the forces acting on individuals are rearranged so that now they see the need for change. According to Edgar H. Schein, when drastic unfreezing is necessary, the following common elements seem to be present : (1) The individuals being changed are physically removed from the accustomed routines, sources of information, and social relationships; (2) All social supports are undermined and destroyed (3) the individuals being changed are demeaned and humiliated so that they will see their old attitudes or behavior as unworthy and thus be motivated to change (4) reward is consistently linked with willingness.

If brief, unfreezing is the breaking down of folkways, customs, and traditions – the old ways of doing things – so that individuals are ready to accept new alternatives. In terms of force field analysis, unfreezing may occur when either the driving forces are increased or the restraining forces are reduced.

Changing

Once individuals have become motivated to change, they are ready to be provided with new patterns of behavior. This process is most likely to occur by one of two mechanisms : identification or internalization. Identification occurs when one or more models are provided in the environment – models from whom individuals can learn new behavior patterns by identifying with them and trying to become like them. Internalization occurs when individuals are placed in a situation in which new behaviors are demanded of them. They learn these new behavior patterns not only because they are necessary for survival, but also because new high-strength needs are induced by coping behavior.

Refreezing

The process by which the newly acquired behavior comes to be integrated as patterned behavior into the individual's personality or ongoing significant emotional relationship is referred to as refreezing. According to Schein, if the new behavior has been internalized while being learned, "this has automatically facilitated refreezing because it has been fitted naturally into the individual's personality. If it has been learned through identification, it will persist only so long as the target's relationship with the original influence model persists, unless new surrogate models are found or social support and reinforcement is obtained for expressions of the new attitudes"

This statement highlights how important it is for an individual engaged in a change process to be in an environment that continually reinforces the desired change. The effect of many training programs has been short-lived when the person returns to an environment that does not reinforce the new patterns or, even worse, is hostile toward them.

What we are concerned about in refreezing is that the new behavior does not get extinguished over time. To prevent extinction, the change agent must schedule reinforcement in an effective way. There seems to be two main reinforcement schedules continuous and intermittent. With continuous reinforcement, the individuals learn the new behavior quickly, but if their environment changes to one of no reinforcement, extinction is much slower because the individuals have been conditioned to go for periods of time without any reinforcement. Thus, for fast earning, a continuous reinforcement schedule should be used. But once the individual has learned the new pattern, a switch to intermittent reinforcement should ensure a long-lasting change.

Stages in a Change Process

Any change process can be seen to involve a series of identifiable stages. There are many such theories and models in the literature, some complex, others simple (Iushman and Romanelli, 1985). One which I believe to have much to commend it since it has great practical utility was orginally devised by Hinings (1983). This model has five stages :

1. Diagnosis
2. Identifying resistance.
3. Allocating responsibility.
4. Developing and implementing strategies.
5. Monitoring.

Planned change needs to be seen as an iterative process. That is, the stages should be seen as a series of steps and, like footsteps, they can be taken backwards and sideways as well as forwards. In reality, the stages will be interwoven into the fabric of the change process and will occur in varying orders with some running concurrently and with many retreats into 'Previous' stages. It is also almost impossible in practice to identify when one stage ends and another begins. What is of critical importance is to recognize that for planned change managed needs to ensure that they are mutually supportive and reinforcing.

Diagnosis

The basic purpose of the diagnostic stage is to reach a clear understanding of the felt need or problem. It involves examining the need or problem in as much detail as possible in order to establish clarity. The basic activities are those of data collection and analysis. What form those activities will take will depend on a number of factors including the nature of the problem or need and whether it is the result of an external or internal source of change. In many cases, the diagnostic stage will involve internal data collection, irrespective of

the laggards. There is another general principle which is equally useful, supported by much evidence in social science theory and research. It is simply that the key to converting laggards and wavers to innovators is involvement. This principle is also be used actively to influence others. There can be allocated leadership roles as part of Stage 3 of the process. In doing so, they are encouraged to actively promote and persuade and so exercise a positive influence on others. Such activity will be very significant in the speed of adoption of those to the right of the mean in the distribution curve which itself will have a form of chain reaction on those on both right and left of the curve close to the mean.

The model also tells us that there will always be laggards, and that they may never adopt the change. In organizational terms, this means that they might choose or be required to leave. Knowing of their existence does mean that realistic targets can be set for implementing change. We should not be surprised or disappointed if 100 per cent commitment from everyone affected does not materialize. It is always likely to be the case.

It is, though, something useful to attempt to convert a small number of laggards to innovators as part of the implementation strategy, especially if they occupy positions of power and influence. This is particularly useful sine laggards are likely to be highly committed to their position, and will therefore seek to influence others.

The application of this principle is widespread in organization and management theory. It forms the basis of many models of effective management style and successful leadership behavior. It is also implicit in many theories of effective teamwork and organization change. The principle has stood the test of time and keeps appearing in different guises in new advice to managers on how to be successful.

In developing and implementing a strategy for planned change, a choice needs to be made on the extent to which to involve those affected by the change. At one extreme, people are merely told of the change and expected to adopt it. This is labeled an information's stragegy, i.e., information about the change is passed on without the opportunity or expectation of a response, apart from adopting the change. At the other extreme, are all (or nearly all) those with determination of the solution. This is termed an involvement strategy. In between are a number of possibilities according to the degree of interaction between decision makers and those affected, and the relative degree of influence on decisions by the same two groups. It is a stage in which there is a lot of scope for choice. The earlier stages are primarily concerned with information collection and analysis and can be aided by developing and implementing an appropriate strategy. that is the provision of training and development. No strategy will work without it.

Monitoring

This brings us to the final part of the process. It appears in some ways the setting of targets, time-scales for achieving them, and setting up and applying the means to assess progress. Doing this in practice relies on Stage I being carried out thoroughly since implicit in monitoring is the need to describe the current position and future desired state. A clear picture of the present is necessary to assess progress towards the future. Also implicit in monitoring is the need for observable and measurable factors to be the focus of planned change. We cannot monitor what we cannot see or measure. The final part of the stage is an assessment of whether the planned change has been achieved and the felt need or problem overcome. But monitoring has to be carried out on a frequent and regular basis until that point, because this stage has a further key element. It is to do with identifying and dealing with unexpected outcomes. Plans and strategies do not always work as intended when put into action, so it is important to be able to respond to the actuality. This is a key purpose of monitoring. It also provides a final illustration of the iterative nature of the process. Unexpected and unintended consequences will mean reviewing and revising earlier stages, often including stage 1.

A common result of monitoring, for example, is identifying resistance (Stage 2) in locations and for reasons impossible to anticipate with a consequent and necessary revision of the original rationale for the change (Stage 1). It is therefore an important stage which, like stage,

I is too often the case that senior decision makers instigate a change without ever checking and therefore ever knowing whether it was implemented or achieved the desired effect, and then carry on doing their jobs in the belief that both have happened. Such behaviour can have detrimental and, on occasion literally disastrous, results for the organization and its members.

Types of Change

For organizations there are particular events and forces that arise from outside the organization and some from inside it. These forces can be changes by the organization or events to which the organization must respond by making changes.

Change Can Affect the Individual

There are four different ways in which change can be experienced by organization, dependent upon the scale of change and the degree of planning involved.

1. **Surprise:** This reflects situations that all unplanned and relatively minor in nature. Change and require the finance managers of a company require the finance managers of a company to adjust loan repayment schedules.
2. **Incremental :** This could reflect situation which are anticipated and relatively minor in nature e.g. the implementation of quality circle recommendations.
3. **Crisis :** This represents both the unexpected and the serious. An extreme example might be the destruction of a factory as a result of a gas explosion or terrorist attack. It contains the potential to destroy the organization.
4. **Strategic :** This represents major planned events that attempts to position the organization more effectively in relationship to its environment: Planned and unplanned change are discussed in detail below.

(a) **Planned Change :-** Plánned change represents those events that management intend to, for which they can provide a predetermined response.

There are many examples of planned change, management may identify that its ability to retain market share is being threatened by competitors with much lower labour cost. Consequently, a package of measures could be developed including the introduction of automation and high technology, the development of flexibility and teamwork practices among, the workforce, the linking of wages to performance; the redesign of the product to make it more lucrative to the customers; the development of a range of customer inducements and support measures. Planning for the many small changes therefore is part of normal managerial experience.

(b) **Unplanned Change :** This category represents the unexpected events that can never be completly alienated. Some parts of California are known to be subject to earthquakes as they lie along faults in the earths crust. Knowing this, measures can be taken to minimize the consequences through building design and emergency planning. However, it is not yet possible to predict with certainty when as how strong a particular tremor will be. They remain random factors and so when they occur, pre-prepared recovery plans must be activated.

Objectives of Planned Change

The planned change is needed to meet the overall objective of the organization. Since, there may be changes in the force (both internal and external) affecting organizational functioning, the organization has to make suitable change to meet its objectives. Thus objectives for such change may be two-fold :(1) modification of the organization's mode of adaptation of changes in its environment, and (ii) modification of structure, technology, attitudes, values, and other behavioral aspect of people in the organization.

1. **Environmental Adaptation :** Organization is basically adaptive – coping system. It has to work in environment which is marked by dynamic characteristics. Every organization has a tendency to maintain balance and equilibrium. Because of change in the environment, the organizational equilibrium is affected. If the

changes are minor and come within the purview of the existing programmes, the organization will accommodate them automatically. However, if the changes cannot be adapted to the existing framework, the organizational equilibrium will be imbalanced and organizational effectiveness is adversely affected. Simply because of this reason, every organization has adaptive subsystem, such as research and development department, marketing research department, and so on.

2. **Individual Adaptation :** The Second objective of planned change is to achieve individual adaptation. The organization cannot reach to the objective of its environmental adaptation unless some basic internal adaptation is achieved. These internal factors may be individuals, organization structure, technology and task. Individuals are the first in this context. For organizational effectiveness, people have to change themselves so that they can cope with the requirement of changed circumstances. Such changes may be required in their attitudes, communication system, way of behaving, leadership and work-styles, and other relevant organizational behaviour. Such changes must be made according to the need for the new situation.

3. **Structural Adaptation :** Organization structure is the pattern of relationships among various positions and position holders. This change may be in the whole set of relationships, work assignment and authority structure. Change in organization structure is required because old relationships and interactions no longer remain valid and useful in the changed circumstances.

4. **Technological Adaptation :** The impact of recent technological development has forced the organization to take into account the role of technology in organizational success. In order to cope with the changed environment which may include technological factors as well, the organization has to adapt new technology. Thus, this technological adaptation forces directly the organization to change its task.

5. **Task Adaptation :** Technological changes may bring many types of changes in organizational task. Task focuses on the job

performed by the individuals in the organization. Since, there may by many new type of jobs, the existing job techniques may not be suitable. Moreover, there may be new job load because of the job enlargement. In such a case, a new equilibrium has to be found out which matches people with jobs. In this matching process, there may by several problems which must be encountered by planned change.

It can be observed that a change will bring disequilibriam in the organization. In order to achieve new equilibrium, the organization has to modify many aspects of the organization. All these aspects are interrelated. This is what the systems approach of organization theory suggests. Thus a system approach to organization change has to be followed. For example, if an organization is not able to face competition in the market because of its old technique of production and competitors with new technique, the only alternative to the organization is to change itself according to the needs of the hour. In this process, the organization will acquire suitable technology. When this technology is put into operation, it may change the job content completely; old jobs may not be able to work with new work environment. Such change may be brought either by recruiting new employees or training them for new jobs. The second alternative may be replacing old employees. Since, the job structure is changed, the internal relationship among people will have to be changed because old relationships may not be suitable. Thus, all these factors are interrelated and simultaneous changes have to be made in all these aspects.

Steps in Planned Changes

Changes are inevitable in any organization – big or small depending upon the environment on the work. Management, therefore has to introduce changes.

In introducing changes, the management has to handle it in such a way that there would be necessary adjustment in various forces. For this purpose, the manager who may act as change agent has to go through a particular process. The planned change process may comprise three steps : Planning for change, assessing change forces, and implementing change.

1. **Planning for Change :** The discrepancy between what is happening and what should be happening creates the necessity of change. When the need for change is identified in the context of analysis of forces lying in this discrepancy, there is a need for identifying alternative solution and appropriate implementation strategy to use in attempting to reduce the discrepancy.

   Effective organization change depends upon certain planning which must be undertaken first. This includes the formulation of objective, polices and other plans which will specify work, the organization is to accomplish, All work done in the organization must be pointed to the accomplishment of predetermined objectives, policies and programmes. Preparation of plan for changes ensures to a great extent the minimization of loss in productivity and the maximization of duration of the benefits of change. Moreover, It makes certain that a really suitable solution of the problem has come which has prompted change.

2. **Assessing Change Forces :** The planned change is not automatic, rather there are many forces in individuals, groups and even in the organization which resist such change. Unless the cooperation of people is not ensured, any change process will not succeed. For this purpose, the management has to create an environment in which change will be accepted by the people. This problem is referred to the problem of overcoming resistance.

   In a group process, there are some forces favoring and some opposing to maintain an equilibrium. This is referred to as 'field of forces' by Kurt Lewin. He assumes that in any situation there are both driving and restraining forces which influence any change that may occur. Driving forces are those affecting a situation by pushing in a particular direction they tend to initiate a change and keep it going. Restraining forces act to restrain or decrease the driving forces equals the sum of the restraining forces. The same type of field of forces applies to cause each Individual's dynamic state of adjustment to his job.

3. **Implementing Changes :** If the driving forces are there or be cause of several efforts the management has been able to bring favorable

condition it can implement the change. The implementation may put various change plan into action. It may reflect into change in putting new machine to work, assigning new jobs, and prescribing new relationships.

Change Cycles

These are four levels of change.

(a) Knowledge changes

(b) Attitudinal Changes

(c) Individual behaviour changes.

(d) Group or organizational performance changes.

Changes in knowledge tend to be the easiest to make; it can occurs as a result of reading a book or an article or hearing something new from a respected person. Changes in individual behaviour seen to be significantly more difficult and time consuming, for example managers may have knowledge about the advantage of increased follower's involvement and participation in decision making and may even feel that such participation could improve theie performance, yet may be unable to delegate or share decision making responsibilities significantly with followers. This discrepancy between knowledge, attitude and behaviour may be a result of their own authoritative leadershes, Level of change become very significant when you examine few different change cycles the participants change cycle and directive change cycle.

1. **Participative Change :** A participative change cycle is implemented when new knowledge is made available to the individual group. It is hoped that the group will accept the data and develop a positive attitude and commitment in the direction of the desired change. At this level an effective strategy may be to involve the individual or group directly in helping to select and form the new methods for obtaining the desired goods. This step is group participation in problem solving.

   The next step will be to attempt to translate this commitment into actual behaviour. This step is significantly more difficult to achieve. An effective strategy may be to identify the informal and formal leaders among the work group (s) and concentrate on gaining their behavioural support for the desired change. Once the behaviour of the group leaders has been changed, individuals change their behaviour after those persons whom they respect and perceive in leadership roles.

2. **Directive change :** Directive change cycle begins when change is imposed on the total organization by some external force, such as higher management. In turn, the change will affect individual behaviours. The new contacts and modes of behaviour create new knowledge, which tend to develop predispositions towards or against the change.

Is There a "best" Strategy for Change ?

Given a choice between the polarities of directors and participative change, most people would tend to prefer the participative change cycle. The appropriate stragegy depends on the situation and these are advantage and disadvantage to each.

Advantage and Disadvantages of Change Cycle

The participate change cycle tends to be more appropriate for working with individuals as groups who are achievement motivated, seek responsibility and have a degree of knowledge and experience that may be useful in developing new ways of operating. A directive change style might be appropriate and productive with individual and groups who are not ambitions, are dependent, and are unwilling to take on new responsibilities unless forced to do so. In fact, these people might prefer direction and structure.

A significant advantage of the participative change cycle is that once the change is accepted it tends to be long lasting. The disadvantage of participative change is that it tends to be slow and evolutionally it may take years to implement a significant change.

An advantage of directive change on the other hand, is speed using position power, leaders can often impose change immediately. A disadvantage of this change strategy is that it tends to be volatile. It can be maintained only as long as the leader has position power to make it stick. It often results in animosity, hostility, and, in some cases overt and covert behaviour to undermine and overthrow.

Reasons of Changes

(1) **Tools, Machines and Equipment :** Technological or mechanical changes in machines, tools and equipment create changes in the organization. For example, installation of an automatic machinery will result in the displacement or replacement of people.

(2) **Methods and Procedure :** When a change occurs in a method or procedure of which the employees have been habitually accustomed to use they have a tendency to resist because their proficiency decrease thereby and they sometimes feel the inferiority complex that they are not performing the job correctly.

(3) **Business Conditions :** Changes in business conditions such us change in the quality of the product, marketing system, practices, business cycles, change in industrial policy etc. create disequilibrium in the organization and need adjustments accordingly.

(4) **Managerial Personnel :** A personnel may retire or a director in the Board of Directors may be inducted or replaced. The policies, practices, procedures and programmes may he changed according to the interest, aptitude, ability etc. of the new incumbent.

(5) **Formal Organization Structure :** A formal organization structure establishes a formal line of authority and responsibility in an organization. There are also created channels of communication and interpersonal relationship along with this line. When changes in this formal organization occur, there would be a change in the relationship which creates disequilibrium.

(6) **Informal Organization :** The informal relationship established between people in an organization becomes a very important point of existence, because many people find their satisfaction in these relationship. Man's urge to belong finds satisfaction in many informal groups and cliques with which he associates, his desire for recognition is satisfied by the accord given to his skill, talent and abilities by various friends in the organization. His needs for prestige, status, achievements and many other basic sociological

and psychological motives depend to a great degree on informal organization for their satisfaction. Hence, when management makes any change that disturbs the informal relationships established between people, there is bound to be a state of imbalance.

(7) **Deficiencies in Existing Organization :** An organization, once established cannot be said to be good for all times. Extension of the plant, change in managerial functions, evaluation of complex organization relationships create so many problems in the organization. Hence change is necessary to remove these deficiencies in the organization.

(8) **Environment :** No organization is an island in itself. Each continually interacts with other organizations and individuals, the customers, suppliers, unions, shareholders, Government and many more. Each organization has goals and responsibility related to others in its environment. An organization dealing with its environment in conducting its affairs, must give consideration lo the goals of others. Changes in social, political, economic, technological and legal environment force organizations to change themselves. Such changes may result in organizational changes like changes in production process, labour-management relations, nature of competition, economic constraints, organization method and other major functions of organization. Organization must change in order to survive in the changing environment.

(9) **Avoiding Developing Interia :** Sometimes, changes take place just to avoid developing inertia or inflexibility. Managers believe that the organization should be dynamic. They take steps to incorporate changes to make the organization dynamic because they think that no single method is the best tool forever. If personnel liking for change is developed, there will be no resistance when major change in the organization is brought about.

Human Reactions to Change

There is a close relationship between change and human attitudes. Attitudes are important in determining the response to change because an employee's perception about the likely impact of a change depends upon his attitudes. Sometimes, attitudes are not a matter of logic, but are entirely different from it. Thus, reaction to a change sometimes, depends not upon logic, but upon feelings of how a change will affect one's need and satisfaction in the organization. This reaction to change may be in following forms :

1. **Acceptance :** If an individual perceives that a change will affect him favourably, he accepts such change.
2. **Resistance :** If the individual feels that the change will affect him unfavourably, he resists it. Resistance to change becomes more forceful when the person concerned has a feeling that through resistance he may eliminate the change.
3. **Indifference :** Sometimes people fail to realize the impact of change or they feel that they will not be affected by the change; either way they remain indifferent.
4. **Forced Acceptance :** Sometimes people are forced to accept the change, though they may resist it at initial stages but when change-forces overpower resistance-forces people have to accept it.

Causes of Resistance to Change

Changes are necessary for successful organizational functioning. These are generally resisted by the people. Individuals tend to resist many types of changes because new habits or sacrifices are required. Similarly, social systems tend to resist change because of homeostasis. Homeostasis implies self-correcting characteristics of organization to maintain equilibrium as a result of change, that is, people act to establish a steady state of need fulfillment and to secure themselves from disturbance of that balance. When change is minor and within the scope of correcting programme, adjustment is fairly routine, but when a change is major or unusual, more serious upsets may occur. This leads to general proposition that people and their social systems will often resist change in organizations. In fact, fear of change can be as significantly disruptive as change itself, because it produces identical symptoms.

People tend to resist change, tendency is offset by their desire for new experience and for the rewards that come with change. Thus, all changes are not resisted. In fact, people want changes which are favourable to them. Moreover, resistance to change is not necessarily an undesirable human response, nor is change always a positive good. Resistance to change forces change agents (managers, specialists etc.) to take a realistic view of change. The main cause of resistance to change are as follows :

(A) Resistance by Employees

1. **Disequilibrium in Situation and Environment :** When change occurs it disturbs the equilibrium of the situation and environment in which indivduals and group exist. To overcome this disequilibrium and to return to a state of balance requires people to go through a period of adaptation and adjustment to the change. Hence change is always resisted though it is beneficial to the employees in the long run. It is impossible to say, how serious situation will be because it will depend upon the nature of the people and the change concerned.

2. **Imbalance in Need Satisfaction :** An imbalance in need satisfaction is cause of resistance to change. It is assumed that prior to change the individual exists within an environment in which the satisfaction of his needs has reached a high degree of stability. when change occurs there is immediately manifested a threat to motive satisfaction. There now occurs the possibility that the change may prevent or decrease need satisfaction.

3. **Insecurity of Jobs :** Where the changes threaten either the status or the job security, reaction is certain to be quick and violently negative. In such a case even minor revision of policies or procedures may evoke profoundly disturbing reactions. Introduction of automatic machinery or technological changes in machines and methods may threaten the security of job. Hence workers resist such changes.

4. **Danger of Economic Disaster :** Some changes may be beneficial such as change in promotion policy but workers fear the danger

of economic disaster in future or the adjustment to the new position or separation from his group etc. Therefore, they resist such changes.

5. **Loyalty to the Group :** Some persons are loyal to their group. They feil that the change should be there if it is inevitable in the present circumstances, yet they resist the change because they are caught between strong forces pushing them to make the change on the one side and equally strong forces deterring them against making the change on the other side. In India, rationalization was opposed by the labour union on this ground.
6. **Ignoring Established Institutions :-** An administration will surely face resistance when he ignores institutionalized patters of work and abruptly attempts to create a new state of affairs which demand that these customs be abolished without further consideration.
7. **Lack of Clarification :** If the nature of change is not made clear to the people who are going to be affected by the change, different people see different meaning in the proposed change, resistance can be expected with some people see the changes as an indication that their office could soon be abolished. Still others think that they are losing some of the power they formerly had.

(B) Resistance by Employer or Management

1. **Resistance by Employer or Management :** The change in the organization brings out problem of adjustment of disequilibrium of situation and environment. The management has the responsibility to restrain the people according to the proposed changes and the responsibility of introducing the change. It increases the work-load and resistance occurs.
2. **Changes Proposed by Government or Labour Union :** Sometimes changes are proposed or forced by the Government or the labour union. The management opposes the change as it thinks it is an insulting matter to it.
3. **Changes on Experimental Basis :-** In some cases, change is introduced on experimental basis. If it is proved beneficial, It is

extended further, otherwise it is abolished. The management does not take interest in such a temporary change and opposes it if it does not suit them.

Factors Influencing Resistance to Change

There are many factors responsible for resistance to change, depending upon degree and force of resistance upon how people felt about change. Thus, there may be real impact of change on people, or it may be an emotional feeling towards the impact of change. People generally resist change because of the following factors.

1. Perhaps the most important factor to resistance to change is the problem of adjustment. When change comes, it requires people to make new adjustment as organization seeks a new equilibrium. Adjustment depends upon how people interpret the impact of change. If a change affects ones position, status, and authority relationships adversely, he resists it. Moreover, in each change he has to change his way of working, which he dislikes because it presents numerous difficulties to him.
2. Another factor which brings resistance to change is the effect of change on individuals' level of need satisfaction. If change abridges or takes away satisfaction of an individuals' economic, psychological and social needs, he will resist the change. Resistance to automation is obvious because people feel that they may lose their jobs if automation is introduced.
3. Sometimes, individuals resist change because the group to which they belong resists it. Though each person interprets change individually, often he expresses it through a group. The degree and force of resistance will depend upon how loyal one is to the group and how effectively group resists the change. Generally the members of a group are influenced by its codes, patterns and attitudes.

Besides, a persons' emotional reasons for resistance to change are also important. Emotional reasons are more of a class interest. For example, if labour treats management as a different class in the organization, It will resist any change by the latter, whatever be the nature of change. However, behind emotional resistance, there are certain fears of adverse effect because of lack of confidence in the change agent. Such factors may be in the following forms :-

Economic Factors : These factors relate to the basic economic needs of the workers like necessities of life, such as job security and safety. These factors are :

(i) Workers apprehend technological unemployment. Generally new technology is expected to reduce the proportion to labour input and therefore, people resist such a change as it will affect the security of their jobs.

(ii) Workers fear that they will be idle for much of their time due to increased efficiency of new technology.

(iii) Workers may fear that they will be demoted if they do not possess the new skills required for the new jobs.

(iv) Workers resist the change of setting higher job standards which may reduce opportunity for bonus or incentive pay.

Psychological Factors : These factors arise when worker perceive that factors relating to their psychological needs will be affected adversely by the proposed change. These needs are his sense of pride, achievement, self-fulfillment, etc. These factors are :

(i) Workers do not like criticism implied in a change that the present method is inadequate and unsuitable.

(ii) Workers may fear that there will be fewer opportunities for developing their personal skill because new work changes will do away with the need for such manual work. This will lead to reduction of their personal pride.

(iii) Workers may apprehend boredom and monotony in the new jobs as a result of specialization brought by the new technology.

(iv) They many fear that harder work will be required to learn and adapt to new ideas.

(v) Workers may resist a change because they do not want to take trouble in learning the new things.

(vi) Workers may not have the knowledge of entire change or they may be incapable of understanding the implications of new ideas or methods.

Social Factors : Individuals to have certain social needs like friendship, belongingness, etc for the fulfillment of which they develop informal relations in the organization. They become members of certain informal groups and act as members of the group to which they belong. The social reasons for resistance to change are :

(i) New organizational set up requires new social adjustment which are not liked by people because they involve stresses and strain. This also means discarding old social ties which is not tolerable to the workers.

(ii) Workers are carried by the fear that the new social set up arising out of the change will be less satisfying than the present set up.

(iii) Workers oppose the people who sponsors and implement the change as they are strangers to them.

(iv) Workers may feel that changes being introduced will benefit the organization or employer, rather than themselves or the general public.

From the above discussions, it is obvious that resistance to change tends to focus on human relations problems, although, it may be related to the technological aspect of change. Workers resist the change which will affect their social relationships, upset their status, and threaten their security. Change may give them a feeling of insecurity since it challenges their way of doing things and may bring less labour oriented processes, moreover it is difficult for the workers to give up their old habits and customs. They also resist change if they do not know it well.

Thus, logical resistance is easier to overcome as compared to emotional one because latter depends upon class interest. Researches show that resistance to change tends to focus on human relations problems, rather than the technical aspect of change, people resist the way change affect them, the force of resistance to change will be determined by the effect of change on people's need satisfaction, and how change agent brings the change.

Role of Change Agents

Any planned change needs change agents. These are the persons who initiate change in the organization. Behavioural scientists have taken frequently somewhat divergent positions on the question of who should initiate an organizational change, what type of person this would be and what methods should be followed. Though management as a whole is involved with innovation as a continuing process, its role is somewhat limited in a planned change, however, the type of requirements may be different and internal management has to take the help of external change agents. Thus, there may be two types of change agents, external and internal.

External change agents are in the form of consultants for change. These are the persons who are normally in the specific area of organizational change. The internal change agents are from the existing organizational personnel, from any level or department, depending upon the needs of the change. Often both these agents work in harmony. A good deal of interaction in early contacts between internal and external change agents is implicitly related to developing a relationship of mutual trust so that each of them can understand the views of others. Afterwards, the internal change agents are trained by the consultants to implement the change as an ongoing process. For this purpose, the consultants devise certain change strategy.

The objective of the change agents is to bring desired change in the organization. However, for this purpose, a specific role is required to be performed by the change agents, both outside and inside. since relative positions of these change agents maybe different in organizational context, their roles may also be different in the change process.

1. **Role of external Change Agent :** The external change agent is in a position to view the organization meant for change from a total systems view point, so that it is much less affected by organizational norms. He is likely to have an easy access to top management since it is the top management on whose initiative the consultant is contacted. Depending upon the situation, the role of external change agent may vary because he is engaged

by an organization for certain specific activities. The role of consultant may include diagnosis of the situation, planning strategy for change, and even the evaluation of the change efforts in the content of various outcomes. From this point of view, the role of consultant may be quite comprehensive. However, the change programme will be successful only when the consultant is given the role of process consultation and the rest of the programme is implemented by the organization itself with the help of the consultant. The consultant has a role in teaching diagnostic and problem-solving skills but he should not work on the actual concrete problem himself. Maheshwari has identified the role of consultant in installing Management by objectives (MBO) programme for organizational change, as follows (i) formulation of implementation strategy, (ii) selection, training, and supervision of MBO advisers, (iii) training of managers, (iv) process consultation at the top level, (v) advice to the chief executive and other top executives on their objective documents (vi) evaluation and innovation, and (vii) integration of MBO process with other management system and techniques.

2. **Role of Internal Change Agents :** There are several difference between internal and external change agents and their roles may not be interchanged. The internal change agents are more likely to accept the system as given and try to accommodate their change tactics to the needs of the organization. By accepting the norms of the organization, these change agents spend little time in helping the organization move towards self-renewal, growth and change, There may be two categories of persons who may act as internal change agents, chief executive of the organization and change advisers from among the organizational managers.

    - **Chief Executive :** The chief executive sponsors the change programme and provides support and leadership for its success. Usually people do not treat a Chief Executive as a change agent in planned change. However, the change programme has greater chance of success if it is sponsored by the chief executive. When the change process proceeds smoothly, the role of the chief executive may gradually reduce and the key members of the organization should also act as change agents in their respective domains. The role of the chief executive was of paramount importance, especially during the initial phase of MBO implementation. He has to be personally convinced about the appropriateness of MBO and must show his conviction not only in the things he says but in the things he does, in the early stages of implementation. He must demonstrate that believes in a participative style of management and provide leadership to his management team in the change process. Unfortunately many of the chief executives and managers do not subscribe this view and the change efforts are not as successful as it should be.

Change Advisers : Apart from the chief executive, the change advisers have important role to play in change process. These are the internal personnel selected to work in close harmony with external consultant. They are trained by the consultant for implanting the change. Their number may be determined by the type of change and the size of the organization. A change advisor communicates to the managers the knowledge of the concepts and methods of various change techniques which he has learned through various training programmes with the help of the consultant. Thus, he helps managers to develop appropriate behaviour and skills for the change process. Thus, the advisor becomes a socio-therapist, trying to help the system itself. The role of change adviser is quite complex in the sense that he has to work now in an advisory capacity where order is given. Now since he cannot issue order, he has to depend more on his persuasive capability. He has to achieve the performance in terms of influencing members of the organization. The change agent needs to develop skills to negotiate, persuade, mobilize, and use power for the process of his role. It suggests that he must be trained as such so that he can find out the alternatives of formal authority in the organization. From this point of view, it is important that change agents are selected carefully. They should have : (i) Diagnostic Skills, (ii) Behavioural Skills in breaking impasses and in interrupting repetitive interchange, (iii) Attitudes of Acceptance, and (iv) Personal qualities to provide emotional support and reassurance.

Organizational Failure to Change : Not only individuals groups within an organization resist change but the organization may also resist many changes because of certain reason. Many organizations are designed to innovation-resisting. To ensure reliability of prescribed operation, the organization may create strong defenses against change. Moreover, in many cases, the change may be counterproductive. It suggests that all changes for a particular organization may not be functional. The following are the major factors because of which the organization does not incorporate change.

1. **Stability of Systems :** The organization may design a system through which it may derive many benefits. The system is stabilized and any change may be perceived a threat by the organization itself. For example, a bureaucratic has certain fixed rules, prescribes rigid authority relationships, and institutes rewards and punishment system. All these work in some circumstances. If the change is required in these aspects. the organization may not bring it easily because it is accustomed to a particular system.

2. **Resource Limitations :** No doubt, the organization has to adapt to its environment but the adaptation has its own cost. If the organization is not fully equipped for meeting such demands, it may not be possible for the organization to bring necessary change. For example, if new technology is adopted, it will require resources to procure machine, building, training for its personnel and commensurate expenses on other items also.

3. **Sunk Cost :** Most of the organizations have sunk cost involved in various assets. Once the assets are acquired, these can be used for specific period. Now, if the change is required, what will

happen to these assets? Naturally an organization will like to make a comparison between the outcomes of changed programme and continuing with the old programme in the light of this sunk cost. Sunk cost cannot be only in terms of various physical things. This can be for people also. If an individual is not making commensurate contribution, it is not necessary that his services are done away with. In such a case, the organization has to pay for his services, though these may not be as useful.

4. **Interorganizational Agreements :** The organization interacts with its environment. In this interaction process, it may enter into agreement with other organizations over certain aspect of working. Thus, If any change is to be incorporated, the organization has to take into account the wishes of other organizations too. It is not necessary that other organizations also agree with the change proposal. For example, the organization may enter into agreement with labour union about not brining technological change. Thus, the organizational is bound by this agreement and technological change is not possible. Similarly, such cases arise when the organization has such obligation. It does not, however, mean that the organization will always resist change. It depends more on the style of top management if it is risk taking, forward-looking, innovative and has zeal for progress, the organization may take change programmes much more frequently.

Overcoming Organizational Resistance to Change

At the core of any O.D. effort is the desire to avert change. However, change introduces ambiguity into the environment, with the con-comitant effects of less predictability and control. Accordingly organizational members resist change because of the undesirable effects it has on individuals yet, paradoxically, the change is regarded as necessary for the welfare at the organization. Resistance to change is a major obstacle in any O.D. effort.

Following are some of the tactics suggested for use by change agents in dealing with resistance to change :-

- **Education and communication :** Resistance can be reduced through communicating with employees to help them see the logic of a change. This tactic basically assumes that the resistance lies in misinformation or poor communication. If employees receive the full facts and get any misunderstanding cleared up, resistance will subside. Communication can be achieved through discussions, memos, group presentations or reports. It does work, provided that management-employee relations are characterized by mutual trust. If these conditions do not exist. the change is unlikely to succeed.
- **Participation and Involvement :** It is difficult for individuals to resist a change decision in which they participated prior to making a change, those opposed can be brought into the decision process. Assuring that the participants have the expertise to make a meaningful contribution, their involvement can reduce resistance.
- **Negotiation and Agreement :** If people or groups are losing something significant in the change and if they have enough power to resist strongly, a manager may use a negotiation strategy. Negotiation before implementation can make the change more smooth, should problems arise later, the conflicting parties can be referred to the negotiated agreement. This is a useful technique when resistance is due to power relationships and group factors.
- **Facilitation and Support :** These are effective in combating problems arising from desires for security and fear of the unknown. When the employees are having difficulty in adjusting to new arrangements or new ways of doing things, a manager may need to arrange for additional training or provide emotional support while employees accustom to the new system. Such facilitation may take time and effort. When employees are struggling with a new machine or technique it is easy for a supervisor to stop by their work area and encourage them to work harder, but it takes more time to sit down with them over a cup of coffee and listen to their problems. Although a discussion over

coffee may not solve these problems. It encourage the employees to work harder to solve the problem.

- **Manipulation and Co-operation :** In situations where other methods are not working or not available, a managers may resort to manipulating information, resources, and favors to overcome resistance. Cooperation may involve including representatives of groups likely to offer resistance in the design and implementation of the change. Whether or not the manager is really interested in their ideas. The manager hopes that inclusion in a planning group will cause the resisters to support the change when it is introduced into the organization. This technique is often used when it is introduced into the organization. This technique is often used when resistance is due to resource allocation, economic factors, and group factors.
- **Coercion :** Managers may resent to coercion to overcome resistance. If all other methods fail or for some reason are inappropriate, compliance can we covered by threats of pay reduction, loss of job or demotion or transfer. Although force may be a quick method of overcoming resistance, it can seriously effect employee attitudes and have adverse consequences in the long run.
- **Use of Group Forces :** Effective change focus not only on the individuals but also on the group itself. The group is an instrument for bringing strong pressure on its members to change. Since behaviour is firmly grounded in the group to which a person belongs, any change in the group will encourage changes in the individual behaviour. The idea is to help the group join with management to encourage desired change. The power of the group to stimulate change in its members depends partly on the strength of their attachment to it. The more attractive the group is to each member, the greater is its effect on the group member. The effect is further increased if members with high status in the group support a change. Change should not disrupt the groups social system more than it is necessary, any change that threatens the group will tend to meet with resistance.

- **Providing a Rationale for Change :** Capable leadership reinforces climate of psychological support for change. It is generally better to provide objective (performance related) reasons for the change. If they are compelling and substantial they should be given, ordinary requests or change should also be in accord with the objectives and vision of the organization. Change is more likely to be successful, if the leaders introducing it have high expectations of success. The expectations tend to get translated into specific managerial behaviors that increase the likelihood of change.
- **Shared Rewards :** Another way to employee support for change is to be sure that there are enough rewards for employees in the change situation. If they see that a change brings them losses and no gains, they can hardly be enthusiastic about it. Rewards give employees a sense that progress accompanies a change. Both economic and psychic rewards are useful. Employees appreciate a pay increase or promotion, but they also appreciate emotional support, training in new skills, and recognition from management. It is desirable for a change to pay off as directly and as soon as positive.
- **Employee Security :** Along with shared rewards, existing employee benefits need to be protected. Security during a change is essential. Seniority rights, opportunities for advancement, and other benefits are safeguarded, when a change is made. Grievance systems give employees a feeling of security that benefits will be protected and differences about them fairly resolved. All these practices help employees, feel secure in the presence of change.
- **Stimulating Employee Readiness :** This approach builds on the premise that change is more likely to be accepted, if the people affected by it, recognize a need for it, before it occurs. It can be induced by management through sharing information with employees. It occurs when workers discover for themselves that a situation requires improvement.
- **Working with the Total System :** Resistance to change can be reduced by a broader understanding of employee attitudes and

natural reactions to change-Managements' role is to tell employees the need for each change and to invite them to participate in it and gain from it. It is also essential for managers to take a systems oriented perspective on change.

Case Studies on Change and Organization Development

1. AT & T adopted to changes in the global economic and political arenas by engaging into 3 separate global companies, laying off 40,000 employees and seizing opportunities for growth in new markets. Following the passage of the North American free trade agreement, AT & T began exploring given optic produced at its Atlanta, Georgia, Plant to Mexico. Nafta is helping AT & T entry into the Mexican Market, which has been dominated by global competitions such as Alcatel of France & Ericsson of Sweden.
2. Michael Yeng, Chairman of Esprit Asia Holding, learned that communication can help overcome resistance to change. Ying, in trying to integrate Esprit Asian and European operations, recognized major differences in the way they managed people and the business. The European Operation was nationalistic, Autocratic and had rigid structures, where as the Asian operation was more open minded and willing to learn. During visits with the European managers, Yeng communicated his common sense approach to problem solving and listened to the Europeans concerns. This communication helped the Europeans to be receptive to Yeng plan of merging into operations.
3. In 1981, partial deregulation of the banking industry led to major changes at Bank of America Corporation. Alternations in banking regulations, fierce competition in the industry and an unstable world economy led to serious problems in the company. In 1986, Bank of America was closing, payment of dividends on common stock had been suspended after November 1985, first interstate bank corporation was threatening a take over and regulators were insisting that Bank of America's deteriorating capital situation be rapidly corrected. In the years since 1986, Bank of America has made a dramatic turn around and has returned to profitability

through a planned program at management led change. The 5 fundamental steps took by bank of America were :-

1. Selected a management team of proven winners and spread the message that corporate survival depended on how well each was alone.
2. Reassessed the entire business and restructured the imagination of the bank and its approach to banking.
3. Focused on generating maximum value for share holders.
4. Managed business to produce immediate and positive results.
5. Communicated credibility, consistently and confidently both inside and outside the organization. In addition, Bank of America developed 2 strategic business objectives to guide the corporate restructuring.

   Through careful planning and implementation at a corporate wide plan for change and through careful attention to goals and it was able to successfully service a deteriorating situation and retake a leadership position in the banking industry.

4. **The Industrial Engineering Change :** An industrial engineer was assigned to an electronics assembly plant to make some method improvement on the assembly operation. They soon recognized that a new fixture might reduce labor costs by about 30 percent. He discussed the situation with the group leader and then with the supervisor. The group leader was indifferent, but the supervisor was interested and offered additional suggestions.

With the permission of the superior, he assigned one assembler to try the fixture. She was co-operative and enthusiastic, and on the first day exceeded the expected improvement of 30 present. When the group leader was shown the results at the end of the day, he assigned an assembler to try the fixture. She was co-operative and enthusiastic, and on the first day exceeded the expected improvement of 30 present. When the group leader had known the results at the end of the day, he claimed that this was one of the fastest workers in the department and that her results could not be generalized for the whole department.

The next day, the industrial engineer asked the supervisor for another operation to help prove the fixture. At this point the supervisor noted that the fixture did not include her ideas fully. The industrial engineer explained that he had misunderstood but that he would include the other suggestions in the next fixture built. The supervisor however contained to be negative about the fixture.

When the industrial engineer attempted to instruct the second woman the way he had instructed the first one, her reaction was negative in fact, when he stopped instructing her it seemed that the woman deliberately stalled as she used the fixture. She also made some negative comments about the fixture and asked the industrial engineer, if he felt he deserved his paycheck for this kind of work. At the end of the day, this woman's production was 10 percent normal production by the old method.

Conclusion

Change Management - Better, Faster Results

Introducing any new technology affects people's emotions and skills during the period of transition. Humans instinctively fear change that they do not understand or feel they cannot influence. Some may believe that their position in the firm is at risk or that the change will put them at a competitive disadvantage. Failing to attend to the "people" side of technology improvements can delay or wreck implementation of the new system. On the other hand, incorporating a change strategy into the project plan can help you to roll out the technology faster and to realize the productivity gains sooner. This chapter focused on three threshold challenges that project managers and change sponsors should consider before initiating any major changes to the firm's technology.

A change strategy is a high-level game plan for altering the organizational structure, work-processes, and behaviors of the people who comprise the organization in order to produce some desired result(s). One threshold challenge in formulating a change strategy is identifying the desired results. Even in the rare organization where its leadership clearly articulates expected results, perceptions of what is meant and what, exactly, needs to be improved vary with the roles and locations of people who comprise the organization. For instance, a senior partner of a law firm might think of the firm in terms of its capacity to add attorneys and develop new clients during the next year, while a legal secretary might think in terms of its capacity to produce documents and support individual attorneys in a predictable and professionally satisfying manner. Similarly, attorneys and managers in a satellite office might have significantly different needs and priorities than their counterparts in the firm's headquarters. The conclusions of each of these groups might differ, but they may be equally valid in their separate contexts. While consensus is often impractical and unnecessary at this stage, taking into account the needs and resistance of various groups and individuals can help the change sponsors to define results or goals that are both attainable and motivating.

A second, related challenge before initiating change is assessing the organization's state of readiness for change. "Readiness" in this context refers to the organization's capacity and willingness to make the desired change. This is determined by much more than the intentions of the Managing Partner or CEO. Firm culture, ingrained habits, client demands, communications concerning the change, and many other factors are strong influences on whether lawyers and other employees will accept the change and integrate it to produce the desired results. To get at these influences and channel them to work for change, successful change managers in a wide range of industries have developed a variety of methods and tools, including the following:

- Quantitative analysis of needs, concerns, expectations, and preferences through questionnaires administered to all employees or representative samples.
- Qualitative analysis of same via interviews or focus groups, or both.
- Work-flow mapping and analysis.
- On-site observation studies to examine work practices and cultural patterns.

While some of these may not seem applicable to the relatively small scale of some law firms, they illustrate the serious approach taken by many organizations to understand and address the underlying drivers of behavior and productivity. Just talking with an experienced and neutral outsider often stimulates employees to spontaneously discover (or rediscover) solutions to a wide variety of productivity and morale issues. The value of the outside consultant is not providing "the answer," but instead asking the right question and providing a neutral sounding board to generate an executable solution.

The results of the readiness assessment enable the project manager to build a more realistic and effective change management plan. The intensity and rate of change can be adjusted to what is likely to be accepted and adapted. It also allows more accurate planning and delivery of initial training and continued education. Finally, the participation of attorneys, administrators, and other employees develops in them an understanding of the change and change process and a sense of influence over the change that empowers them to integrate it and produce the desired results.

A third threshold consideration is communication planning. Lawyers know well the power of "framing the argument" to conduct the negotiation or dispute within a context that is logically related to the intended conclusion. Similarly, communications by the change sponsors (including everything they say and do, or not) can be framed in a manner that supports the desired outcome. Conversely, communicating without forethought can inadvertently raise expectations or fears that are unrealistic and counterproductive. Therefore, change sponsors and project managers should carefully plan what, how, and when the proposed change and change management process will be communicated to those who will be affected by it. This does not mean being secretive. On the contrary, it means developing in the change team a common understanding on the key messages they should be consistently and openly transmitting.

In conclusion, a change management plan cannot guarantee that all employees will readily accept the change and adapt their ways of working. It can, however, help set realistic, achievable goals and then help achieve the desired results much sooner. It does that by addressing the underlying needs of the "critical mass" of people in the firm and encouraging and empowering them to realize the results by removing structural, procedural, and cultural barriers.

References and Further Reading

1. Adrian Thornhill, et. al. (2000), Managing Change – A Human Resource Strategy Approach, Prentice Hall.
2. Drucker. P. et. al. (1995) – Managing in a Time of Great Change.
3. Kaila H.L. (2003). Human Factors in Organisational Management. Mumbai: Himalaya Publishing House.
4. Martin J., Organizational Behaviour, An International Thomson Publishing Company.
5. Muchinsky. P. Psychology applied to work, Wadsworth Thomson Publishers.
6. Newstrom. J. , Davis. K. Organizational Behaviour, Tata Mc-Graw Hill Publishing Co. Ltd.
7. Parveen S. (1997) – Organizational Behaviour, Mumbai: SMS Publishers.
8. Paul H. et. al. (2001) – Management of Organizational Behaviour, New Delhi, Prentice Hall of India Pvt. Ltd.
9. Robbins. S. Organizational Behaviour, Prentice Hall India.
10. Steward. J. (1996), Managing Change through Training & Development, Kogan Publishers.

14

Total Quality Management (TQM)

In today's global competitive market place, the demands of customers are forever increasing as they require improved quality of products and services but are prepared to pay less for their requirements. Continuous improvement in total business activities with a focus on the customer throughout the entire organization is one of the main means by which companies meet these demands.

Quality: "Quality is now a familiar word, however a variety of interpretations are placed on its use and meaning". Many people say that they know what is meant by quality; they typically claim, 'I know it when I see it' (i.e. quality by feel, taste, smell) This simple statement, and the interpretations of quality made by lay people, marks the need to define quality in an operational manner. Infact, quality as a concept is quite difficult for many people to grasp and understand, and much confusion and myth surround it.

In a linguistic sense, quality originates from the Latin word 'qualis', which means 'such as the thing really is'. There is an international definition of quality: 'Totality of characteristics of an entity that bears on its ability to satisfy stated and implied needs'.

Meaning : Competitive environments demand a better quality product or service at lower rates. Only those organizations which manage productivity and quality on a continuous basis are in a position to compete in increasingly global market place. The impact of poor quality on any organization is graphically presented.

Quality is a customer's determination and not manufacturer's or marketer's determination. The modern view of quality is that products should totally satisfy the customer's needs and expectations in every respect on a continuous basis. This new concept of quality calls for :

- Well-designed product with functional perfection, first time right;
- Providing satisfaction beyond customer's expectation;
- Excellence in service;
- Absolute empathy with customer;

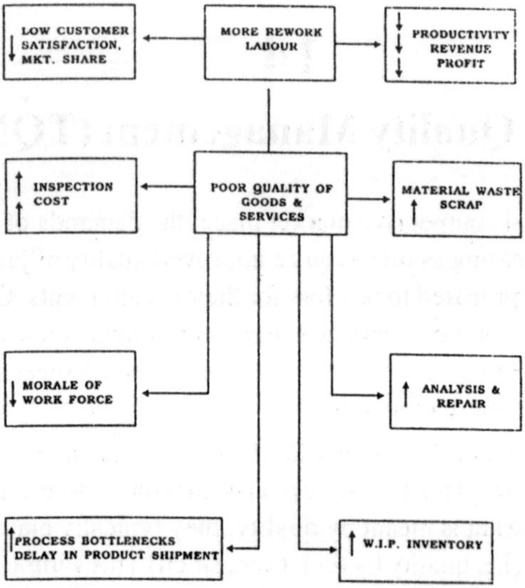

Several definitions of quality exist, depending upon the recognition of need to be included in the assessment of quality – the true requirement of customer's needs and expectations. There are several definitions of quality by experts and authors on quality :

Definitions of Quality

'Fitness for purpose or use' ——— Juran

'Quality is conformance to requirements' ——— Crosby

'Total composite of product and service characteristics of marketing, engineering, manufacturing and maintenance through which the product and service in use will meet the expectation by the consumer'——— Feigenbaum

'Quality should be aimed at the needs of the consumer, present and future' — Deming

'Quality is the degree of excellence at an acceptable price and control of variability at an acceptable cost' ——— Broh

'The totality of features and characteristics of a product or service that bear on its ability to satisfy stated or implied needs' ——— ISO 8402: Quality Vocabulary

Origin of TQM

Developed in Japan: Total Quality Management is a new technique developed first in Japan in the 1960's. Japanese were the first to enlarge these principles and use them to corporate strategy. The idea of involving all employees, not just quality control staff and management in quality control, was made popular first in Japan. Japanese organizations believe in total quality control. In Japan, the idea of quality circle was further extended to another concept called total quality management. Now TQM has gained popularity all over the world.

Contribution of Deming and Juran: The credit of introducing quality revolution in Japan goes to two Americans, Dr. W. Edwards Deming and Dr. J.M. Juran, both 'gurus' of Japanese in the field of quality management. It is interesting to note that they became heroes in Japan long before America realized their importance.

Commitment to Quality : Under the influence of Juran and Deming, commitment to quality became a part of every plant's culture. This commitment was reinforced by the introduction of quality circle for improving quality and reducing costs. This deeply embedded commitment to quality is known as total quality management (TQM). The Deming Prize is the highest TQM award in Japan and is given to most respected and successful corporations. Toyota and Matsushita are the winners of highest TQM awards in Japan.

Meaning of Total Quality Management

Total quality management is a comprehensive concept and not related only to the quality of goods and services. TQM is a preventive approach and not a corrective one. It aims at producing best possible product and service through regular innovation by doing right things every time.

The concept of TQM is closely related to the concept of quality circles. They have made substantial contribution in making Japanese industries quality and cost conscious. Quality circles create proper background for the concept of total quality management.

Total quality management reflects the culture of an organization. It indicates consumer-oriented management philosophy. It is a commitment to quality by all managers and workers. TQM is a philosophy for achieving customer satisfaction, which involves all – managers, employees and users. It is management by commitment and not management by control.

According to John Gilbert, Total Quality Management is "A process designed to focus on customer expectations, preventing problems, building commitment to quality in the workforce and promoting open decision-making."

Total Quality is defined as, "..... a people-focused management system that aims at continual increase in customer satisfaction at continually lower cost. TQ is a total system approach (not a separate area of programme), and an integral part of high level strategy. It works horizontally across functions and departments, involving all employees, top to bottom, and extends backwards and forwards to include the supply chain and customer chain."

Total Quality Management (TQM) is a continuous process of improvement for individuals, groups of people and total organization. Unlike other methods, TQM is the concentrated focus on continuous improvement. TQM is about changing the way things are done within the organisation's life time. People, must know what to do, how to do it, have the right methods to do it, and be able to measure the improvement of the process and current level of achievement in order to improve the process.

Advantages /Need /Importance or Is TQM the Need of the day ? Reasons :

Satisfaction to Customers : The main aim of TQM is to provide satisfaction and welfare to the customers. It satisfies the needs and expectations of the customers. It pays special attention to the customers. TQM provides the best quality goods and services to the consumers. It provides them with zero defect goods. TQM does not make profit by exploiting the customers.

Reduction in Customer Complaints : TQM results in less or no complaints from the customer. This is because TQM helps to produce a very good quality product. TQM makes a zero defect product. TQM is never satisfied with the quality of the product. It goes on improving the quality. Therefore, the customer is always happy. So he does not complain.

Increases Goodwill : TQM helps the company to produce good quality goods at low prices. It continuously tries to improve quality and to reduce costs. It tries to give maximum satisfaction and welfare to the customers. Therefore, the name, image and reputation of the company increases. This results in higher goodwill.

Reduces Internal Rejection : TQM improves the Quality. Quality improvement reduces the rate of internal rejections. That is, very less products are rejected by the Internal Quality Control department.

Better Facilities to Employees : TQM results in higher profits for the company. These profits are used to provide better facilities to the employees. So, the employees get higher salaries, better working conditions, canteen facilities, transport facilities, recreation facilities, etc. So, TQM also results in Employee Satisfaction.

Helps to Face Competition : TQM helps the company to produce a good quality product at low cost. It helps the company to increase its market share. It also helps the company to face both national and international competition. It helps the company to become a global leader. Japan is a global leader in so many products only because of TQM.

Motivates the Employees : TQM motivates the employees to work willingly and efficiently. It motivates them to give suggestions about quality improvement, wastage elimination, cost reduction, etc. The employee who gives the best suggestion is rewarded. So, TQM motivates the employees by giving them recognition and rewards. It gives them cash awards, merit certificates, invitations to lunches and dinners, promotions, higher salary, higher status, etc. All this motivates the employee to give their best for the company.

Expansion and Diversification : TQM increases the name, image and reputation of the company. This helps the company to become bigger. It can introduce new products in the market. The satisfied customer will purchase these new products. So, TQM helps the company to expand and diversify.

Features of TQM

Stress on Quality Management: In TQM, collective efforts are made for improving quality of goods and services to give higher satisfaction to consumers. Quality improvement is also useful for facing market competition and for earning market reputation. TQM covers all functions, activities and people who are instrumental for raising the competitiveness of an enterprise.

Continuous Process : TQM is a continuous process as there is an ample scope for using new methods and techniques for improvement in the quality standards and performance. "Steal ideas constantly and shamelessly" is the rule in TQM. Implementation of innovative ideas or taking benefit of new opportunities is an integral aspect of TQM. In fact, TQM is a never-ending quest for achieving new levels of performance.

Stress on Quality Assurance System: The aim of TQM is to give maximum satisfaction to consumers by providing goods, which are best in quality (zero defects). The present ISO 9000 series is a set of well-recognised standards for quality assurance system.

Linkage of Quality and Productivity: The TQM technique is useful for improving quality as well as productivity. The methods used in TQM programmes (e.g., zero defect production and making all employees responsible for quality maintenance and improvement) bring quality improvement as well as yield higher productivity. Similarly, the TQM programme creates a feeling of participation among the employees. There is positive improvement in the morale and approach of employees.

Gradual Process: Introduction of TQM is a gradual process. It is self-improvement and group improvement programme through team building. A mental revolution among the employees is required for the execution of TQM. However, such change in the mental make-up of managers and employees is time-consuming. This suggests that TQM is a gradual process and not a timebound programme. There are, in fact, four broad phases in the introduction of TQM. These are : (a) Awareness Phase, (b) Planning Phase, (c) Implementation Phase, and (d) Institutional Phase.

Focus on Customers : Focus on customers is the central idea of TQM. It aims at producing goods as per the expectations of consumers and supplying them at fair prices. Consumer satisfaction is the base around which TQM concept moves. Customers are the source of all the revenue that flows through the corporation. Their satisfaction is essential to keep the money flowing especially in an open market where competitors are wooing them. According to British Quality Association (BQA), TQM is a corporate business management philosophy, which recognized that customer's needs and business goals are inseparable.

Employees Involvement : TQM is possible only through participative management. Under TQM, employees will be motivated to participate actively in the proccss of quality improvement through incentives, rewards and recognition. TQM creates teamwork where workers are trained and motivated properly.

Formation of Quality Improvement teams : A cornerstone of TQM is the team building that leads to commitment to improvement. There are several types of such teams such as quality steering teams, corrective action teams and so on. Special importance is given to teamwork in TQM.

Management's Involvement : TQM is a systems approach in managing business and improving overall performance. It needs total commitment from the top management to provide viable leadership to the whole approach. Top level management has to take number of initiatives in order to start the process of TQM. In fact, TQM cannot have a good take off without total commitment of CEO and other senior executives. (Draw a pyramid chart)

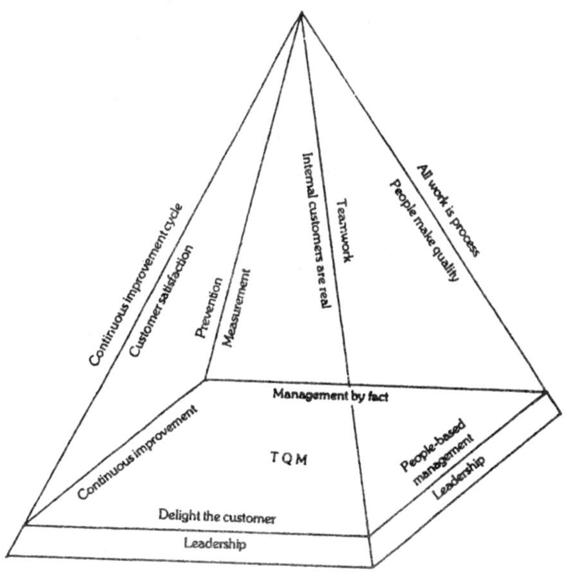

Elements /Approach Plan for TQM

Role of Top Management Personnel : The success of TQM largely depends on personal initiative shown by top management personnel. They must lead by example. This will motive the employees. Employees look forward to their superiors to provide right guidance and direction. When employees know that their bosses do not make any compromise on quality matters, they tend to become careful in providing best quality of work.

Management of Change : Traditionally, Indian business is run as per the whims and desire of the owners of the business. TQM is a change. Some employees who have creativity, they are encouraged to display their caliber.

Zero Defects : TQM puts emphasis on preventive action rather than corrective action. Defects are created because of human and mechanical malfunctioning. When human and mechanical errors are controlled, it is possible to attain zero defects production.

Education and Training : There are several additions and deletions made in TQM. Management should impart regular education to all the employees. Training improves efficiency and makes employees confident and competent.

Joint decision–Making : success of TQM depends on mass participation. Inter–departmental participation brings about all round progress, which is key to the success of TQM.

Objective Treatment : Employees should not be treated like a cog in a machine. Employees should be made to feel that they are part and parcel of the organization. Objective treatment to employees will guarantee success of TQM.

Recognition and Rewards : Recognition and rewards are a good combination providing psychological and financial benefits. Recognition is provided through compliments, appreciation for efforts, certificate of merit, letter of thanks etc. Rewards are mostly monetary benefits. TQM combines recognition and rewards focusing on quality improvement.

Performance Feedback : Periodic performance evaluation keeps the managers and subordinates alert. Such evaluation indicates where they stand vis-à-vis other colleagues.

Bench Marking : This element defines the best features of the competitor's products. Efforts are made to adopt those features in one's products.

Reduced Inventory : Just–in–time inventory management became popular during early 1970's in Japan. It was established that as inventories grew smaller, quality improved. Improvement of quality depends on having right quality of inventory, which is one of the elements of TQM.

Limitations of TQM

Slow Moving Process : TQM is a slow moving process. It requires total change in the outlook of management and employees. Its benefits will be available only after a long period. Naturally, the TQM is not useful for solving immediate problems.

Difficulties in the Implementation of TQM : The implementation of TQM is not easy / quick particularly in developing countries due to the unfavorable attitude of management and employees. For the introduction of TQM, a total charge in organizational culture, shifting of responsibility by management and continuous participation of employees in the quality improvement process are required. This is rather difficult in many developing countries including India.

Limited Initiative from Employees : Participative management is necessary for the introduction of TQM. In India, workers and trade unions show limited interest in quality improvement. Even adequate training facilities are not provided to workers. This creates difficulties in the introduction of TQM.

Position of TQM

TQM–Neglected Area of Management for Long : For a very long time, quality was a neglected area of production management in India. This was natural as everything produced had ready customer in the market. One of the common questions of Indian businessman was, how low may we go in quality without losing customers ?

Present Position of TQM : India is now entering the global markets. Economic reforms and liberal economic policies of the government are encouraging. In this context, quality management has special significance. Quality management is the only philosophy, which can help Indian Industries in promoting exports. For this, the concepts of quality circle and TQM must be used purposefully in all aspects of Indian economy particularly in the industrial field.

Indian industries can face competition in the world markets only by improving quality and reducing costs. The benefit of current liberal economic policy needs to be taken seriously for raising quality and competitive capacity of Indian industries.

It is rightly said that quality is the price for entry into global markets and also for survival in the global market. To meet the challenges created by globalization of Indian economy, new initiatives will have to be taken in the industrial sector. One such initiative is total quality management programme.

Application of TQM Technique : Several Indian companies are taking steps to improve quality beginning with company–wide training programmes. However, quality improvement is difficult unless we reform our attitude as TQM is all about attitude. The Confederation of Indian Industry (CII) is playing a major role in spreading the message of total quality management in the industrial and service sectors in India. The need of TQM programme is accepted and many Indian companies are taking positive steps in the execution of TQM programmes. Such companies include TELCO, TISCO, SAIL, Bajaj Auto, Godrej, L & T and so on. Along with industrial sector, total quality management is equally important in the service sector in India. In addition, international standards may be made applicable to services in the near future. Such services include hospitality service, technical and professional services, maintenance services and utilities. The TQM concept should be introduced to this sector for providing better service to customers and for overall prosperity.

Problems of Implementation of TQM

Conservative Outlook : Conservative, traditional and profit – oriented outlook and approach are common to Indian business. In addition, there is lack of consumer–focus in business. Indian business community is not willing to adopt changes taking place in the environment. This creates problem in implementation of TQM in Indian industries.

Unsound Relations : Absence of cordial labour management relations in many industrial enterprises creates problems in implementation of TQM. Effective use of TQM presupposes presence of conflict–free relations between employers and employees.

Unions Non-supportive attitude : Negative approach of trade unions and their leaders as regards TQM techniques. Limited interest and initiative of trade unions in regard to quality control, quality improvement and TQM. Mostly unions are politically – oriented. They are more interested in achieving their political objectives and in the process interest of workers suffer.

Inadequate Training : Inadequate training facilities to employees and lack of good trainers is a common feature of Indian business. Training results in dramatic effect on the skill and knowledge of employees. The success of TQM in Indian business is restricted because of lack of training.

Lack of Incentives : There is absence of liberal incentives to employees and failure of management to appreciate good work. Good work done by workers is not recognised by the management instantly. This makes workers disheartened. Their involvement to make TQM successful remains superfluous.

Lack of Communication : There is an ineffective communication with employees and low morale of employees. Lack of communication widens the gap between management and employees. TQM cannot succeed unless there is an adequate communication between all the parties involved.

Domestic Environment : TQM cannot succeed in India unless it is widely supported and adopted by the government and customers. Incidentally, government does not consider TQM on priority basis. There is negligence of TQM by the government. Customers are price–minded and not quality–minded. Because of this typical situation, implementation of TQM has become difficult.

Limited Participation : There is limited efforts on part of management for introduction of participative management at the business unit level. Most of the managements are opposed to introduction of participative management. TQM is a form of participative management.

Lack of Teamwork : In order to make TQM effective, it is necessary to create teamwork. At times, management wants to weaken the trade unions and follows the policy of divide and rule.

Indifference of Top Management : In addition, there is lack of top management leadership and participation in TQM programme. The top management maintains the position of supremacy and treat employees as their servants. Moreover, feedback from employees is not taken seriously.

Making TQM Popular in Industries

The Traditional Approach to Quality Should be Given Up : The traditional approach to quality has to be changed. We have to accept quality standards, which are best in the international market and try to reach that level.

The Management Style Must Change : The management style needs to be open and transparent. Our management style continues to be somewhat like the game of 'Three cards' where everyone keeps the cards close to his chest. It is necessary to have open "flush" system in preference to the blind game.

Dissemination of Accurate Data : For effective TQM, accurate data should be provided to all. Managers must learn to have free communication if they want to bring out the best in their people. Inaccurate data do more harm to the future prospects of the company.

Participative Management : The practice of TQM calls for a participative style of management. All problems should be discussed with facts and figures. This facilitates best solutions. Such approach to problem solving facilitates introduction of TQM.

Provision of Education and Training : Education and training are integral components of TQM. For the introduction of TQM programme, managers and workers should be given training regarding quality awareness, team building, time management and effective delegation. This will improve the quality of people, which is essential for the introduction of TQM. It is rightly said that "TQM begins with Education and ends with Education."

Provision of Recognition and Rewards : Employees should be given full freedom to express their suggestions for quality improvement, cost reduction and elimination of wastages. Those who take keen interest in these aspects through useful suggestions and participation should be rewarded suitably.

Positive Change in Attitude of Workers and Unions : For introduction of TQM, the attitude of employees and their unions must change considerably. To say that quality is management's problem is not favourable to TQM process. Similarly, the argument that we are not going to participate in TQM programme as we are not going to get direct monetary benefit must be given up by the workers and their unions.

Importance of Lower Level Employees : It is necessary to give more attention to the requirements of employees working in different departments. This is necessary for raising quality. For example, Sony furnished their factories beforc their offices. The present attitude of managements in this regard must change.

Collective Approach : Quality flourishes if all players are offered even playing surfaces. 'Do as decided' is a rule that everyone in the company has to follow. Such collective approach is necessary for the success of TQM.

Conclusion

TQM is to give maximum satisfaction to the customers. It tries to improve the quality of goods and services. It tries to produce goods with zero defects. TQM believes in preventing mistakes rather finding out mistakes. The management and the employees must come together and try to improve the quality. If not, TQM will fail.

TQM believes in giving maximum satisfaction to the customers. IT provides them with the best quality of goods and services at low cost. According to TQM, if the customers are not satisfied, they will go to the competitors.

TQM also improves the total performance in the organization. It reduces wastage. It reduces cost. It also increases productivity and profitability. TQM increases profits by improving the performance of the employees.

References and Further Reading

1. Barrie.G.Dale and Gary.L.cooper and Adrian aitkinson, 2001, Continuous Improvements in Managing Quality and Human Resource. 1st edition, Mumbai.
2. N.G.Kale and Mehtab ahmed, Management and human resource development. 9th edition, Manisha publication, mumbai.
3. Parag diwan, 1995, A manager's guide to TQM and ISO 9000, Deep and Deep Publications, New Delhi.

15

Organizational Behaviour-Emerging Reality for Workplace Revolution

Introduction

"Organizational Behaviour is a human tool of extraordinary versatility".

—*Pradip Khandwalla.*

Organizational Behaviour has a long powerful contributor to each business success. It has become a very important tool to meet the fast pace of the world. The study of Organizational Behaviour facilitates to meet the outcome of upcoming of industrial revolution such as merger, downsizing, and corporate reorganization and so on. In this way it remains the ultimate prize to employer and employee.

Organizational Behaviour is nothing but the outcome of interaction between. Organizational policy, rules, culture, values with that of individuals ethic, values, and behaviour which results in employee and employer satisfaction and benefit or otherwise it causes employee and employer dissatisfaction and losses to both.

In this chapter we are going to see how Organizational Behaviour is important to meet the current trends for workplace revolution with reference to Indian context.

Definitions of Orgnizatiional Behaviour

There are many definition of the organizational behaviour, few worth quoting are as follows: -

"Organizational behaviour is the study and application of knowledge about how people act within organizations. It is a human tool for human benefit. It applies broadly to the behaviour of people in all types of organizations such as business, school and service organization." —Keith Davis 1985

"Organizational behaviour is directly concerned with the understanding, prediction, and control of human behaviour in organization." —Fred Luthans 1985.

"It is a field study that investigate the impact that individual, group, structure have on behaviour within organizations for the purpose of applying such knowledge towards improving an organization's effectiveness." — Stephen Robbins, 2001

"Organizational behaviour is the study of organizational components and their impact on human behaviour and organizational performances. Such study can benefit from various behavioural and social sciences." —Chung and Leon, 1981

"Organizational behaviour means the study of the behaviour of individual and groups in organization, and organizations themselves, as they act and interact to attain desired outcome."

— H. Bobbitt Jr., 1978.

All of these definitions emphasise on three main features, viz:

1. Organizational behavior is the study of human behaviour;
2. The study is about behaviour in organizations; and
3. Knowledge about human behaviour would be useful in improving organizations effectiveness.

An analysis of definition reveals that Organizational behaviour is the study of human behaviour in organizations; the interface between human behaviour and the organizations itself. Organizational behaviour is concerned specifically with employment related situation and it mainly focuse on behaviour related to job, work, absenteeism, turnover, productivity, human performance, management, quality of work-life, organizational stress and so on.

Fundamental Concept of Oraganaizational Behaviour

Organizational behaviour is based on a few fundamental concepts that revolve around the nature of people and organizations.

The following are the features on which the organizational behaviour is based

- There are differences between individuals in physique, intelligence, personality, coping, mechanisms etc.
- A whole person means when individual is hired along with his skill he carries his social background- likes, dislikes, pride and prejudices- are also hired.
- Behavior of an individual is caused.
- An individual has dignity.
- Mutuality of interest among organizational members mean organization needs people and people need organization.
- Organizations are social system.
- Holistic organizational behavior, it implies the whole person, whole group, whole organization, and whole social system.

Importance of Organizational Behaviour

1 It helps an individual to understand himself and others better. Hence it improves the interpersonal relationship considerably.

2. Organizational behavior helps to understand management when and how to motivate employee.
3. It will be useful to maintain cordial industrial relationship, means relationship between organization and employee. It also helps to know the cause of problem, predict its course of action and control its consequences.
4. The field of organizational behavior serves as the basis for modern human resources management.
5. The subject of organizational behavior is useful in the field of marketing.
6. An organizational behavior predicts the human and organizational behavior and applies it in some meaningful way to make organizations more effective.
7. Finally, organizational behaviour is a discipline that enables a manager to motivate his subordinate towards higher productivity and better results.

Organizational Behaviour an Emerging Reality for Workplace Revolution

The following are the areas of workplace revolution in which organizational behavior can play effective role.

1. Golbalization.
2. Work-force Diversity.
3. Changing Demographics of Work-force
4. Changed Employee Expectation
5. Empowering People
6. Corporate Reorganization
7. Improving Quality and Productivity
8. Stimulating Innovation and Change.
9. Improving Ethical Behavior

All these factors lead to organizational effectiveness and increasing its productivity.

Globalization

Growing internationalizations of business and application GATT act has its impact on people management. The management is required to cope with its problem of unfamiliar laws, language, practice, competitors, attitude, management style, work ethics and more. Hence personnel function, hiring, training, compensating, maintaining, firing and the alike require global perspective. To face this challenge, the management must be flexible and proactive. Being flexible and proactive the management can make significant contribution to company's growth. All these can be achieved by qualified and best people.

The internalization of business or globalization present four challenges to survive as follows

(a) It requires increasing number of managers and professionals;

(b) It emphasise on certain qualities and competency (skill);

(c) Strong teamwork devoted to one mission;

(d) Management of career in the context of globalization gives many companies peculiar difficulties.

Globalization affects a manager's people skill in at least two ways. First, a manager require frequently to do foreign assignments or he may be transferred to operate division subsidiary in other country. In such situation a manager has to manage a workforce that is likely to be very different in needs, aspiration and attitudes from those he is used to back home. Secondly, what is motivating him may not be motivating them and a manager may find difficult to cope with this situation in the absence of peers, family and so on.

In this context organizational behavior explains to work effectively with these people, you will need to understand their culture, how has its shaped them, and how to adapt your management style to their differences.

The following descriptions of International Business trends will explain the importance of organizational behavior in context of international management.

More and more companies big and small, are entering international market place. Infosys, a Bangalore based company for example, is earning 75% of its sales from overseas markets. Business transactions are also becoming more and more blurred across national boundaries. Ford owns 25% of Mazda, GM and Toyota have joint venture in California, Honda and British sterling have one worldwide. Sooner, some of these MNC's lose their identity and become truly global corporations.

Secondly, Unification of Germany, emergence of single European market, emergence of WTO and movement of the Eastern block towards a free–market economy, will provide new opportunities and challenges to business in the years to come. It is therefore necessary to understand the basics of organizational behavior and the dynamics of international management.

Work-force Diversity

One of the important and broad based challenges currently facing organizations is adapting people who are different, and the work-force diversity describes and provides a solution on this situation. Work-force diversity addresses the differences among people within given countries. Workforce diversity means organizations are becoming more heterogeneous in terms of gender, race, and ethnicity. It includes women, physically disabled, gay and lesbians, Asian, American. Managers in Canada, Australia, have to adjust large influxes of Asian workers.

Historically, there are two approaches to the culture differences –

1. Melting pot conception where culture differences are homogenized and an individuals gets along to adjust to their culture differences as time passes

2. Multiculturalism conception, this approach accepts the presence of cultural differences and proposes to improve relationship by teaching people to appreciate the culture of others.

Organizational behavior suggest the need of cultural diversity training- to the individual assigned to an international position ; in order to reduce the relatively high failure rate of manager in such assignments. It also suggests of including one's spouse and other family members in cross-cultural training to preview of their new environment. However the failure of international assignment has little to do with employee's technical skill; it's largely concerned with host's country geography, political system, history, religion, custom, and habits. Thus cultural diversity training mainly emphasise on increasing awareness of different-ness as people.

Changing in Work-force Demography

The major challenge from demographics of workforce relates to the dual-career couple, who are pursuing professional careers. Organizations have been accustomed to using job and physical relocation as important means of development of talent. The increasing number of dual career professional limits the individual flexibility in accepting role-differentiating assignment and may hinder organizational flexibility in acquiring and developing talent.

Another change in workforce demography relates to the growing number of employees who are young. People who join to fill vacancies are fresh graduate or diploma holder. These personal needs are to be handled with case. Organizational behavior suggests the need of mentoring to these people in order to handle the experience and expertise to young people.

Increasing number of working mothers and steadily decline of blue collar employee giving a place for the-white collar employees are the other demographic changes. These developments have their own implication in personnel management in organizations.

Changed Employee Expectations

The early part of the 19th century is significant because it was during this period that the industrial revolution took place that resulted in the total transformation of then industrial environment. Prior to the 19th century the plight of an average worker was miserable. He had to work under the inhumane condition, as he had no option. He had to live.

Then came the industrial revolution which brought about materialism, discipline, monotony, boredom, job displacement, impersonality, work interdependence and related behavioral phenomenon. However the industrial revolution leads to potential improvement. Industry created surplus of goods and knowledge that eventually gave workers increased wages, shorter hours, and more work satisfaction. In western world it came in view of the Robert Owen work when he refused to employ the young children.

In India around this time, J.N.Tata took special interest in the welfare of his workers. But ideas of these personalities led to more paternalistic, do-good-approach than to genuine recognition of the importance of people at work. This a challenge to the Organizational behavioral filed.

Empowering People

Change in industrial revolution leads to the change in employee expectation and attitude. Traditional allurements such as job-security, attractive remuneration, housing.

Employee demands empowerment and exact equality of status with management. Expectation of equality breaks up the traditional relationship between employees top to bottom.

Secondly, there is a increasing need and demand of flexi-time and opportunity to work at home. Alvin Toffler estimates that the information revolution will shift the million of jobs out of the factories and offices and to back home. This is precisely what has happened at Veri-fone, Bangalore. All the 100 employees of the transaction-solution company are used to work without secretaries, very little paper work and just three organizational levels. All have computer at home, and link to the offices and their customers.

The firm practices flexi-time, managers manage their own time, as they deliver.

They are turning their home into surrogate office. Employee loses exclusivity and freedom. The pleasure of spending at least Sunday with families is lost. Any time a message can be faxed and he/she may be required, employees virtually become a bounded laborer, chained to the companies 24 hours, 365 days in a year.

Also, today's employee demand better treatment, challenging jobs and career advancement. For instances- union of Otis, Hindustan Lever, ICI, Blue star, Central Bank.

Hence, it is the necessity of today's manager to redraw the profile of the worker and discover new method of hiring, training, remuneration and motivating employees.

Changed Employer View and Expectation

Changed in employee expectation leads to the change in employer expectation and views about the employees. The employers not only expect a hard work from their employees but also active participation in increasing productivity, more commitment, various suggestion and innovation and creation. The employer thinks employees have capability and strength to achieve a goal created by company and hence emphasise on following employee development programmes.

(A) Improving People Skill and Empowering People : Recently many organizations have emphasised on developing people skill through introducing various training programmes, also the organizations are giving importance on empowering employees. Empowering people means putting employees in charge of what they do. Empowerment results in redefining jobs, both in the shop-floor as well as in board-room. As a workman is given more control over their jobs, a whole class of supervisor becomes redundant as there shall be no need for them. Nowadays, managers are being called as coach, adviser, or facilitators and workman are being called as associates.

(B) Helping Employees Balance Work/Life Concepts : A number of forces have contributed to blurring the lines between employees' Work life and personal life. First, the creation of global organization means the world never sleeps. At any time, any day you would need.

Second, communication allows people to do their work at home, this leads employees to put more hours at work and cause no freedom and enjoyment.

Third, organization asking employees to put more at work.

Finally, fewer families have a single bred winner. Today's married employees are playing a role of dual career couple role. This makes increasingly difficult for married employees to find a full commitment to home, spouse, children, parents and friends.

Employees are increasingly recognized that work is squeezing out personal lives and they are not happy about it. In addition next generation employee is likely to show similar concern. Organizations that don't help their people achieve a work life balance will find increasingly hard to retain and motivate most capable and potential employees.

The field of Organizational behavior offers a number of suggestions to guide manager in designing workplace and job that can deal with work life balance.

(C) Emphasis In Emotional Intelligence : Emotional intelligence has been defined as the "mental ability we are born with which gives us our emotional sensitivity and our potential for emotional sensitivity and our potential for emotional learning management skill which can help us maximize our long term health, happiness and survival."

In organizations Emotional Intelligence (EI) has taken a pivotal place in strategy formulation for business performance improvement. EI provides a structured pathway to improve the employees' self development, self-management, and the way they interact with people and develop relationship. Higher EI leads to better leadership and interpersonal relationship, which, in turn, results in improved business performance.

On one hand, India's liberalization of its economy, privatization, globalization and thrust towards information technology is encouraging more and more MNCs to make investment in the country. Secondly to cope with the high speed of changes and increased stress in life, Recently, Cadbury and Cap Gemini Ernst and Young have started given importance to EI.

(D) Quality of Work Life Programmes (Qwl) : Quality of work life programmes have been designed by OD practitioners to create work situation that enhances employee's motivation, satisfaction and commitment factor that may contribute to high levels of organizational performance, collectively called quality of work life (QWL) programmes, these are designed to remove drudgery associated with any work situation-an attempt is to humanize the work place. There are two approaches to humanize the work place.

One such approach to improving QWL involves work restructuring–the processes of changing the way jobs are done to make more interesting to workers. It includes job- involvement and job enrichment.

Another approach to improving QWL is quality circle (QCL). These are small group of employees who meet regularly on voluntary basis to identify and solve problems related to quality of the work they perform, a condition under which they perform their jobs. To help them work effectively, member in QWL receives training in problem solving.

QWL programmes benefit organization in at least three ways. The most direct benefit is increased job satisfaction, organizational commitment, and reduced turnover among workforce. A second benefit is increased productivity. Finally, organizations stand to gain in the form of profitability and goal attainment.

Organizational behavior provides an effective strategy for implementing the QWL programmes and helps in removing the constraint in adopting QWL programme.

(E) Employee Assistance Programme : The success of implementing Employee Assistance Programme (EAP) largely depends upon the Organizational behavior. EAP is more defined as a company sponsored programme designed to assist employees with personal problem due to substance abuse, domestic problem, financial crisis and other psychiatric and medical problem. (Byars and Rue, 1987). The central goal of EAP is to impact the well being of employees. The benefits that organization acquires through the implementation of EAP are in terms of a cost effectiveness, compatibility to management goals, improved labor management relations and enhanced corporate image.

Some of the Indian companies that both in public and private sector have adopted EAP are Bharat Electricals limited, Larsen and Tubro (Powai Plant); Madura Coats Ltd and few more.

In this way organizational behavior helps to maintain the balance between the changed employee and employer expectation.

Responding to Labor Shortage

Economic ups and down are difficult to predict. The world economy in the late 1990s is generally very tight and robust to the labor market. The demand for unskilled labour comes down and the demand for skilled labor is rising. Organizational behavior has a direct implication on this economical and political calamity.

Competition from MNCs and domestic industries has compelled many companies to restart the downsizing and flattening the structures. To survive in new revolution occurred it is necessary to adopt the flatter structures. A Business Today Survey (Dec.7-21, 1993) revealed that more than a dozens of biggest companies were busy in reducing the number of management grades, eliminating the layers, and rewarding the lines within their organizations. ITC, HLL, Godrej and Boyce, PG enterprise, Raymond Woolen Mills, Shaw Wallace, Ballarpur Industries and Crompton and Greaves are only some of the companies which have embarked on flattening exercise.

Reorganization is beneficial because they offer following benefits.

I. Increased growth opportunity for performers.

II. Faster decision making and market response.

III. Up-gradation of skill within ranks.

IV. Better internal communication and interaction.

V. Reduced manpower cost.

However the flattened structures have following pitfalls.

I. Reduced promotion chances for employees

II. Increased workload as layers gets trimmed.

III. Reduced morale during the transition phase.

IV. Increased training and development needs.

V. Rigorous manpower attrition

Coping with Temporariness

People in the earlier period were habituated to the stability and interrupted occasionally by short period of changes. On the other hand, managing today would be more accurately described as ongoing change, permanent change and temporariness. The actual job workers are performing in a state of flux; so the worker needs to update their knowledge and skill. Finally the organizations themselves are in a state of flux. They continually reorganize their various divisions, sell of poor performing business, downsizing operations, sub-contract service and so on.

Today's managers must learn to cope with temporariness. They have to learn to live with flexibility, spontaneity, and unpredictability. The study of organizational behavior can provide an important insight into helping better understand a work of a continual change, how to overcome the resistance of change, and how best to create an organizational culture that thrives on change.

Corporate Reorganization

The past three to four years brought us news about corporate merger, and massive reorganization to fend off hostile take over bids. It is difficult to imagine the circumstances that are a greater challenges to organizational behavior than the reorganization resulting from the acquisition, merger, take-over threat. The reorganization will have a impact on the organizational level as well the employee level. The employees of both taken-over as well as taking-over will have the anxious movement because of-

- Fear of job loss.
- Job changes including new role and assignment.
- Transfer to new geographic locations.
- Changes in remuneration and benefits.
- Changes in career possibility.
- Changes in organizational power, status and prestige.
- Staff changes including new peers, subordinate, and supervisor.
- Changes in corporate culture and loss of company identity.

Hence it is necessary to concern the management of human resources. Otherwise there are greater chances of failure of merger or it may have greater disastrous effect on employee and employer. For instance— Take-over of Poysha industries Ltd, by Tinplate Co., of India Ltd. in 1991 broken down in 1994.

Secondly, the merger between Procter and Gamble – Godrej failed due waste culture difference. Godrej was a "career company" where Procter and Gamble was a result oriented MBA bastion. Here Godrej found Procter and Gamble is a ruthless company and Procter and Gamble found difficult to work at slow pace and get frustrated.

Improving Quality and Productivity

As organizations are exposed to competition, managers are seriously thinking of improving the quality and productivity. For this purpose they emphasise on the programmes like TQM means total

Quality Management and Re-engineering programmes that require extensively employee involvement and teamwork.

Total Quality Management (TQM) is a philosophy of management that is inspired by the constant attainment of customer satisfaction through the continuous improvement of all the processes. Specifically TQM involves-

- Intense focus on the customer
- Active leadership
- Concern for the continual improvement
- A corporate culture
- Improvement in the quality of everything the organization does
- Accurate measurement of a statistical technique
- Recognition of suppliers
- Empowerment of employees

Re-engineering means radically rethinking and re-designing those processes by which we create the value for customer and do work. It requires manager to reconsider how work would be done and their organization structured if it starts from scratch.

To make this intervention successful, an organizational behavior helps manager to ensure people's participation and teamwork.

Stimulating Innovation and Changes

In today's competitive environment, organization must foster innovation and manage successful changes or if they are not flexible enough towards the changes they will become the candidate for extinction. Victory will go to the organization that will beat their competition to marketplace with a constant innovation and changes in their product and services. For instances- Domino's market strategy which is always ready for change in order to attract the customer.

Employees are the key to innovation and change. The challenge for manager is to stimulate the employee creativity and tolerance for change. The field of organizational behavior provides ideas and technique to help realize these goals.

It emphasises on teamwork and transformational leadership

- Recently almost every organization emphasised on teamwork in order to meet the changes organization wants to introduce and to reduce the resistance towards the new changes including merger, strategy, policy, adopt new culture and so on. In addition team environment constantly challenges teams to innovate and solve problems creatively. Organization improvements are certain to result.

Companies diverse as Titan, Tata Information System, Ltd ;(TISL), GE plastic India, Philips are empowering employees both front lines and bottom lines.

- **Transformational Leadership :** The current trend gives a lot of importance on the transformational leadership that implies a process whereby an individual attempts to elevates his or her consciousness so that various common place conflict and dualities begin at a higher level of synthesis. Transformational leadership attempts to change the whole organization from one "style" or "culture" to another. Transformational leadership has ultimate aim of raising the level of human conduct and ethical aspiration of both the leader and the led. The leaders' main thrust is to elevate, inspire and evangelize his followers to higher things in life.

  The late J.R.Tata comes under transformational leadership. His qualities of head and heart moved everybody who so ever came in contact with him.

Our economy is now thrown open for global competition. Foreign companies are entering our country in a large number. In order to maintain our own identity and sustain our ethos and at the same time to accept what is good for our business, we need more transformational leaders.

Improving Ethical Behavior

Managers and employees in Today's organization are always under pressure to register increased turnover, and strengthen the bottom lines. They therefore are tempted to cut the corners, bend rules, and restore to questionable practices.

The findings of KPMG's fraud survey for 1998 has estimated the loss of 200 corers in corporate India

Ethics is important for the organization due to following reasons.

- To correspond the basic human needs.

- To create the creditability with public.
- To bestow the management with creditability before employees.
- To improve the decision making process.
- No law can protect the society but ethics can.

Hence, it is the duty of every manager to create an ethically healthy environment for his or her employees, where they can do their work productively and with clear conscience.

Hence, Organization resorts to different ways to enforce ethical behavior on their employees. They draw elaborate codes of conduct and expect all employees to adhere to the guideline. They offer seminars, workshop, and conduct training programmes to improve ethical behaviors. Organizations provide in-house advisors who can be contacted for assistance in dealing with ethical issues. They are also providing protection to those who reveals internal unethical practices.

Conclusion

Organizational Behavior not only studies the human behavior in context of organization but also it studies the organizational culture, policy, structure, which have ultimate effect on organizational growth rate, production, profit or loss rate.

Organizational Behavior suggests the ways to create flexibility in order to meet the new challenges of forth coming years.

Organizational Behavior is the study of human behavior in organizations. Knowledge about human behavior is useful to improve organizational effectiveness.

The Organizational Behavior has a certain fundamental assumption like any other subject these are (i) individual difference, (ii) Whole person entity, (iii) Caused behavior, (iv) Human dignity, (v) mutuality of interest and, (vi) Holistic approach.

A study of Organizational Behavior is useful in more than one way. It enables an individual to understand human behaviors, which contribute to, improved interpersonal relations. The subject enables manager to motivate his employees for better results. It will help to improve the industrial relations. For successful marketing of goods, this subject is highly useful. To pursue one's career, organizational behavior is useful.

Organizational Behavior is helpful to meet the next million challenges such as work-force diversity, changed employee and employer expectation, globalization and corporate reorganizations.

Hence, we must welcome the future, remembering that soon it will be the past; and we must respect the past, remembering that it was once all that was humanly possible.

References and Further Reading

1. Byres S.S and Rue L.W.(1987), Human Resource Management, Homewood, IU: Irwin.
2. Effective Executive magazine. August 2004 pp. 33 to 39.
3. Fred Luthans, (2000) Organizational Behavior; 6th edition, New York McGraw Hill.
4. K. Aswathappa. (2000) Organizational Behavior, 5th revised edition. Himalaya publishing house.
5. Keith Davis and Newstrom, (1998) Human Behaviour at work Organizational Behaviour, New York: McGraw Hill, p-7.
6. Muchinsky, P (1998) Psychology Applied to Work: Industrial Psychology and Organizational Behaviour, Brooks Cole, Wadsworth, New Delhi.
7. Stephen P.Robbins. (2004) Organizational Behaviour 10th edition, Pearson Education, Inc.
8. Steven L.McShane and Mary AnnVon. (2003). Organizational Behaviour at workplace. Irwin Mc Graw—Hill, ISBN.
9. Walsh D.C. (1982). Employee Assistance Programs: Health and Society, Englewood Cliffs: Prentice Hall.

16

Organizational Survey Research

Introduction

"Human resource development has two main purposes to provide employees with greater opportunity to grow and succeed within a company and to strengthen management and professional teams at all organizational levels." —J.J. Famularo

Different types of development programmes are used to build varied skills of human resource. These include organizational development, career, employee and management development. (R.S. Dwivedi).

Many changes occur naturally as organizations pass through their life cycles.Generally these changes are initiated and directed by those who hold power, such as top management in a bureaucratic organization. Organizational development (OD), however, is a process of data collection, diagnosis, action, planning, intervention and change and evaluation of results applied to a whole organization or a large component of it. (Miner, 1992).

In the last 40 years, researchers as well practitioners have been interested in organizational development (OD), considered it as a response to accelerated changes in the technological, political and institutional dimensions of our societies. Although much discussions about the concept remains, OD has not disappeared from organization literature and practice and it is still considered as a part of those disciplines directed toward using behavioral science knowledge to assist organizations in dealing with the problems of change. (Anderson and Viswesvaran, 2002)

Organization development as an approach to planned change in organizations has been very widely used in recent years. Several writers have defined OD in different ways.

According to historic research by Clark and Krone (1972) the term organizational development was used for the first time in the 1960's, and in their article, the authors go over the main phases of the development of this discipline.

Bennis (1962) defines OD as "a response to change, a complex educational strategy intended to change the beliefs, attitudes, values and structure of organizations so they can better adapt.

Beckhard (1962) defines OD as "an effort (1) planned, (2) organization-wide, (3) managed from the top, (4) increase organization effectiveness and health through (5) planned interventions in the organization's processes, using behavioral science knowledge." (Neil, Ones, Viswesvaran, 2002).

Although there are several points of agreement in these definitions, special emphases are also reflected in them.

OD is a planned effort, initiated by process specialist(s) to help an organization develop its diagnostic skills, coping capabilities, linkage strategies in the form of temporary and semi permanent systems, and the culture of mutuality.

There are several important dimensions of OD contained in this definition. Some elaboration of these dimensions may be useful.

A planned Effort : OD is a planned effort, and therefore, requires a great deal of thinking and planning on the part of the OD export

Initiated by process specialists: The knowledge and skills of applied behavioral sciences are used in OD. An expert who has both the knowledge of applied behavioral science, and the skill of applying this knowledge in the organizational situations can therefore, properly initiate it. This effort may be taken over by the organizations in the long run, and internal resource in the organization can be developed to carry on this work. However, in the beginning mostly behavioral science consultancies from outside are used for this purpose.

Diagnostic Skills: The emphasis of OD is on planning change on the basis of data. As a part of OD, data are continuously collected about several aspects of the organization and its problems. OD tries to develop the capacity of organization to diagnose its problems. The emphasis of OD is not only on the diagnosis of the current problems, but also on developing these skills in the organization, so that it can use these skills to diagnose its problems as a part of its regular functioning.

Coping Capabilities: the main thrust of OD is on problem solving abilities of the organization. The organization helps to develop the ability to confront and cope with the problems it faces. OD certainly deals with the problems, the organization is facing currently, but does not stop there.

Linkage Strategies : OD emphasizes building of linkage between the individual goals and the organizational goals, amongst the individuals who work in the various roles, and amongst various groups which function in the organization. Problems of the organization can be resolved only through collaborative effort. One emphasis of OD, therefore, is on building such collaborative effort in the organization. This is done, amongst several other ways by setting up temporary systems, like task forces, and by creating structural changes which may ensure continuing collaboration in the organization.

Culture and Mutuality : OD is based on certain values which are important for the development of the organizations as open and proactive systems. The client organization should know it clearly that OD fosters a set of specific values. OD makes an effort to develop OCTAPAC culture. OCTAPAC stands for seven important values, which OD tries to develop in the organization. These are: openness, confrontation, trust, authenticity, pro-action, autonomy and collaboration. Openness implies confronting the problems rather than avoiding them. Confrontation means facing the problems and exploring ways of improving relationship amongst individuals, and searching for solution to the problems the organization faces. Trust is both the result of these values as well as helps in generating mutuality in the organization. Authenticity is the value underlying trust. It is the willingness of the person to acknowledge the feelings he has and accept both him as well as others who relate to him as person. This value is important for the development of the culture of mutuality. Another value emphasized is pro-action. Instead of merely reacting to the situations, the organization should take the initiative in influencing the situation. Autonomy is the next value. An individual who does not feel threatened in seeking help from others in coping with the various problems is an autonomous person. Collaboration is emphasized as a value so that individual instead of working independently in solving their problems, work in teams and develops commitment to their roles and to the organization. (Udai Pareek, 1996).

Methods of Data Collection

In the analysis phase of the information system's development process, the system analyst relies on specific techniques for gathering study facts. At a glance through the methodology of OD, research methods and techniques widely used in recent years include: content analysis, interviews, questionnaires, participant observation, taskforce report, case studies, archival research, survey reports, simulation techniques, action research and many more.

The consultant needs to collect information or data in order to find the problems in the organizations and to go into more details about those problems. The usual way of data collection is to use some instruments to be filled out by the individuals. Such instruments may give data about the individual as well as group processes. The instruments used may focus on such aspects of the organization: the climate, the motivational patterns, perceptions of leadership styles, perception as various kinds of problems, delays, etc., work satisfaction and role tension. Such instruments are either available as standard instruments (Pareek and Rao, 1996) or these instruments are specially prepared by the consultant in order to collect data. Data collection through structured instruments helps in getting things which may not come out in the interview can be known from such data. In many cases it may not be possible to interview such a large number of person in the organization, and data collection may be more convenient.

After data collection, the consultant tries to diagnose the main problems. Diagnosis takes into account not only the data collected through the instruments but also the data from interviews with the people, as well as several observations and notes kept. The consultant has his preliminary understanding of the diagnosis, he prepares notes on it and has some understanding of what the problems are, which of these are more important than the others. (Udai Pareek).

Organizational Survey Research

Survey research is popular in industrial and organizational psychology. In fact, the use of surveys has increased tremendously over the past half-century (Kraut, 1996), with millions of employees being asked to complete at least one organizational questionnaire each year (Gallup, 1998).

Organizational survey research typically proceeds through five stages:

- Identification and documentation of the purpose and scope of the survey effort.
- Construction of the instrumentation.
- Survey administration and data collection.
- The analysis of information obtained.
- The reporting of results to key constituents.

While the level of emphasis in particular stage may differ depending on the nature of research agenda and the survey modality used, the process of conducting survey research itself can be generally described as having these five components.

All organizational survey efforts fundamentally possess the same broad goal- to collect information from one or more people on the same set of organizationally relevant constructs. However, in practice, survey can serve a variety of specific purposes. Purpose refers simply to the intended use or ends to which the information gathered will be directed. Survey purpose determines survey scope. Survey scope represents the methodological requirements dictated by the purpose- namely, the number and type of respondents needed, the content areas to be covered, logistical requirements, and the timing of the survey effort.

The next element in a survey effort is to determine the type of instrument to be used. This would, of course, be driven directly by the purpose of the research. In some instances, standardized survey measures may exist, such as the Job Descriptive Index (Blazer et al, 1977), while in other situations, existing survey tool will need to be modified or anew measure be created. It is important for the survey researcher to remember that the quality of data collected is largely dependant on the quality of items, instructions and response scales used in the instrumentation.

Survey administration and data collection represent the third stage in the survey process. The data collected from the employees through some formalized process occurring via paper-and-pencil, email, interactive voice response, internet, intranet or fax. This aspect of survey research is for many the least stimulating, yet most detailed, because it is concerned largely with communication, document reproduction, scheduling, guaranteeing access, tracking response rates and working with technology-based systems (Kuhnert and McCauley, 1996; Macey, 1996)

The fourth component is the analysis of data obtained. Often the majority of the analysis, time and effort in survey research work is focused on the identification and exploration of significant trends by various individual level demographics, as well as across different business units, functional divisions, and other relevant variables. The analysis of write-in commentary, vis-à-vis a content analysis approach, is also fairly common practice. A less common approach that may be quite powerful in applied research involves data-linkage.

Finally, the analysis of survey data should include some considerations for the potential presence and analysis of non-response bias (Rogelberg and Loung, 1998; Rogelberg and Cristol, 2000).

The fifth element in any survey research effort is the presentation of findings. The favored approaches by researches and practitioners alike still include bar graphs, pies, radar charts, and line graphs, tables of mean and distribution, and related display techniques. The only element that has, arguably, changed significantly in the last decade is the actual method of delivering the findings. A less readily used potentially meaningful and powerful presentation approach involves presenting the data within the context of a framework or model of organizational change and development.

There is a critical sixth step- taking action- which is in fact a requirement for an effective organizational survey process. This sixth element concerns the extent to which changes in the organization are made as a direct result of the data obtained.

This general survey research process typically holds true regardless of the modality in which the survey is conducted. However, the survey modality can affect the detail underlying a number of the steps in the model. This is particularly true when survey research is conducted via the internet/intranet.

The internet/intranet holds great promise for survey researchers. Some of the positives include reduced research costs, enlarged sample size, and improved access to typically hard to reach populations, enhanced interactivity of research materials and adaptability of research materials. An additional advantage is that it allows viewing surveys in a new light, as real-time decision-making tool; because it allows data collection-analysis-presentation cycle, time for an internet/intranet survey can be so short. It is possible to design a short survey, post it and have the data analyzed and reported in a few days or even a few hours if necessary. As a result, it is possible to systematically and immediately gather opinions regarding a pressing informational need through the use of internet/intranet surveys. This is not only important from the perspective that the research is addressing organizational needs in timely manner, but it may help to enhance the importance and criticality of I-O psychology in the workplace.

Interviews

In many instances, the best way to obtain critical study facts is to conduct a series of interviews. Simply stated, the interview is face-to-face exchange of information. It is a communication channel between the analyst and the organization. Interviewing is used to gain information concerning what is required and how these requirements can be met. The interview can be used to gain understanding from the user for a new idea or method. (John, Felix and Gary, 1983).

An interview is called unstructured if questions asked by the psychologist do not follow a pre-determined course and largely if not exclusive, depends on the person's responses and own interjections. Today most assessment views are semi-structured or fully structured. In the first case, the interviewer is guided by a schedule of questions or topics, with varying degrees as how the psychologist may chose to follow up the person's responses. Fully structured interviews follow an interview schedule containing all questions to be asked, often with detailed rules about which question to ask next depending on a person's response to previous questions. (Pawliks and Rosenzweig, 2000).

The typical components of organizational research using interviews are sampling, instrument design, conducting the sessions, and analyzing the results. Interview is one-on-one session between an interviewer and interviewee, typically for the same purpose. The research can be subject matter experts, key stakeholders in a project, or more randomly selected employees who can contribute to the research. Interviews can provide rich source of qualitative information when development or testing of new theories is needed or when in-depth discussion would provide clarity on an issue. Interviews are often used prior to a quantitative study to identify critical topics to include in the research or at the conclusion of a quantitative study when findings need further exploration. Interviews are also useful for gaining a general understanding of an issue without involving the number of people needed for a statistically representative survey.

Interviews can be used for stand-alone research, generally they are not methods intended to provide representative data for a large population. Therefore, the findings must be used within the confines of their limitations by avoiding weighting single comments too heavily or generalizing findings too broadly.

Ideally, the number of sessions conducted should be enough to achieve theoretical saturation (Lee, 1999), which is the point at which new sessions are not adding new knowledge. Practical considerations include the number of people available to conduct sessions and the amount of time available for the project. Key subgroups should be identified and it should be determined whether to conduct sessions with them separately. Recruiting participants is often the weakest link in the process (Morgan, 1998). Participants should be chosen randomly if possible and if needed.

A facilitator's guide is the script for conducting interviews. Structured guides will include introductory statement, directions for participants, an ice breaker exercise, and questions to ask participants and close information. In addition, the format of the guide should be structured with more general questions first, followed by more specific or more sensitive questions later in the session (Gumesson, 1991)

Dates and sites for the session must be chosen, invitations should be sent 7-14 days prior to the session, and responses from the participants must be managed. Excellent facilitation skills are critical for conducting successful interviews, and, often subject matter expertise is required (Morgan, 1998). The facilitator should be objective, avoid engaging in a dialogue with participants, and maintain the flow of the discussion. Lee (1999) recommends three approaches for facilitators: retiring participant's comments, asking a participant to clarify the point, and summarizing statement to keep the discussion moving. A live note-taker can be used, or sessions can be audio-or video taped where verbatim comments are later transcribed. Privacy laws vary ÿaround the world with regard to gathering information via interviews and specifically, to the recording of sessions. Locals laws and company policies must be followed, and permission to tape must be obtained from all participants prior to each session. If recording devices are not allowed to be used, the following list of recommendations should be considered: 1) draw a map of participants, assigning a number to each so comments can be associated with the individuals, thereby avoiding weighting verbose participant's comments too heavily: 2) record much verbatim as possible and do not try to summarize or formulate conclusions during the session; 3) record relevant non-verbal behavior.

After each session, the facilitator should summarize the major messages. These notes, written when memory is fresh, will be useful during report writing. After the interview is over, a "thank you" not and later summary of the findings from the research are critical. (Rogelberg, 2002).

Interviewing is an art, and accordingly, does not always proceed as planned. Normally, people react to an interview in different ways, some favorable and some unfavorable. The following material includes a spectrum of reactions the system analyst is likely to encounter, along with some suggested stop gap activities to offset them. (John, Felix and Gary, 1983).

Questionnaire

A questionnaire can be used at various times by the systems analyst in the systems development process. It can be used in systematic work to obtain a consensus, to identify a direction or area for in-depth study, to do a post implementation audit, and to identify specific but varying requirements.

For fact-finding, the questionnaire is a somewhat restricted channel of communication and should be employed with great care. Analyst must know, structure the questions that they desire to know, structure the question that will result in the answers to these needs, and prepare and submit the questionnaire to the individual who is to complete it. Unfortunately like the interview, the analyst has no immediate opportunity to readdress comments that are vague and unclear. Moreover, the analyst cannot follow up tangent comments that might well lead to additional facts or ideas.

The questionnaire can be used best as a fact-finding tool when the recipient is physically removed from the analyst and travel is prohibited, where there are many potential recipients and when the information is intended to verify similar information gathered from other sources.

The reasons for recommending a limited use of the questionnaire in system analysis are numerous. First, it is extremely difficult to structure questions without anticipating a certain response. Second, the in-ability for immediate follow-up tends to limit the real value of this type of communications. Finally, it appears that "blanket" style documents, especially questionnaire, are assigned low priority and importance by most people.

When the analyst decides to use questionnaire a few, but important, guidelines should be followed:

Explain the purpose, use, security and disposition of the responses.

Provide detailed instructions on how you want the questions completed.

Give a time limit or deadline for return of the questionnaire.

Ask pointed and concise questions.

Format questions so that responses can be tabulated mechanically or manually.

Provide sufficient space for a complete response.

Phrase questions clearly. For example, "has your processor stopped to answer for the respondent whose processor has never malfunctioned?" can be very frustrating to answer for the respondent whose processor has never malfunctioned.

If a question cannot be responded objectively, provide an opportunity for the respondent to add a clarifying comment.

Identify each questionnaire by respondent's job title, department, etc.

Include a section where respondents can state their opinions and criticisms. (John, Felix and Gary, 1983).

Observation

Another technique available to the analyst during fact finding is to observe people in the act of executing their job. Observation as fact-finding technique has widespread acceptance by the scientists. (John and Felix, 1983). Observational research in organization is an extension of ethnographic approaches used by anthropologists and sociologists. (Rogelberg, 2002).

Observational research is a process of watching and listening. Perhaps an organization wants insight into the practices of a manager who has been particularly successful retaining critical talent. Breg (1998) provides four general steps:

Taking in the physical setting is accomplished by walking around, taking some initial notes, and perhaps mapping out the physical layout of the organization. This process is intended to help with preliminary logistics, getting to know members of the organization, and drawing some first impressions.

Developing relationships with inhabitants is a process of identifying potential guides and informants. Often the guide may be the primary contact for the research project. However, the initial walk through the location may be having relationships simply through a smile and an informal greeting. This initial relationship can then be used to most important source of information. Senior members of the department may provide unique and valuable insights into the climate and or culture of the department

Tracking observing, eavesdropping and asking questions is the next step. Tracking involves following a guide or informant and observing interactions and behaviors. Although eavesdropping is generally frowned upon, much can be learned from what is overheard in the course of a day. Ethical considerations must again be weighed against the value the observation will bring to the research.

Locating subgroups and stars is matter of identifying cliques (groups that tend to spend more time together) and social networks. The central figures in these sub-groups have been called stars, and developing relationships with stars can be very valuable source of data for the researcher.

The data collection format for observational research can take on many forms, but the two most frequently used methods are checklists and field notes. The key to both approaches is to be as systematic as possible. If the research is intended to verify the existence or frequency of certain behaviors or events, detailed checklist can be created and used by the researcher. The Position Analysis Questionnaire (PAQ) (McCormick, Jeannere and Mecham, 1972) is one example of a very detailed list that can be used for job analysis. The use of a checklist reduces not only focuses the attention of the researcher; it also reduces the masses of data that might be collected. The researcher's hypothesis may drive the development of behavioral checklists that can be used by multiple raters. The use of multiple raters also allows for reliability checks during data analysis and is one of the methods to accomplish triangulation.

When the research questions are more exploratory, or the research location and context preclude the use of checklist, field notes are the primary means of recording data. Some researchers suggest writing complete records immediately after leaving the research site (Bogdan, 1972), while others suggest jotting down notes on site and later creating the complete record (Festinger, Riecken and Schacter, 1956).Burgess (1991) stated that note-taking is a function of the research context, the researcher's objectives, and the relationship with informants. The researcher should try to take down as much as possible and aim for verbatim accounts of conversations. Whenever possible, accounts of the times of events or conversations should also be part of the notes. The researcher's opinions, impressions, and feelings are also worth recording.

Whichever note taking method is used, several problems arise. The selective memory of the researcher creates validity problems. Experienced researchers develop tricks to enhance their memory. Berg (1998) recommends the following memory enhancing steps:

Record key words and key phrases while on location. These words and phrases will act as cues later to recreate the conversation. Carrying a small notepad can facilitate this process without being too disruptive.

Make notes about the sequence of events. The sequence of events facilitates the identification of important patterns that may be critical in final data analyses.

Limit the time you remain in the setting. To facilitate memory and emphasize the importance of note reconstruction, Berg (1998) suggested a 1:4 ratio of field time to subsequent note-writing.

Write the full notes immediately after leaving the location to minimize the opportunity for memory erosion.

Get your notes before sharing them with others to avoid forgetting and unintended embellishment of actual events. Especially if working as part of a research team, your memory of events can be influenced by what your teammates might share3 with you about their observations.

Hand-held personal computers that are easily transported and concealed hold particular promise for facilitating data recording ion the field. And again, ethical and legal issues must be considered in using any technology-based recording equipment. (Rogelberg, 2002).

Observation can be used to verify what was revealed in an interview or as a preliminary to the interview. Observation is also a valuable technique for gathering facts representing relationships. Observation tends to be more meaningful at the technical level of data where tasks can be more easily quantified. Technical activities include tasks related to data collection, accumulation and transformation. Decision making activities can be best understood through the process of interviewing. (John, Felix and Gary, 1983)

Management by Objectives (MBO)

Donaldson Brown and Alfred Sloan in 1920s and Edward Hagenin in 1930s contributed the ideas that led to MBO.

Peter Drucker, a noted management writer introduced the term MBO in 1954. Drucker first made the use of this term in his book "Practice of Management" in the same year.

George Odiorne defines MBO as "a process whereby superior and subordinate managers of an organization jointly define its common goals, define each individuals major areas of responsibility in terms of results expected of him and use these measures as guides for operating the unit and assessing the contribution of each of its members."

Humble considers MBO as dynamic system which seeks to integrate the company's need to clarify and achieve its profit and growth with the managers' needs to contribute and develop himself."(Nirmal Singh, 2000).

Dale D.McConkey has defined it" an approach to management planning and evaluation in which specific target for a year or some other length of time are established for each manager on the basis of result which each must achieve, if the overall objectives of the company are to be realized. At the end of the period, the actual results achieved are measured against the original goals, that is, against the expected results which each manager knows, he is responsible for achieving."

MBO which is also called as" management by results" has a central focus on the "objectives" in the management process and emphasizes performance improvement as the goal.

Some experts have styled MBO as a simple but quite a powerful system of management. They have gone further to the extent of saying that MBO is neither a tool nor a technique but it is management itself. (Nirmal Singh, 2000).

Management by Objectives essentially is a collaborative goal-setting process through which organizational goals systematically cascade down through the organization. It is implemented through a series of discrete steps. The following discussion describes the steps in a general way; many organizations have adopted variations to suit their own purposes.

Starting MBO: MBO must start at the top level to be successful. Top management must stand behind the program and take the first step by establishing overall goals for the organization.

Establishment of Organizational Goals: the upper level managers of course, set the initial goals. Goals might relate to sales growth, market growth, costs, productivity, absenteeism or any other area important to the organization.

Collaborative Goal Setting: Next, superiors and subordinates collaborate in setting goals. First, the organizational goals are committed to everyone. Then each manager meets with each subordinate, during this meeting, the manager explains the unit goals to the subordinates and the two determine together how the subordinate can most effectively contribute to those goals. The manager acts as a computer and helps ensure that the subordinate develops goals that are verifiable. Finally manager and subordinate ensure that the subordinate has the resources needed to reach his or her goals. The entire process spirals downward as each subordinate meets with his or her own subordinate to develop their goals.

Periodic Review: During the time frame set for goal attainment (usually one year), the manager periodically meets with each subordinate again to check progress.

Evaluation: Finally, at the end of the specified time period, managers hold a final evaluation meeting with each subordinate. At this meeting, manager and subordinate assess how well goals were met and discuss why. This meeting often serves as the annual performance review as well, determining salary adjustments and other rewards based on reaching goals. Finally this meeting may also serve as the initial goal-setting for the next year's cycle. (Moorhead and Griffin, 2000).

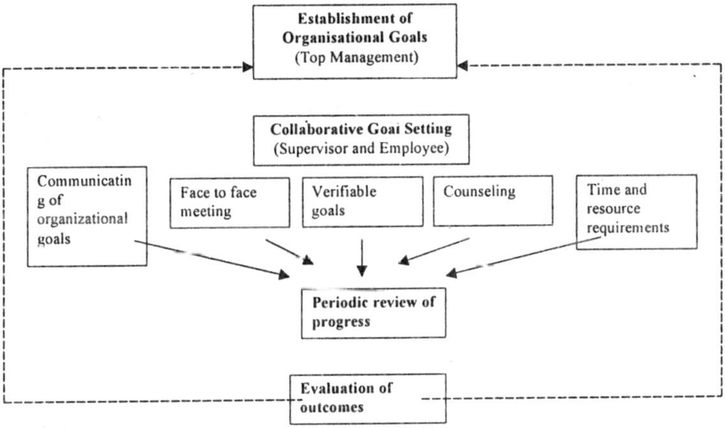

Effective Implementation of MBO

Basic steps in setting up an MBO system have already been defined and stated above.

Let us now examine in more detail what important steps does an MBO programme involve. These are:

Specifying Objectives: In implementing an MBO programme, the first step is that of specifying objectives.

Objectives, it may emphasize here are the central focal point in MBO process. These objectives should include the three types of inter-related objectives, namely:

- Purpose of an organization,
- Strategic and long-term objective, and
- Short-term objective.

Objectives both for the organization and its units are essential as otherwise individual manager's contribution cannot be identified within the area of his operation.

Along with specifying the objectives of the programmes, it is also important that the names of the departments and units that will be participating should also be specified together with inter-relationship that exists between the departments coming within the operation of MBO. While being sure of job descriptions, responsibility for MBO activities at each level is to be assigned, time limits have to be prescribed for each phase of activity and necessary check-up if these activities have been performed within time limit is to be exercised.

Setting objectives: The next crucial step in this process is that of setting objectives. This is as important as the output (results).

The objective should be specific, clear and without any ambiguity. They should be attainable, that is, within the reach of the person concerned. They should be stimulating, motivating and challenging. They should be in keeping with the organizational policies, procedures and plans. They must correspond to the exact requirements of the enterprises and participative sprit should prevaiỹ in these objectives.

With regard to the nature of participation, it may be stated that participation of manager lends added strength to commitments to organization objectives; autocratic management style is least helpful in successful working of any MBO activity; participation to be effective must be voluntary.

The objectives should be measurable and have to be set at all levels of the organization.

Maintenance of hierarchy in setting objective is important, that is, before lower level objectives can be set, it is necessary that specific and clear top management objectives must be set and then further on, such objectives should be set throughout the organization.

There is no harm in assigning priorities in case of objectives, should there seem a possibility of all set objectives not being accomplished.

Reviewing and Validating Objectives: As a useful and an advantageous measure, reviewing and validating the objectives and performance is important. Research in MBO and behavioral science suggest that any programme works better if its performance is reviewed and objectives validated, regularly through feedback not necessarily after a year but quarterly and even monthly.

Existence of objectives without a system of review of performance and validation of these objectives carries no value.

Implementing Objectives: while implementing the objectives, it becomes essential to have a correct assessment of the present position in respect of management rules, procedures, systems, managers (their attitudes) and external environment.

Those managers that are authoritarian and result-oriented will tend to accept MBO. While bureaucratic managers tied up with the system, rules and procedures, not desirous of laying any focus on performance, may not be very enthusiastic, rather shirk to show any affinity with MBO and might even resist objectives taking any concrete shape in their application. In such situations, objectives are not likely to show any progress.

Organization structure and past performance of an organization are very much linked with the implementation strategy.

If structural changes, modifications needed in an organization for creating a favorable and acceptable atmosphere, are possible, MBO objectives implementation will work speedily and with success.

Similarly, past performance has important implication for the future. If the past overall performance has been good and satisfactory and of an acceptable nature, people in the organization are likely to be confident of doing better in the future.

Those essential factors in objectives implementation that really matter are: commitment, sincerity of purpose, hard work, good understanding, time effect, patience and planning.

The personnel who are most concerned with MBO implementation are:

Top Executives : who initiate and sponsor the programme, lend their full support and leadership and want to see it getting through, the second type of personnel are MBO advisers who carry specified and onerous duties of helping managers in the organization accept and practice MBO and third type of personnel are consultants from outside who make available their experience and expertise to the top management by fully supporting and endorsing executive efforts in the direction of MBO objective implementation

Controlling and Evaluating Objectives: Here objectives are matched against performance. If there are any errors detected, corrective action is taken and guidance on future achievements is provided.

MBO tends to emphasize quantitative rather than qualitative aspects of performance in terms of goal achievements (Nirmal Singh, 2000).

MBO- Its Use and Applicability

Initiative of use and applicability of MBO in India came from multinational parent companies based in Britain to their major Indian subsidiaries who emphasized on the adoption of MBO. They supplied necessary literature, manuals, forms, etc. but due to non-availability of expertise nothing much could be gained.

However, MBO got an impetus in its awareness, knowledge and learning to Indian managers with the holding of the first top management seminar organized by Administrative Staff College of India, Hyderabad with the "management by Objectives" in July 1969.

MBO gradually gained much recognition with the Indian managers who have been studying this technique, gaining increased knowledge of it and trying to bring in use and its applicability by practicing it. With organizations MBO has become even a fad in India. For a better overview of Indian experience with MBO, we do better examine its introductory and development stages.

In the early stages, say up to 1973, it was more or less a learning, knowledge gathering, trying to find ins and outs, 'learning or doing" and "trial and error" stage. During this period MBO received setbacks. However, in the second stage, since 1974 Indian industry and business, both public and private sectors took to MBO seriously. By this time expertise and consultancy also grew in strength. MBO practice came in increasing use and applicability. Big organizations in both the sectors, to name a few such as, Madura coats, Bharat Bijlee, Hindustan Copper Ltd., Bharat Heavy Electricals, and Blue Star came within the fold of MBO.

So much so that even the Government like Tamil Nadu and Gujarat also brought in the use and applicability of MBO in various organizations and establishment in their respective states.

Advantages of MBO

It forces managers to think of planning for results rather than merely planning work; this is very important, because only result-oriented planning makes any sense.

It increases commitment throughout the company to the aims of the organization, because everyone should be working towards definite target which are all well coordinated.

It forces companies to clarify internal structures and organizational roles.

It helps in development of effective control system as well as leading to more effective planning. (Rob Dixon, 1997).

As with other approaches, MBO too has been criticized. One comment made against the approach is that it is not applicable to all jobs in all organizations. Jobs with little or no flexibility, such as assembly-line work, are not compatible with MBO. An assembly-line worker usually has no little job flexibility that the performance standards and objectives are already determined. The MBO process seems to be the most useful with managerial personnel and employees who have a fairly wide range of flexibility and self-control in their jobs. Besides, when the results of an MBO system are to be used to allocate organizational rewards, employees may be less likely to establish challenging goals-goals they are confident that they can accomplish. Further, the allocation of merit pay on a semi-annual basis may encourage the setting up of goals with short term horizons to the disadvantage of important long-term goals. (K.Aswathappa, 2002).

Summary

Organizations develop over a period of time. Many changes and modifications occur naturally. This process of change is what leads to organizational development. Organizational development, however, is a process of data collection, diagnosis, action, planning, intervention and change and evaluation of results applied to a whole organization or a large component of it.

Organizational development has certain dimensions such as a planned effort, Initiated by process specialists, Diagnostic skills, Coping capabilities, Culture and mutuality and Linkage strategies.

Organizational development seeks and often leads to new organizational arrangement, power relationship and structure that break with traditional bureaucratic patterns.

To implement better methodologies, techniques and training programmes in an organization to increase the productivity, the management needs to obtain information or data for this purpose. Data collection can be achieved with the use of many different techniques such as interview, questionnaire, observation and survey.

Within an organization, interviewing is the most significant and productive fact finding technique available to the analyst. The interview is a face-to-face exchange of information. Interview is conducted at all levels within the organization. Several points have to be kept in mind before interviewing:

- Arrange for an appointment ahead of time.
- Identify the interviewee's position and job responsibilities.
- Prearrange the time and place for the interview.
- Prepare outline of the forth coming interview, along with pertinent questions.
- Explain who you are, what the purpose of the interview is and what contribution the interviewee will make.
- It is important to attempt to ascertain the interviewee decision making model.
- As much as possible, try to ask specific questions that allow for the quantitative responses.
- Avoid buzz words, meaningless jargon and broad generalization.
- Develop an awareness of the feeling of the person being interviewed, learn to listen well.
- At the end of the interview, summarize the main point of the sessions, and thank the interviewee.

A questionnaire can be used at various times by the system analyst to obtain a consensus, to identify a direction or the area for in-depth study, to do post implementation audit, and to identify specific but varying requirements

The survey process can be quite involved, regardless of the modality used. Survey research passes through five stages.

- Identification and documentation of the purpose and scope of the survey efforts.
- Construction of the instrumentation.
- Survey administration and data collection.
- Analysis of the information obtain.
- Reporting of the results to keep constituents.

Another technique available to the analyst is to observe the act of executing their jobs. The purpose of observation is multifold. It allows the analyst to determine what is being done, how it is being done, who does it, when it is done, how long it takes, where it is done and why it is done. Before observation begins, the analyst should:

- Identify and define what it is that is going to be observed.
- Estimate the length of time this observation will require.

- Secure proper management approval to conduct the observation.
- Explain to the parties being observed what will be done and why.

It was Peter F. Drucker who first gave the concept of MBO to the world in 1954.

MBO can be described in four steps:

- The first step is to establish the goals each subordinate is to attain. In some organizations, superior and subordinate work together to establish the goals.
- The second step involves setting the performance standard for the subordinate in a previously arranged time period.
- In the third step, the actual level of goal attainment is compared with the goals agreed upon. The evaluator explores reasons for the goals that were not met and for the goals that were exceeded.
- The final step involves establishing new goals and possibly new strategies for goals not previously attained. At this point, superior-subordinate involvement in goal setting may change.

MBO is often an effective and useful system for managing goal setting in organizations. Most organizations would tailor it to their own unique circumstances. MBO has the potential to motivate employees because it provides unambiguous objectives for them to work toward. It also clarifies the basis for rewards, and it can spur communication. Performance appraisals are easier and more clear-cut under MBO. Further, managers can use the system for development purposes.

References and Further Reading

1. Gregory Moorhead and Ricky Griffin: Organizational Behavior-Managing People and Organization. (2000) 3rd edition. Jaico Publishing House, Mumbai.
2. John Burch, Felix Strater and Garg.G. : Information Systems: Theory and Practice (1983) 3rd edition. John Wiley and Sons, Inc. New York.
3. John.B.Miner: Industrial Organizational Psychology. (1992).
4. Kurt Pawliks, Mark.R.Rosenweig: The International Handbook of Psychology.(2000) Sage Publications Ltd. London.
5. Neil Anderson, S.Ones and C.Viswesvaran: Handbook of Industrial, Work and Organizational Psychology. Volume 2. (2002). Sage Publications, London.
6. Neil Anderson, S.Ones and C.Viswesvaran: Handbook of Industrial, Work and Organizational Psychology. Volume 1. (2002). Sage Publications, London.

7. Nirmal Singh: Principles of Management. (2000) Deep and Deep Publications Pvt. Ltd., New Delhi.
8. Paul.M.Muchinsky: Psychology applied to work. 2000 (6th edition). Wadsworth Publishing, Thompson Asia Pvt. Ltd., Mumbai.
9. R.S.Dwivedi: Personnel Management in Indian Enterprise. (1997). Galgotia Publishing House.
10. Rob Dixon: The Management Task. (1997) 2nd edition. Butterworth Heinemann, division of Reed Educational and Professional Publishing Ltd.
11. Stephin Robbins : Organizational Behaviour, 1996 (7th edition), Prentice Hall of India Pvt. Ltd., New Delhi.
12. Steven.G.Rogelberg: Handbook of Research Methods in Industrial and Organizational Psychology. (2002) Blackwell Publishers.
13. Udai Pareek: Organizational Behavior Processes. (1996) Rawat Publications. Jaipur and New Delhi.